Come Out, Come Out, Whoever You Are

Come Out, Come Out, Whoever You Are

ABIGAIL C. SAGUY

OXFORD
UNIVERSITY PRESS

OXFORD
UNIVERSITY PRESS

Oxford University Press is a department of the University of Oxford. It furthers
the University's objective of excellence in research, scholarship, and education
by publishing worldwide. Oxford is a registered trade mark of Oxford University
Press in the UK and certain other countries.

Published in the United States of America by Oxford University Press
198 Madison Avenue, New York, NY 10016, United States of America.

CIP data is on file at the Library of Congress
ISBN 978–0–19–093166–7 (pbk.)
ISBN 978–0–19–093165–0 (hbk.)

3 5 7 9 8 6 4 2

Paperback printed by LSC Communications, United States of America
Hardback printed by Bridgeport National Bindery, Inc., United States of America

For Claire and Jonah

Contents

About the Authors

Abigail C. Saguy is professor of sociology with a courtesy appointment in the Department of Gender Studies at the University of California, Los Angeles.

Laura E. Enriquez is assistant professor of Chicano/Latino Studies at the University of California, Irvine.

Nicole Iturriaga is a postdoctoral fellow at the Max Planck Institute in Göttingen, Germany.

Michael Stambolis-Ruhstorfer is assistant professor of American and Gender Studies at the University of Bordeaux, Montaigne.

Preface

This book is about how and why people use the concept of coming out as a certain kind of person to resist stigma and collectively mobilize for social change. It is about how metaphors like that of coming out evolve as people adopt them for varying purposes—across time, space, and social context. There have been countless books written on coming out but—whether fiction, academic, or memoir—almost all of them focus on the experience of gay men and lesbians in the United States. This is the first book to examine how a variety of people and groups use the concept of coming out in new and creative ways. It examines how the use of coming out among American lesbians, gay, bisexual, transgender, queer (LGBTQ+) people has shifted over time. It also examines how four diverse US social movements—the fat acceptance movement, the undocumented immigrant youth movement, the plural-marriage family movement among Mormon fundamentalist polygamists, and the #MeToo movement—have employed the concept of coming out to advance their cause. Doing so sheds light on these particular struggles for social recognition while also illuminating broader questions regarding social change, cultural meaning, and collective mobilization.

The idea to trace the use of the concept of coming out across different social contexts came to me when I was doing research for my previous book, *What's Wrong with Fat?* (Oxford, 2013). As part of this research, I conducted a series of in-depth interviews with leading activists in the fat acceptance movement—a social movement that promotes appreciation of body size diversity and confronts weight-based stigma and discrimination. In one of the very first of these interviews, in response to a question I asked about how she got involved in fat acceptance activism, eminent fat liberation activist and author Marilyn Wann spontaneously began telling me her coming-out-as-fat story. I was struck by her choice of language—that she spoke about *coming out as* fat—and soon found that other fat acceptance activists used this same phrasing. I wondered: Why talk of "coming out as fat" as opposed to, say, simply "getting involved with fat rights activism"? What was being accomplished by using the concept of coming out—so tightly associated with LGBTQ+ activism? Did it mean the same thing in this context? Coming out as gay, for instance, often means disclosing an unknown fact about one-self, but is it not obvious when one is very fat? What, if anything, is being disclosed? I put these questions aside for a while, as I pursued other questions related to disputes over the medical, political, and social meaning of fat-ness. Ultimately, however, I returned to these questions, publishing (with Anna Ward—then a graduate student in the UCLA Department of Gender Studies who helped with the literature review for that paper) "Coming Out as Fat: Rethinking Stigma" in *Social Psychology Quarterly* in 2011. Chapter 3 draws on this article.

As I was working on this paper, I discovered—talking to UCLA graduate students—additional cases in which a variety of people were using the lan-guage of coming out to resist stigma and mobilize for social change. Nicole Iturriaga had written a senior thesis at UC-Berkeley about Mormon fun-damentalist polygamists and told me that they too spoke of coming out as polygamist. Michael Stambolis-Ruhstorfer suggested that a comparison be-tween how gay men and lesbians in France talk about coming out with how gay men and lesbians living in the United States discuss it. Michael also told me to talk to Laura E. Enriquez, who was studying the undocumented im-migrant youth movement, where there were flyers and events focused on "coming out as undocumented and unafraid." Finally, Rebecca DiBennardo reported that adult children of gay men and lesbians have their own coming out stories as people with one or more gay parents.

From 2011 to 2013, the five of us met weekly to create a joint interview guide, discuss coding strategies and emerging findings, and workshop drafts of four stand-alone articles—published in the subsequent years.[1] Parts of Chapters 2, 4, and 5 draw on interviews and analyses in these previously published articles. Michael Stambolis-Ruhstorfer, Laura E. Enriquez, and Nicole Iturriaga conducted all the interviews with the gay men and women (we only use the ones with Americans in this book), undocumented immi-grant youth, and Mormon fundamentalist polygamist activists, respectively. I am grateful to all the people who agreed to be interviewed for this research. While Rebecca DiBennardo and I ultimately decided that the interviews with people who have at least one lesbian, gay, or queer parent required a different kind of analysis and were not a good fit for this book, the book has benefited from the valuable insights Rebecca DiBennardo provided as part of the original research team.

An anonymous reviewer for Oxford University Press suggested that I add a chapter on the #MeToo movement, which emerged after I submitted a book proposal and sample drafts. I am grateful for this suggestion, which has allowed me to extend my early and ongoing research on sexual harassment.[2] The Oxford reviewers and editor James Cook made several other helpful suggestions during the review process, for which I am most grateful. My literary agent, Jill Marsal, read every chapter of the book and provided brilliant feedback, for which I am deeply grateful. Ian Patrick patiently worked with me over several sketches to create the beautiful original illustration on the book cover.

As I was writing the conclusion to the book, UCLA Gender Studies professor Juliet A. Williams and I were conducting interviews with leading LGBTQ+ rights activists for another research project. While we had no questions about coming out in our interview guide, several people spoke spontaneously about the political importance of coming out and shared their own coming out experiences. I am grateful to Juliet for encouraging me to use this material in the conclusion to this book. More generally, I am grateful to Juliet for providing me with intellectual inspiration, support, and camaraderie over the past several years, as well as for helpful comments on several of the chapters in this book. All of my work is better thanks to our ongoing conversation about gender, sexuality, culture, and politics. Juliet has also made the process of research and writing more fun. I am lucky indeed to have Juliet as a colleague and friend.

The analysis presented in this book benefited from feedback on earlier co-authored articles. Specifically, Jeffrey Alexander, Jessica Cattelino, Lieba Faier, Hannah Landecker, Purnima Mankekar, Damon Mayrl, Paul McLean, Vilma Ortiz, Gabriel Rossman, David Paternotte, Thomas Pineros-Shields, Adam Slez, Bruce Western, and anonymous reviewers from the *American Journal of Cultural Sociology, Social Problems, and Sociological Forum* offered helpful feedback on at least one book chapter. Gabriel Rossman consistently communicated his interest for this project, forwarding me countless instances of coming out. I regret that I could not systematically explore them all in this book. Christine Williams generously read an earlier version of this manuscript and provided insightful comments that inspired important revisions to Chapter 6 and the Conclusion. Several colleagues expressed enthusiasm for the project idea, cheering me on when I was having doubts. This helped keep me on track and for that I am most grateful. Rachel Lee has been a longtime supporter of this project, and as the director of the UCLA Center for the Study of Women (CSW), generously organized a colloquium on the topic in February 2016. James Schultz was tasked as respondent, and this book benefited enormously from his comments as well as from comments from Kristen Schilt, who presented related work at the symposium. Chan-Mi Lee provided research assistance.

I could not have finished writing this book if former Sociology chair Darnell Hunt and former Social Science dean Laura Gomez had not both approved my request for a sabbatical leave for the full 2017–2018 academic year. The UCLA Academic Senate Council on Research and several UCLA centers—including the Center for American Politics and Public Policy, the Center for European and Eurasian Studies, and the Center for the Study of Women—provided essential funding for this research. The National Science Foundation (grant #1734340) is funding the research I am doing with Juliet A. Williams, on which I draw in the conclusion to this book.

Finally, I am grateful to my friends and family—including my late father Charles W. Smith, my mother Rita Cope Smith, my brother Jonathan Cope Smith, and my extended family and in-laws—for their loving support. I benefited from several conversations I had with my father—a fellow sociologist—about this project before he died on May 31, 2017. He continues to influence me in myriad positive ways, despite his painful absence.

After 26 years of marriage, my husband Dotan Saguy continues to encourage me when I falter and celebrate my triumphs. Dotan—who is having a second career as a photographer[3]—conceptualized the design of the book cover and worked with Oxford and Ian Patrick to execute it. In winter 2018, Dotan convinced me—despite my better judgment—to welcome an 8-week-old puppy into our home. Not initially a dog person, I am now smitten with this little being whom we call Beau and am grateful that Dotan pushed me beyond my comfort zone. I dedicate this book to my teenage children, Claire and Jonah, who continue to surprise and delight me. I hope that they will come into their most authentic selves and help make this a more just, equitable, and kind world.

1

Introduction

"Come out! Come out! Wherever you are!" I bellowed after counting to 100. Despite my order, I knew that none of my playmates would reveal themselves willingly. I was 6 years old and playing the popular game of hide and seek. As seeker, my job was to find the others. Theirs was to stay hidden at all costs. The first one found would be the next seeker. The last one found would be the winner of that round.

In contrast, in the 1970s, gay rights activists discovered that coming out could offer a key to greater social acceptance and civil rights. In 1978, openly gay elected government official Harvey Milk famously made "Come Out, Come Out, Wherever You Are" the slogan of his campaign to defeat the Briggs Initiative, or Proposition 6, which would have banned gay teachers from working in public schools in California. The idea was that if enough gay men and lesbians told their friends they were gay, Californians would realize that they had friends, co-workers, and family members who are gay and—out of solidarity—would oppose the proposition.[1] Harvey Milk implored gay men and lesbians:

> Come out to your relatives . . . come out to your friends . . . if indeed they are your friends. Come out to your neighbors . . . to your fellow workers . . . to the people who work where you eat and shop. . . . Come out only to the people you know, and who know you. Not to anyone else. But once and for all, break down the myths, destroy the lies and distortions. For your sake. For their sake. For the sake of the youngsters who are becoming scared.

The campaign helped defeat the initiative.

Since then, coming out—as a cultural concept and political tactic—has spread within and well beyond gay rights activism. A search for the terms *coming out* and *closet* in the keywords of major papers, indexed by Lexis-Nexis, yields examples of people coming out as asexual, celibates, male heterosexuals, Jews, Republicans, Scots, Kiwi males, witches (coming out of "broom closets"!), shopaholics, minivan aficionados, slackers, knitters,

Come Out, Come Out, Whoever You Are. Abigail C. Saguy, Oxford University Press (2020).
© Oxford University Press.
DOI: 10.1093/oso/9780190931650.001.0001

homemakers, Christian musicians, and men with erectile dysfunction.[2] The undocumented immigrant youth movement has used the idea to encourage undocumented immigrant youth—who fear the consequences about being open about their immigrant status—to "come out of the shadows" as "undocumented, unafraid, and unapologetic," which has, in turn, helped shift popular understandings of undocumented immigrants. More recently, the #MeToo movement has encouraged people not only to come out as having experienced sexual harassment, assault, or rape but also to *out* their abusers—resulting in material implications for many of those accused and a shift in public attitudes about harassment, assault, and rape.

This book is about how and why folks "come out" as specific kinds of people and the various forms this takes across different identities. It examines the distinct social and political implications for the specific groups that come out and for the broader society. This book assesses how the term's origins in the gay rights movement inform what it means to "come out" as, say, fat, undocumented, or Mormon fundamentalist polygamists. It shows that identity-based movements, in responding to oppression and advocating for rights, challenge negative stereotypes and sometimes seek to overcome internalized shame. This can involve reclaiming stigmatized terms such as *black, queer, dyke, fat,* or *slut*. It can also involve groups using new terms, such as *undocumented, DREAMers,* or *plural-marriage families*. Both approaches represent attempts to counter stigma and discrimination, while pursuing a desire to have one's authentic self recognized and valued.[3]

The close association of *coming out* with gay people informs the term even when it is used in other contexts. For instance, when fat liberation activist Marilyn Wann speaks about how she "came out" as fat, she is not just speaking about a turning point in her personal biography when she decided to politicize her body size. She is also staking a broader claim about what it means to be fat. Simply by using the term *coming out*, she implies that being fat is like being gay and that, just as it is good to be "out and proud" regarding one's gayness, so it is good to be "out and proud" about one's fatness. In this context, in which social stigma—or unwanted difference[4]—is plainly visible rather than hidden, coming out as fat means *owning* one's fatness or *refusing to apologize* for it.[5]

This book points to how social movement tactics travel between and among different movements, and how different causes—while seemingly distinct— get connected through political strategies and rhetoric. For instance, the civil rights movement—centered on racism and racial equality—provided legal tools, political strategies, and language for the women's rights and gay rights movements, which followed in its wake.[6] In the 19th century, the abolitionist movement inspired a women's rights and suffrage movement. In the 1960s, the Civil Rights Act of 1964, which was originally conceived to address employment discrimination on the basis of race, was extended—through the legislative process—to also prohibit discrimination on the basis of sex.[7] In subsequent decades, these actions provided feminist legal activists with the basis to develop a robust body of case law on gender discrimination and sexual harassment.[8] Feminists in the 1970s adopted many of the same political strategies—from sit-ins to marches—used in the civil rights movement, in which many had taken part. Even the term *sexism* was inspired by the earlier term *racism*.

The way various social movements have drawn on coming out politics—originally developed in the gay rights movement—is a more recent example of this same phenomenon. By the 1970s, the gay rights movement showed that by coming out to their friends and co-workers, gay men and lesbians could change hearts, minds, and laws. Since then, other groups have used the same strategy to gain sympathy for their cause while also implicitly likening themselves to members of sexual minorities—the group most associated with this tactic. Just as Harvey Milk urged gay men and lesbians to overcome their fear of disclosure and provide a model for "youngsters who are becoming scared," so too the undocumented immigrant youth movement has used talk of coming out as undocumented and *unafraid* to mobilize fearful constituents by trying to change their deepest feelings.

In other words, coming out has become what sociologists call a "master frame," or a way of understanding the world that is sufficiently elastic and inclusive that a wide range of social movements can use it in their own campaigns.[9] The equal rights and opportunities frame is one such master frame, originally developed in the US civil rights movement of the 1950s and 1960s and since deployed by countless other movements. Coming out is another master frame. This book is about how and why it has proven so powerful and how it has evolved as it has been used in distinct ways across different social contexts.

This book also addresses the process by which the concept of coming out has diffused beyond the gay rights movement. Work by social movement scholars suggests that social movement tactics are most likely to travel between movements that have common members or whose members are connected through social networks.[10] Both the fat rights movement and the undocumented immigrant youth movements have members who identify as lesbian or queer themselves or are connected to gay rights activists, links that would be expected to facilitate diffusion of talk of "coming out" from gay-rights to these contexts.[11] Yet other groups—such as Mormon fundamentalist polygamists—are, for reasons that are examined in Chapter 5 engaging in coming out politics despite being largely disconnected from gay rights activists. Moreover, by likening themselves to gay men and lesbians, a few develop feelings of solidarity and a sense of linked fate with gay men and lesbians despite religious opposition to homosexuality.

Scholarship on identity politics tends to focus on single issues or identities or to address the topic in abstract terms that are not grounded in empirical research. In contrast, this book takes a broad view, covering groups as varied as gay rights activists, fat rights activists, undocumented immigrant youth activists, Mormon fundamentalist polygamist activists, and people denouncing sexual violence. This book teases out important differences across these disparate groups while also noting commonalities. It grounds this wide-ranging discussion in careful empirical research conducted over several years. Specifically, this book draws on participant observation, textual analysis, and a total of 146 in-depth interviews.[12] All interviews were transcribed verbatim and interview excerpts were lightly edited for clarity. I identify by first and last name those people who requested this—typically public figures, prominent activists, or authors. I refer to all others with pseudonyms, using first names only.

Before examining how the concept of coming out has moved beyond the gay rights movement, evolving in the process, the next chapter—Chapter 2, Come Out, Come Out, Wherever You Are—shows how gay men in pre–World War II urban communities first spoke of coming out *into* gay society.[13] By the 1970s, that coming out had become a political tactic in which gay men and lesbians revealed their sexual orientation to friends, neighbors, and co-workers or—in the case of celebrities—more publicly via the mass media in an effort to challenge harmful stereotypes and gain sympathy. This helped establish an identifiable group of people that could be legitimately categorized as a minority group, following the adoption of the civil rights movement model of activism.[14]

Chapter 2 examines the ways, in the 1980s and 1990s, coming out was set up in explicit relation to the metaphor of the closet, conveying the shame associated with hiding one's homosexuality. It examines how the mantra "Come Out, Come Out, Wherever You Are," used by lesbian and gay activists in the 1980s and 1990s, became as much a demand for gay men and lesbians to declare their sexual orientation as an assurance of safety and community—bringing forth the notion of the "closet case" and the tactic of "outing." The *closet case* is a term of derision for someone who hides his or her sexuality; *outing* is publicly exposing those who are in the closet (usually people in the public eye such as politicians and celebrities). Chapter 2 also considers various criticisms of the imperative to come out and reviews assertions that gay men and lesbians have moved "beyond the closet,"[15] while suggesting that the closet may also be moving beyond sexual orientation—the topic of subsequent chapters.

Coming out as gay to family and friends can help other people realize that they already know and like people who are gay. But what if one's difference is hyper visible? Chapter 3, Coming Out of Glass Closets, examines this question, focusing on the case of coming out as fat. We learn that talk of coming out as fat originated with fat lesbian feminists, who were already steeped in talk of coming out as lesbian and extrapolated from that experience to talk of coming out as fat. We learn that coming out as fat is less about disclosing one's fatness than refusing to downplay one's weight in the hopes that others will not notice it. It means politicizing body size in order to challenge negative stereotypes. If fat people are apologetic about their size or refuse to identify as fat ("I'm a thin person trapped in this fat body"), they are unlikely to challenge negative stereotypes that others have of fat people. If, in contrast, they refuse to apologize for their weight and embrace it as part of their identity, they are more likely to stand up against weight-based oppression. Herein lies the political potential of coming out.

Considering what it means to come out as fat opens a broader question about the role visibility plays in coming out generally. We typically speak of coming out as gay or lesbian to refer to revealing to family and friends (or others) that one is gay. This is what Harvey Milk had in mind when he urged people to come out. Yet many people—particularly those who are gender nonconforming—may be assumed, rightly or wrongly, to be gay or lesbian. Effeminate men, for instance, are often assumed to be gay, while masculine-presenting women may be presumed to be lesbian. Queer theorist Eve Sedgwick uses the term *glass closet* to refer to people whose gender nonconformity makes them visibly gay despite failed attempts to conceal their sexual orientation.[16] Stated differently, coming out has never been *only* about revealing a hidden identity. It is about *proudly* claiming this identity.

Thus community and pride—and not just disclosure—are an integral part of coming out.

Repression and persecution, as well as internalized shame, keep many people in the closet. People identifying as queer, lesbian, or gay have made legal gains that offer some protection from discrimination and stigma, and some social milieus have become more accepting of these groups, arguably making it easier to come out as queer, lesbian, or gay; however, it remains extremely risky to come out as an undocumented immigrant. Undocumented immigrant youth recognize that by revealing their immigration status to others, they risk their own—and potentially their undocumented family members'—deportation.[17] Rising deportation statistics only deepen these fears.[18] Chapter 4, Overcoming Fear, examines how the undocumented immigrant youth movement—recognizing this—has evoked "coming out as undocumented and unafraid" to mobilize fearful constituents. The undocumented youth movement has advocated a range of local- and state-level legislative changes, including the federal DREAM Act.[19] First introduced in 2001, the DREAM Act would allow undocumented young adults under the age of 35 to legalize their immigration status if they entered the United States before the age of 16, have lived in the United States for at least five years, have obtained a high school diploma or equivalent, and have spent at least two years in higher education or in the military. The DREAM Act would make approximately 2 million undocumented youth eligible to legalize their immigration status, but each Congress fails to pass it.[20] While the DREAM Act never passed, the undocumented immigrant youth movement arguably led President Obama to sign the Deferred Action for Childhood Arrivals (DACA) executive order in June 2012, which deferred deportation for "Dreamers" who meet certain criteria on a two-year renewable basis. The undocumented immigrant youth movement has also successfully challenged cultural understandings by offering an alternative image to that of "illegal immigrants" sneaking across the border—that of educated and talented "DREAMers."[21]

Previous research suggests that social movement tactics flow between those movements with overlapping memberships and social networks. Indeed, as we see in Chapter 3, lesbian feminist fat rights activists first spoke of "coming out as fat," extrapolating from their experience of coming out as lesbian. Over time, the concept caught on and took on a life of its own within this new context. Likewise, as we see in Chapter 4, the "undocuqueer," who identify both as undocumented and as queer, played a central role in the diffusion of coming out tactics to mobilize undocumented immigrant youth. In contrast, Mormon fundamentalist polygamists are not socially connected to the LGBTQ+ rights movement. As Chapter 5, Producing a Sense of Linked Fate, shows, they are socially conservative and disapprove of homosexuality. Yet they have nonetheless self-consciously and explicitly borrowed the tactic of coming out from LGBTQ+ rights movements as part of a broader political strategy of likening polygamy to same-sex marriage.

Chapter 5 examines how and why they have done this. It argues that it has been politically expedient for Mormon fundamentalist polygamists to liken polygamy to same-sex marriage, an analogy that has also been evoked by powerful people and organizations in public forums. The linking of these two issues has created a sense among some Mormon fundamentalist polygamists that their fate is linked to that of sexual minorities. For a small minority of Mormon fundamentalist polygamists, this link seems to be generating some sense of solidarity with members of sexual minorities. In other words, while being socially conservative in other ways, Mormon fundamentalist polygamists generally support same-sex marriage and LGBTQ rights for strategic reasons, which—in some cases—is generating deeper empathy and solidarity, pointing to some of the unexpected ways in which different identity movements are being connected. Likewise, the fact that many Mormon fundamentalist women identify as feminists may make them more supportive of other feminist causes, such as opposing sexual violence—the topic of Chapter 6.

Chapter 6, Airing Dirty Laundry and Squealing on Pigs—focusing on the #MeToo movement—examines how contemporary feminists have used coming out tactics to draw attention to sexual violence. In late 2017, over three dozen women accused Hollywood producer Harvey Weinstein of sexual harassment, assault, or rape. Shortly after—following the lead of actress Alyssa Milano—millions of women posted "Me Too" on Twitter, Snapchat, Facebook, and other social media platforms.[22] While some left it at simply, "Me Too," others provided wrenching detail about abuse they had sometimes never shared publicly before. Similar media campaigns erupted across the globe. In France, a social media campaign under the hashtag of "balance ton porc"—loosely translated as "squeal on your pig" or "out your pig"—began the day *before* Milano launched #MeToo.[23]

Chapter 6 argues that #MeToo was the culmination of earlier social movement tactics focused on sexual violence. These include African American activist Tarana Burke's Me Too movement, founded in 2007 to let sex abuse survivors, especially girls and women of color, know that they were not alone, and the Clothesline Project, which, since 1990, has sought to "break the silence of violence" about incest, domestic violence, and sexual violence by publicly displaying in the center of college campuses clotheslines full of T-shirts that speak of such violence.[24] It also includes Take Back the Night marches, which have happened on college campuses since the 1970s to draw attention to the issue of sexual violence, and "slutwalks," organized for the first time in 2011 in Toronto and since then going viral and global.[25]

While all of these initiatives could be thought of as outing the *issue* of sexual violence, they have varied in the extent to which they disclose either the victims'/survivors' or perpetrators' identity. As Chapter 6 discusses, naming one's harasser, assaulter, or rapist has been controversial, hearkening back to debates over outing in the 1990s. Some have expressed concern that people will be falsely accused or judged in the court of public opinion, rather than in a court of law. Others counter that the cards are stacked against victims of sexual abuse and that they need to use whatever means possible to protect and defend themselves.

Most of the interviews for this book were conducted during Barack Obama's first presidential term. Chapter 7, Conclusion, examines the extent to which the claims of the book still hold when taken in the context of Obama's second term and the first half of Donald Trump's administration. Drawing on interviews I conducted with Juliet A. Williams in April 2018, it shows how transgender rights activists were able to use the politics of coming out to make important gains during Obama's second term. It also shows that while Trump has worked to reverse LGBTQ+ rights during his presidency, the LGBTQ+-rights movement has gained power and influence, and public opinion has shifted in ways that are not easily or quickly reversed. Having felt the relief and joy of exiting the closet, people are not willing to return so readily. Likewise, Dreamers have refused to retreat into the shadows, and the undocumented immigrant movement continues to encourage coming out as a strategy to garner sympathy and support. At the time of this writing, under nationwide injunctions issued by the US District Courts for the Northern District of California and the Eastern District of New York, the United States Citizen and Immigration Services (USCIS) is still required to accept, and is currently processing, DACA renewal applications despite President Trump's having rescinded the executive order.[26] Meanwhile, the Trump administration seems to have provided a catalyst for feminist organizing—including but not limited to the issue of sexual harassment and assault—while also emboldening members of the "alt-right," or white nationalist movement, to "come out of the woodwork."[27]

As this books shows, affirming specific group identities can be an effective way to cast off negative stereotypes and internalized shame, draw attention to injustice, gain public sympathy, mobilize fearful constituents, and enact social change. While there are important differences in the experiences of distinct kinds of stigma and oppression, the fact that many of the tactics developed by one group have also resonated among members of other groups speaks to some of the universal qualities of stigma and stigma resistance.

* * *

This book examines how the concept of coming out has traveled well beyond its origins in the gay rights movement. But before we tell that story, we must examine its origins and evolution within the social movement from which it emerged. It is to this we now turn.

2

Come Out, Come Out, Wherever You Are

At the end of the 19th century and the beginning of the 20th century, gay subculture thrived in many large American cities, as chronicled in historian George Chauncey's groundbreaking *Gay New York*.[1] There were "Pansy Balls," in which gay men "came out" into "homosexual society" or the "gay world, a world neither so small, nor so isolated, nor often, so hidden as 'closet' implies."[2] For instance, in 1931, the *Baltimore Afro-American* ran a story that explicitly and unselfconsciously drew the parallel between enormous drag balls and the debutante and masquerade balls of the dominant culture on which they were patterned. Under the headline "1931 Debutantes Bow at Local 'Pansy' Ball," it announced "the coming out of new debutantes into homosexual society."[3] This vibrant and visible pre–World War II situation belies the myth that gay people's lives were much worse in the past or, at the very least, that they kept them completely underground. Instead, although their codes and rituals were different from today's, many Americans who loved and had sex with members of the same sex embraced a positive identity, rejected the idea that they were perverted aberrations, and skirted around oppressive legislation.

The 1930s witnessed the beginning of a backlash against this visible gay world, but—with the help of industrialization, urbanization, and World War II—it nonetheless continued to grow in the 1940s and 1950s.[4] The social upheaval caused by mass mobilization for the war effort allowed a generation of American men and women to spend time in single-sex environments on the front or in factories far from their towns and families, where they explored their same-sex desires.[5] After the war, they moved to cities where they joined local gay subcultures. Yet political anxieties linked to social change in the context of demobilization and anti-communist fervor during the Cold War made gay people targets of heightened repression. As Larry Gross, a communications scholar and one of the founders of Gay and Lesbian Studies, explains: "From the late 1940s through the 1950s, actual and suspected homosexuals were the targets of witch-hunts, just as real and suspected communists were; in fact, the categories were often collapsed into the

Come Out, Come Out, Whoever You Are. Abigail C. Saguy, Oxford University Press (2020).
© Oxford University Press.
DOI: 10.1093/oso/9780190931650.001.0001

commie-queer bogeyman."[6] Thus, on April 27, 1953, President Eisenhower issued Executive Order 10450, banning gay men and lesbians from working for any agency of the federal government.[7]

In response to this backlash, the gay world became more secretive. The stakes rose for people who were known to be gay. The earliest important organization of what was known as the homophile movement, the Mattachine Society, was founded in Los Angeles in 1950–51.[8] Its name came from "mysterious mediaeval figures in masks . . . [who] might have been homosexuals."[9] It symbolized the society's members as masked, unknown, and anonymous.[10] Indeed, many used pseudonyms so that no one who knew them outside of the organization would suspect their activism on behalf of such a stigmatized group. This tradition of secrecy was faithfully observed for the following two decades.[11] Historians dispute whether the Mattachine Society's organization was modeled on the Communist Party[12] or on Freemasonry, which the founder Harry Hay devotedly served for many years.[13] Both enjoined secrecy and had hierarchical structures and centralized leadership. In April 1951 in a one-page document, the Mattachine Society articulated their goals and their ideas about homosexuals as a minority.[14]

In October 1955, four lesbian couples in San Francisco formed the first lesbian organization in the United States—the Daughters of Bilitis, named for the heroine in a 19th-century collection of French erotic, lesbian poetry. Though independent, Daughters of Bilitis jointly sponsored discussion sessions with the Mattachine Society. The organization also produced a monthly magazine, *The Ladder*, which published stories, verse, biographies, history, and columns discussing problems of concern to its lesbian readership. Daughters of Bilitis was "a tiny group," made up of white-collar semiprofessional women but not professionals or workers.[15]

Over time, the homophile movement expanded and deepened the self-awareness of lesbian and gay people as a distinct, self-conscious, and embattled minority.[16] The process of coming out was central to this awareness. For this movement, coming out meant acknowledging one's sexual orientation to oneself and to other gay people, *not* to the world at large. In fact, it was nearly universally taken for granted that this information was to be kept within the group. Such selective sharing relied on code phrases that could be used in mixed company to designate someone as homosexual. These included "family," "a club member," "a friend of Dorothy's," "a friend of Mrs. King," or "gay."[17] Like *coming out*, the term *gay* was derived from women's culture and specifically from the slang of female prostitutes, who used the term *gay* to refer to female prostitutes before it came to refer to gay men.[18] Of course, "gay" was ultimately "outed" itself when the gay rights movement adopted it in 1969.[19] Thus, prior to 1969, coming out primarily meant coming *into* a community that is much like a secret society. The dangers of this secret club were accompanied by attendant pleasures, including "in-group knowledge and solidarity of locations and codes, the excitement of shared risk, and the pleasures of gossip."[20] Daughters of Bilitis was, from its inception, "cautious, apologetic, and conformist."[21] The Mattachine Society became more assimilationist after 1953.[22]

Still, as early as the mid-1960s, a few movement leaders—most notably Franklin Kameny—planted the seeds for the more political gay rights movement that would come at the end of the decade. Forming with others the Mattachine Society of Washington, DC, in 1961,[23] Kameny rejected the homophile movement's traditional concern with medical theories of the causes of homosexuality and its possible cure. He noted that we do not see "the NAACP [National Association for the Advancement of Colored People] and CORE [Congress of Racial Equality] worrying about which chromosome and gene produced a black skin, or about the possibility of bleaching the Negro."[24] Talk of black as beautiful inspired Kameny's own slogan "Gay is Good." He explained: "I remember sitting here one day watching Stokely Carmichael on television talking about how 'Black is Beautiful,' and that started me thinking we needed some sort of slogan. I fooled around awhile with 'Gay is Great,' but finally settled on "Gay is Good."[25] Kameny took the position that "not only is homosexuality . . . not immoral, but that homosexual acts engaged in by consenting adults are moral, in a positive and real sense, and are right, good, and desirable, both for the individual participants and for the society in which they live."[26]

Indeed, the civil rights movement and racial minority models of social movements of the 1960s provided a new paradigm for collective action.[27] Despite the differences that some scholars point out between racial and sexual identity, one being presumptively visible and the other invisible, the civil rights movement provided a template for political organizing and a way of conceptualizing gay identity. As sociologist Steven Epstein explains, "This 'ethnic' self-characterization by gays and lesbians . . . [permits] a form of group organizing that is particularly suited to the American experience, with its history of civil-rights struggles and ethnic-based, interest group-competition."[28]

Through the slogan Gay is Good, Kameny sought to cultivate gay pride and the worthiness of gay men and lesbians. Kameny and others contended that only a movement "openly led by homosexuals themselves" could achieve these goals.[29] He and others led political demonstrations that foreshadowed the gay rights movement to come later in the decade. For instance, on July 4, 1964, Kameny and Barbara Gittings of Daughters of Bilitis led the first ever public demonstration for gay rights—at Independence Hall in Philadelphia.[30] Kameny and the Mattachine Society of Washington also organized meetings with government officials, challenged the government's discriminatory policies in court, and picketed the White House, State Department, Pentagon, and Civil Service Commission. Their efforts led to the American Civil Liberties Union's reversal, in 1964, of its 1957 policy statement supporting the constitutionality of anti-gay discrimination and, in 1965, to the US Court of Appeals ruling that the dismissal of a gay job applicant rested on overly vague charges of unfitness.[31]

How *Coming Out* Became Political

Resistance became more confrontational in the late 1960s.[32] Riots against state oppression around gay establishments, including those at the Black Cat Tavern in Los Angeles in 1967 and—most famously—the 1969 Stonewall Riots in New York City, propelled the movement forward. The Stonewall Riots—or Stonewall Rebellion—are often treated as the turning point between the homophile movement and the more radical gay rights movement.[33] These began at the Stonewall Inn in New York City, a popular, members-only bar on Christopher Street in Greenwich Village. Like other establishments catering to lesbian, gay, bisexual, and transgender (LGBT) people, the Stonewall Inn had often been the target of police raids.[34] Policing of LGBT people was harsh and included tactics such as entrapment. However, the patrons of the Stonewall Inn fought back against the police on July 27, 1969. The officers' especially rough clubbing and hauling of patrons, many of whom were young, trans and gender nonconforming people of color, was part of an uptick in police violence against gay venues in New York in the summer of that year.[35] But patrons did not go passively, and observers outside joined the fight. The police, who had stormed the bar, barricaded themselves inside as the growing crowd on the street pelted them with bottles and stones, preventing them from escaping until reinforcements arrived. At that time, the police made a few arrests, and the crowd dispersed. When word of the riots spread throughout the Village, many LGBT people joined the resistance, which continued off and on for several days. Gay people confronted the police and some were clubbed. Others engaged "in the minor sort of property destruction known as 'trashing,' shouting 'Gay Power!' as their slogan."[36]

The commemorative parade that took place in New York and other cities on the first anniversary of Stonewall and subsequent annual parades across the globe, now known as Gay Pride, commemorate the Stonewall Rebellion. Historians of gay history often refer to the pre- and post-Stonewall periods, despite the fact that there were similar events earlier and elsewhere that were not institutionalized into gay rights history or popular imagination.[37] After the Stonewall Rebellion, the gay rights movement—taking inspiration from the New Left, many of whose leaders were veterans of the civil rights and anti-war movements of the 1960s—spread like wildfire. At the first Christopher Street Gay Liberation March in New York City in June 1970, one of the organizers stated that "we'll never have the freedom and civil rights we deserve as human beings unless we stop hiding in closets and in the shelter of anonymity." Gay periodicals emerged with titles including *Come Out!* And *Out*.[38]

Sociologist Laud Humphreys described the scene the following year, at the second Christopher Street Liberation Day March in Greenwich Village, New York City:

> The initial images are those of a carnival: shouting, happy people, colorful banners spanning the street, hundreds of balloons, confetti, costumes, and noise-makers . . . but it is also apparent that these thousands are assembled for protest. Banners and posters proclaim a serious purpose: "Gay Liberation!" There are buttons insisting "Gay is Good" and asking "Equality for Homosexuals.[39]

These marches were themselves a public and dramatic enactment of coming out. As an article in the *San Francisco Chronicle* pointed out more than 20 years later, the first march was itself "the coming out of the movement on the national political agenda."[40]

It is at this time that coming out was set up in explicit relation to the metaphor of the closet—from skeletons in the closet—conveying the shame associated with hiding one's homosexuality. Journalist, historian, and gay rights movement leader Jim Kepner first used the expression *in the closet* in a speech at a movement conference in 1966 and noted that most of the audience did not know its meaning.[41] The expression, in the context of sexual orientation, first appeared in print in Wainwright Churchill's 1967 book *Homosexual Behavior among Males*.[42] By the end of the 1960s, lesbians and gay men who pretended to be heterosexual were said to be "in the closet" or labeled a "closet case" or—in the case of gay men—"closet queens," a play on the association of male homosexuality with femininity. People also "came out" to varying extents. They could come out only to themselves, to a few select people, or to the gay world more generally. By the 1970s, mainstream journalists were already using the term in contexts without a sexual connotation, speaking of "closet conservatives" and "closet gourmets."[43] Other terms emerged at this time as well. *Gay* replaced *homophile* or *homosexual* as the code word of choice, and *community*—with its left-wing popular associations—replaced *minority*, the "legalistic concept of the old gradualist elite."[44]

The civil rights movement provided a model for unapologetic public action, but it was challenging to create a 1960s-style mass movement from a group that had long learned to hide its identity from view. Political necessity largely drove the new movement to make coming out of the closet a public as well as an individual act. As historian John D'Emilio explains:

> Gay liberationists . . . recast coming out as a profoundly political act that could offer enormous personal benefits to an individual. The open avowal of one's sexual identity, whether at work, at school, at home, or before television cameras, symbolized the shedding of the self-hatred that gay men and women internalized, and consequently it promised an immediate improvement in one's life. To come out of the "closet" quintessentially expressed the fusion of the personal and the political that the radicalism of the late 1960s exalted.[45]

Coming out also provided a strategy for encouraging people to join the movement, as visible lesbians and gay men served "as magnets that [draw] others in" and once out of the closet cannot easily fade back in. Coming out thus provided the gay liberation movement with "an army of permanent enlistees."[46]

This new formulation of coming out was both public and political. As sociologist Joshua Gamson notes, "Coming out in public, especially through major institutions such as schools, the workplace, and communications media, is a way of asserting the public relevance of what others deem private."[47] Indeed, gay liberation movements critiqued the same bifurcation of the public and private sphere that feminists targeted. As sociologist Steve Vallocchi explains, "No longer [can] oppression be seen as purely 'public' in nature; the personal, sexual, the domestic [are] now sites for the creation and reproduction of social injustice. Personal 'authenticity' now [requires] a public 'coming out of the closet.' "[48] The public nature of this new formulation of coming out was explicitly politicized. "Anyone who adopts a gay or lesbian identity but ignores the political implications of this action," argues philosopher William Wilkerson, "has not fully grasped the meaning of the coming out experience."[49]

The making public of lesbian and gay identities was also part of a public relations campaign intended to change attitudes; it showed straight people that there were gay people whom they already know. The person coming out says: "I'm the same person. You liked me before. Why not now?" It also helped establish an identifiable group of people that could be legitimately categorized as a minority group, following the adoption of the civil rights movement model of activism. Sexologist Alfred Kinsey's popularized (and since contested) statistic that 10 percent of men are homosexual fueled the homophile movement's early claims for tolerance.[50] Gay liberation movements beginning in the late 1960s sought greater mobilization to effectively ground claims for legal and political rights and protections. Remaining in the closet in this context was a luxury that gay liberation movements could ill afford. Thus, the gay liberation model of the closet and of coming out moved away from the idea that coming out is a purely social or psychological journey to the idea that coming out is political.

In the early 1970s, gay and lesbian rights activists scored victory after victory. In 1973, after Frank Kameny staged a zap action—or raucous public demonstration designed to embarrass a public figure while calling attention to issues of gay rights—at the American Psychiatric Association (APA) convention, the APA removed homosexuality from its list of psychiatric disorders. In 1973, the New York Court of Appeals ruled that the New York bar association must admit an openly gay member. Homophobia became "unfashionable among sophisticated, avant-garde heterosexuals."[51] Police harassment relented and in 1972, New York City's mayor forbade police entrapments, which had run to over 100 each week in 1966. Blackmail also abated.[52] Meanwhile, gay neighborhoods spread and, by 1992, nearly 30 cities were holding their own Gay Pride parades, visibly and publicly celebrating the new ethos of coming out collectively.[53]

When, in 1978, the Briggs Initiative, or Proposition 6, threatened to ban gay teachers from working in public schools in California, a coalition of activists—including openly gay elected government official Harvey Milk—organized the "No on 6 Campaign." The campaign's slogan—"Come Out! Come Out! Wherever You Are!"—was an imperative that gay men and women come out to show Californians that they have friends, co-workers, and family members who are gay.[54] As reviewed in the previous chapter, Harvey Milk implored gay men and lesbians to "come out" to their relatives, friends, neighbors, "fellow workers," and to "the people who work where you eat and shop," to those "you know, and who know you" with the goal of "break[ing] down the myths [and] destroy[ing] lies and distortions." To come out, in this context, meant purposefully signaling one's gay identity—conceptualized as a central component of social and personal identity—to others. The power of this visibility was so successful that anti-gay activists, such as Anita Bryant—the famous Baptist singer whose success in repealing an anti-discrimination ordinance in Florida inspired the Briggs initiative—accused LGBT people of "recruiting" children.[55] Behind this malicious stereotype that gay men are pedophiles was an acknowledgment that growing pride encourages people, including youth, to lead openly gay lives.

Coming out was also about providing role models for other LGBT youth and adults. Sociologist Robert Merton coined the term *role model* in a 1957 study of medical students, arguing that medical schools teach students how to perform the role of doctor.[56] It has since become integral to gay pride.[57] By coming out, people—especially those in positions of authority—encourage and empower LGBT and questioning youth and adults by showing that it is possible to be gay and to be successful and happy. Some early examples of role modeling include Christine Jorgensen, whose male-to-female transition was reported on the front page of the *New York Daily News* in December 1, 1952.[58] More recently, NBA player Jason Collins came out in April of 2013, prompting out-athlete Martina Navratilova to declare: "One of the last bastions of homophobia has been challenged. How many LGBT kids, once closeted are now more likely to pursue a team sport and won't be scared away by a straight culture?" [59]

In the 1980s, under conservative leadership, the Christian Right and AIDS (acquired immune deficiency syndrome) crisis created an increasingly hostile climate for members of sexual minorities—galvanizing the gay and lesbian rights movement. Increasingly, a hostile, homophobic mainstream culture was blamed for the creation of the closet, but individual closeted people were blamed for its maintenance. Thus, the mantra "Come Out, Come Out, Wherever You Are," used by many activists in the 1980s and 1990s, can be understood as just as much a demand for people to declare their homosexuality as it is an assurance of safety and community for homosexuals. The AIDS epidemic itself also outed several public figures who contracted what was "tragically identified as the gay disease."[60]

In the 1980s, the coming out narrative became central to the formation of gay and lesbian identity and community within the gay liberation model, generating numerous anthologies of coming out stories in the 1980s and 1990s, such as *Like Coming Home: Coming-Out Letters*, *The Coming Out Stories*, *Testimonies: Lesbian Coming Out Stories*, and *Does Your Mama Know?—An Anthology of Black Lesbian Coming Out Stories*.[61] The coming out narrative became a rite of passage, something to be shared with others, and the centerpiece of gay liberation movements.

In 1987, the single-issue organization AIDS Coalition to Unleash Power (ACT UP) was formed; it was a radical direct action advocacy group working to bring about legislation, medical research, and treatment and policies to help people with AIDS and bring an end to the disease. It disseminated posters and stickers with a black background, a pink triangle, and the words "silence = death" (see Figure 2.1) and engaged in acts of civil disobedience and marches, for which many members were arrested. For instance, in 1989, seven ACT UP members chained themselves to the VIP balcony of the New York Stock Exchange to protest the high price of Azidothymidine (AZT)—the only approved AIDS drug at the time, leading the price of the drug to be dropped from $10,000 per patient per year to $6,400 per patient per year.[62] The 1980s witnessed some gay rights setbacks—including the US Supreme Court decision *Bowers v. Hardwick* (1986), in which the Court ruled that states could continue to outlaw sodomy, even in private. The *Bowers* decision created a significant roadblock because lawmakers used it as a justification—homosexual sex remained technically illegal in many states—to deny LGBT people protection from violence and discrimination. The movement nevertheless continued to see gay rights advances in some parts of the country on issues including child custody, adoption, spousal rights, employment, housing, and protection against hate-mongering.[63]

The radical organization Queer Nation split off from ACT UP in March 1990 in order to organize direct action focusing on a wider range of problems confronting lesbians and gay men—not exclusively AIDS.[64] The term *queer* had begun as a derogatory term for homosexuals in American criminal slang

Figure 2.1. ACT-UP's iconic pink triangle with the simple and devastating message: silence=death.

in the early 20th century, becoming common in British English in the 1950s and 1960s.[65] Queer Nation reclaimed the term in the same way the Black Power movement had reclaimed *black*, thereby inverting the associated stigma. They also deliberately recouped anti-gay myths—such as the idea that homosexuality is a choice or contagious—and rejected assimilationism. Members called themselves "queer nationals" and chanted, "We're here, we're queer, get used to it!"[66] They saw themselves as "militantly visible—wearing T-shirts and stickers with blatant slogans in unavoidable Day-Glo colors: PROMOTE HOMOSEXUALITY. GENERIC QUEER. FAGGOT. MILITANT DYKE." They organized "Nights Out," in which members

entered heterosexual bars in New York and San Francisco wearing their con-
spicuous T-shirts and staged "kiss-ins." "Queer Shopping Networks" visited
suburban shopping malls outside these same cities and chanted, "We're here,
we're queer, we're fabulous—and we're not going shopping!"[67]

The concept of *the closet* began to include a somewhat different meaning
in this context than it had in the 1960s. Increasingly, it referred to someone
pursuing same-sex desire in private but maintaining a homophobic political
stance in public. Such a character is hypocritical in a way that was not true for
the "closet case" of the 1960s, however pathetic he or she may have been. The
recognition that the veil of the private sphere had to be lifted for effective political mobilization brought forth the tactic of "outing"—*or* publicly exposing
those who are in the closet (usually public figures such as politicians and
celebrities)—that developed in the late 1980s and early 1990s.[68] Support for
this controversial tactic was fueled in the late 1980s and 1990s "by the anger
of those working furiously to counter the ravages of AIDS against those who
seem to be more concerned about retaining their membership on society's
A list."[69]

Outing

In February 1988, the National Gay and Lesbian Task Force organized a "war
conference" to debate political options. Although the attendants did not ultimately decide to pursue outing, the strategy was the object of lively debate.
While the executive director of the task force maintained that "our movement should [not] be about the business of dragging other people out of the
closet," the head of the Human Rights Campaign Fund—the leading gay
political action committee—retorted that "those who participate in the gay
community and then vote against it are guilty of hypocrisy—hypocrisy that
causes harm to a whole class of people." He likened them to Jews "who put
other Jews into the ovens. . . . Their duplicitous, devious, harmful behavior
ought to be exposed."[70] The more radical organizations took the initiative.
The following year, an ACT UP chapter in Portland, Oregon, carried out the
first outing, that of Senator Mark Hatfield, who supported various homophobic initiatives. Thereafter, outing became a favorite tactic of both ACT
UP and Queer Nation.[71]

One of Queer Nation's first actions consisted of altering bus kiosk ads
for Gap clothing featuring country singer k.d. lang by changing the p to y,

transforming *Gap* to *Gay*. Queer Nationals showed up at a promotional appearance by Olympic diving champion Greg Louganis, announcing that they were there as members of the lesbian and gay community and would love to have him as an out member.[72] In the spring of 1991, Outpost, a group formed from *OutWeek* and Queer Nation, blanketed New York City with street posters modeled on Absolut vodka ads that read "Absolutely Queer" under the faces of various celebrities (see Figure 2.2).[73]

Time introduced "outing" to the larger American public in an article published in its issue of January 29, 1990, showcasing divisions among LGBT activists and their allies over this controversial tactic.[74] It quoted Chicago *Windy City Times* associate editor, Susan Craig, saying: "Really, you're only using the same bludgeon used to injure you to injure someone else."[75] The article pointed out that if outing ends someone's career, that person will be unlikely to support the movement and often have no opportunity to be

Figure 2.2. A billboard riffing on advertisements for Absolute Vodka by outing Boy George as "absolutely queer."

effective. Lambda Legal Defense and Education Fund executive director Tom Stoddard suggested, "The gay movement is actually based upon two principles that collide. One is privacy, and the other is disclosure, the process of coming out."[76]

According to Larry Gross, "The continued secrecy of most gay people keeps alive the belief that gay people are much fewer than they really are, and that they are confined to inner city 'gay ghettos' and to stereotypically gay professions."[77] In this context, outing may be justified by three related considerations, including (1) the costs of homophobia; (2) evidence that personal contact with someone gay reduces homophobia and that "for media-fixated Americans, vicariously knowing openly gay celebrities would be the next best thing to personally knowing openly gay people";[78] and (3) that those who engage in frequent, voluntary same-sex conduct are gay regardless of their state of political awareness and that gay people are a minority group coming into self-realization. It is this last aspect—that "all homosexuals are members of a community, whether they admit it or not, to which they owe a measure of accountability and allegiance"—that Gross considers the most radical.[79]

The controversial New York City periodical OutWeek, which began publishing in 1989 on the eve of Gay Pride Day, did the most outing. Taking a stand against the myth that all public figures and celebrities are heterosexual, it aimed to convince the younger generation that they were not alone. With the support of publishers, editor Gabriel Rotello refused to employ a double standard when writing about public figures he knew to be gay, reasoning that if we do not gloss over celebrities' heterosexuality we should not gloss over their homosexuality.[80] Outweek writer and "arch-outer"[81] Michelangelo Signorile admitted that people who have to be forced out of the closet are poor role models, since they are filled with shame and have not accepted themselves. Still, he maintained that the visibility they provide is valuable and that they could serve as negative role models. Signorile insisted that privacy as a basis for gay rights belonged in the 1950s, when outing meant ruin, and that in the 1990s, "our community 'should be making itself as public as possible for visibility.' The Queer Nation must be able to take a census of its citizens!"[82]

Still, for outing to have maximum impact it required the active participation of the mainstream media, which largely refused to participate in outing, while actively constructing closets for the rich and famous. "Like the proverbial noise made by a tree falling in a forest, outing a politician requires an audience."[83] Even when the "ACT UP generation" of the 1990s—"a generation that has lived its entire life in the age of mass media gossip and infotainment"[84]—was willing to break the code of silence surrounding sexual orientation, many out-gay journalists continued to "proclaim the primacy of the right to privacy when it comes to gay people who are not egregiously hypocritical, conveniently ignoring the double standard revealed by singling out this one area in which to protect a right to privacy that is routinely trampled in the interest of the public's 'right to know' everything about the private lives of celebrities and public officials."[85]

Outing continued to be a controversial tactic beyond the 1990s, with activists and journalists focusing primarily on public figures whose actions or personas hurt LGBT people. The 2009 documentary *Outrage*, directed by Kirby Dick, detailed the politics of outing at the turn of the 20th century.[86] At a time when a critical mass of celebrities and politicians had revealed their gay, lesbian, or bisexual identities, such as Congress members Barney Frank and Tammy Baldwin, those who had private gay sex but public anti-gay positions stood out as malicious hypocrites. Activists such as the blogger Michael Rogers, whom the film chronicled, gathered enough source materials to make public the clandestine sexual encounters of politicians including Representative Edward Schrock (Republican of Virginia), Representative Mark Foley (Republican from Florida), and Senator Larry Craig (Republican from Idaho). Despite their sexual behaviors—or perhaps to dispel any doubt about their heterosexuality to their conservative constituents and their families—these politicians consistently voted against same-sex marriage, anti-discrimination laws, funding for HIV, allowing gays and lesbians to serve openly in the military, hate crime protections, or any other legislation that might help LGBT people. Many of the politicians Rogers and his supporters targeted resigned, retired, or otherwise changed their political trajectories. These outings sent the message that a politician could not take advantage of the sexual and social pleasures of homosexuality and simultaneously cause harm to those who live openly. According to Representative Frank, lawmakers in a democracy must be subject to the laws they create. By outing them, activists forced closeted conservative politicians to abide by this democratic duty.

Critiques of Coming Out and Competing Identities

People of color and white women critiqued the "out and proud" mandate for privileging sexual identity over all others, including race, class, gender, or gender identities.[87] They resisted the notion that sexual behavior should dictate a person's identity and political priorities, especially in a context dominated by white gay men. In the early post-Stonewall gay liberation movement, lesbians insisted on the distinctiveness of their experience and oppression and resisted being lumped in with a broader male gay population.[88] Although the term *gay* had been used in the 1950s and 1960s inclusively to refer to gay men and lesbians, lesbians insisted that the term *lesbian* be added to the name of pride marches held in the 1970s and 1980s to emphasize their specific struggles.[89]

Meanwhile, people whose sexual identity was more fluid or less salient critiqued the idea of coming out as acknowledging an intrinsic quality just waiting to be discovered and accepted.[90] They claimed not to identify with the sense of permanency signaled by coming out and to not necessarily view their same-sex desire as their defining characteristic. In response to bisexuals' claim of an independent and valid identity, *bi* was added to the name of the marches held in the 1990s. Before long, demands were heard to expand the movement further to explicitly recognize transsexual and transgender people, and *transgender* was added at the turn of the century.[91]

But reliance on the acronym LGBT glosses over glaring differences between (and within) the populations it designates and supposedly joins together, further contributing to a false sense of uniformity. It is not clear how the metaphor of the closet—which reifies the binary between heterosexual and homosexual—operates for bisexuality, which blurs this binary. Nor is it clear that "coming out" functions in the same way within transgender communities as it does within lesbian and gay-identified communities. Coming out among the transgender population can signify coming out *as* transgender—or non-binary (someone who identifies as neither male nor female but somewhere in between or beyond), but it can also signify coming out as belonging to the sex category with which one is comfortable identifying.[92]

Meanwhile, people of color have pointed out that an unexamined prioritization of white experiences within the gay rights movement has meant that "coming out" often amounts to coming into whiteness.[93] Facing both racism within the gay community and rejection from their racial and ethnic communities because of their sexuality, people of color experience multiple dimensions of marginalization that defy simplistic characterizations of the closet and coming out.[94] If coming out means supporting the prioritization of white gay men's political concerns, it fails LGBT people of color. For this reason, many navigate disclosure of their sexual and romantic attractions in ways that allow them to create systems of support within their own communities that challenge discrimination on multiple fronts.[95] Given these dynamics, some organizations have called for organizing around alliances (e.g., homosexuals and other groups) rather than prioritizing one identity over another.[96] By recognizing how people have multiple identities—based on, say, race, class, and gender—such organizations help bridge differences within the movement and build coalitions beyond it.[97]

Coming Out Narratives

As coming out has become more central to gay identity and political organizing, models of the coming out *process* emerged in the 1980s. While there is some variation, the themes of assorted models, whether developed by lesbian and gay psychologists or activists, are strikingly similar. The model of the organization Parents, Families and Friends of Lesbians and Gays (PFLAG) is arguably the most representative of mainstream lesbian and gay organizations and the scholarly literature.[98] PFLAG talks of a five-step process: (1) self-recognition as gay, (2) disclosure to others, (3) socialization with other gay people, (4) positive self-identification, and (5) integration and acceptance.[99] PFLAG specifies that this model should not be understood as a linear process or the same for everyone.

Social scientists call these narratives "sexual scripts."[100] In order for people to make sense of their desires, understand what to do with them, and decide if and how to act on them, they use these scripts—consciously or not—as guides. Sexual scripts are instructions that tell a person how to interact with others. Going on dates or making special plans on Valentine's Day are examples of scripts that people commonly use to guide their romantic behavior. In the United States, people who realize they are attracted to someone of the same sex can now draw on the commonly available script of coming out that activists and the media popularized in the 1980s. Movies, TV shows, books, magazines, blogs, and Twitter feeds all offer representations of what coming out looks like. Gay men, lesbians, and bisexuals get a sense from these materials about what they "should" do with their identities.

As with PFLAG's five-step process, Larry Gross affirms, "The initial stage of 'coming out' tends to be a private, individual recognition that often occurs long before any physical homosexual experience. It requires confronting the prejudices that everyone acquires as a member of a sexist and hetero-sexist society."[101] Resonating with this model, Jazzmin, a 57-year-old lesbian from Maryland with short-cropped salt and pepper hair who used to drive a taxi for a living, talks about self-discovery as the first step. "There's a distinc-tion between coming out to myself and coming out," she explains, "because I guess, you know, that coming out is kind of an internal thing, and some-times people mean that when they're talking about coming out, and then sometimes people mean an external thing, which is like when they came out to their parents, they came out to the world." Before telling anyone else, Jazzmin first had to acknowledge her sexual desires. After dating men, she began to explore intimacy with women involved in local feminist organizing. "So I came out to myself, even though I've been a lesbian my whole life. I just didn't know it," Jazzmin says with a laugh.

Gross's next stage consists of joining "whatever gay subculture the person can find and muster the courage to join," PFLAG's third stage.[102] Gross explains, "At this point, there are skills to learn and codes to master: where to locate potential partners, how to identify likely candidates, how to negotiate with them, and, if successful, where and how to conduct these potentially dangerous activities."[103] In the past, finding other people usually entailed going to places where other gay people congregate, such as bars, clubs, bookstores, neighborhoods, and cruising grounds. White gay men have fre-quently dominated popular urban gay neighborhoods, making them less welcoming for women and people of color. Furthermore, as urban renewal leads to gentrification the early 21st century, the LGBT people who estab-lished these neighborhoods are leaving.[104] For people who live far from cities or in the Bible Belt, or feel rejected by mainstream gay culture, they some-times have other local places they can go.[105] In the age of the internet, finding other LGBT people is easier than it ever was in the past.

After finding others, according to Gross, comes "going public"—PFLAG's second stage—which can itself be categorized in phases, "although there is no standard sequence followed by most people and few traverse the entire territory."[106] These include revealing one's homosexuality to family, friends, and co-workers, becoming an activist, and—in some cases—being publicly identified in the media. All sorts of variations are possible. People residing in large cities with concentrations of gay people may be out at work and where they live but still closeted to their parents and others in their hometowns. A few may end up being publicly identified in the media before coming out to family members.[107]

Going public is now institutionalized in mainstream American culture. National Coming Out Day, on October 11 each year, was founded by gay rights activists in the 1980s and is now a widely followed event when teachers, students, public figures, and other people publicly reveal or confirm their identities. Yet, although coming out is often scripted as a one-time event, most gay people have to constantly decide to come out or pass as they interact with new people.[108] For instance, when a lesbian takes a taxi and the driver casually asks her about her husband, she must decide whether to correct him or not. Sometimes going against the universal assumption of heterosexuality is dangerous or not worth the effort. Thus, most gay people pass some of the time, since no one can come out over and over, day after day, in opposition to the universal assumption of heterosexuality.[109]

Whether focused on personal or political transformation, coming out narratives tend to conform with specific narrative conventions, including (1) a sad, dark past of being "in the closet"; (2) the decision to come out; 3) redemption. This is true in the case of Kendell, a short and well-dressed African American gay man in his mid-20s, with excellent posture, a ready smile, and a musical voice. When Michael Stambolis-Ruhstofer interviewed him, he was working for marriage equality as a senior fellow with an American civil rights organization while also completing a master's degree and applying for law school. He described the period before he revealed his sexual orientation to others as "a very difficult period" of his life, when he could not be himself. He said he does not like to talk about this time, and, when asked to provide one word that would encapsulate it, he says "*dark* or *shame*." He described being bullied by high school classmates and not understanding why since he had not yet fully internalized the idea that he was gay.

Like others, Kendell said it was important to come out, which he defines as "basically presenting yourself as a member of the LGBT community unabashedly." He says he does not think "you need to make a grand proclamation to the world" but that "it's important to have someone that you can feel that you can share that part of your life with." Other gay men and lesbians similarly demarcated the period before and after coming out. They spoke of feeling less isolated and more comfortable interacting with others after the disclosure.

Gay men and lesbians speak about how coming out also provides a "teaching opportunity" that can create empathy. Ace's story of telling his family for the first time is a good example. Ace is a tall and imposing white 32-year-old retail manager who is active in the Baltimore community theater scene. He grew up in the white working-class suburbs around the now defunct steel mill but attended the magnet arts high school for acting. On National Coming Out Day in one of his final years in school in the late 1990s, Ace called his brother from a pay phone to tell him about being gay. Ace's father, who was secretly listening in on the conversation, said over the line, "Do you think I'm an idiot? Of course I know!" Surprised by this reaction, Ace understood that he still needed to explain the situation. When his father picked him up from school, Ace took the opportunity to describe his attractions, his feeling unsatisfied dating girls, and the new elation he had with his first boyfriend. His dad, reflecting on his divorce from Ace's mother and the fickleness of relationships, said he was happy that Ace did not wait until he was too old to fully realize the kind of love he wants. By teaching his father about his sexuality, coming out created new ties between the two.

Beyond the Closet?

As social circumstances change, so do the narratives that people use to articulate their identities. Whereas the script of coming out created a "narrative generation"[110] in the late 20th century that set it apart from early generations of gay and lesbian people, we may be witnessing a new shift. Some argue that growing legal equality, social tolerance, and institutional visibility has made the closet less relevant for young gay men and lesbians living in more progressive regions of the United States; in other words, some have moved "beyond the closet."[111] Thus, many young members of sexual minorities report not having ever felt compelled, as those who came of age in the 1970s and earlier did, to pass full time as heterosexual. Instead, those living in urban centers evoke a sense that it is normal and expected to reveal their sexual identity.[112]

Yet, even if homophobia has arguably diminished over time, coming out—whether one-on-one or more publicly—remains a high-risk proposition for many. Many young people who come out to their parents as gay find themselves homeless, contributing to statistics that—in 2012—40 percent of all homeless youth were lesbian, gay, bisexual, or transgender (LGBT), even though they made up only 10 percent of their age group.[113] People who come out to their co-workers may find themselves ostracized or even fired, as discrimination based on sexual orientation is still legal in more than half of US states. The barriers to coming out as transgender are arguably even greater.

A different question from whether or not we have moved beyond the closet is whether the closet has moved beyond sexual orientation. It is to this topic we now turn.

3

Coming Out of Glass Closets

I first met Marilyn Wann—a leading fat liberation activist and author—in 2001 at an annual convention of the National Association to Advance Fat Acceptance (NAAFA). I was excited to meet the author of the irreverent and funny book *FAT!SO? Because You Don't Have to Apologize for Your Size*. Marilyn Wann beckoned me to sit next to her on a comfortable sofa in the lobby of the Cherry Hill Hilton, where the conference was being held. Her eyes twinkled behind a pair of black cat eyeglasses and below hot-pink cropped hair. She wore a hot pink top and jacket with a feathery collar, a black skirt, fishnet stockings, and hot pink boots. I thought back to the page in *FAT! SO?* dedicated to reasons "why you should dye your hair hot pink." These included: "Because being fat sets you apart from the crowd. But being fat and having hot pink hair makes you flabulous," "Because little kids will love you for it. They'll say, 'Mommy, look at the lady with the hot pink hair!' instead of 'Mommy, that lady is fat.' Better still, they'll believe you when you tell them that being fat is cool," and "Because just think of all the people who will smile when they see you."

Smiling myself, I asked Marilyn Wann to tell me about how she got involved in fat acceptance activism. She described a turning point after a "Really Bad Day," during which a romantic interest told her he was embarrassed to introduce her to his friends because of her weight, and she received a letter from Blue Cross refusing her health insurance because she was "morbidly obese." At that point, she realized that

> living in the closet is not working. Skirting this issue is not working. . . . I just decided to come out as a fat person and tried to do it really publicly and really loudly because I just decided that I wasn't going to put up with exclusion. And I wasn't going to put up with it internally, for myself—self-limiting, and that I wasn't going to put up with it in the world, that I was going to confront it and try to do it in a fun sassy way. . . taking a lot of inspiration from drag queens and every fabulous thing like that.

Come Out, Come Out, Whoever You Are. Abigail C. Saguy, Oxford University Press (2020).
© Oxford University Press.
DOI: 10.1093/oso/9780190931650.001.0001

I was struck by Marilyn Wann's choice of words—"living in the closet" and "come out as a fat person"—that were so tightly connected to the gay rights movement. By using this vocabulary, Wann was implicitly making an argument that being fat was somehow similar to being gay. As we talked more and as I spoke to other fat rights activists, I understood that she was arguing that—like sexual orientation—body size is largely determined by biology and that "fatphobia," not fatness itself, is a social problem. Moreover, she was claiming fatness as an identity and politicizing it. On a personal level, just as it is good to be "out and proud" regarding one's gayness, so it is good to be "out and proud" about one's fatness. Such personal politics were intimately linked to a collective goal of reversing weight-based discrimination and stigma.

The fat acceptance movement demonstrates the process by which human traits, such as fatness, become politicized. Like others, Marilyn Wann spent years trying to downplay her difference from others and ignore how people were mistreating her because of her body weight. But her "Really Bad Day" led to an Aha! moment when she decided she needed a new approach. Instead of minimizing her fatness hoping that others would not notice it, she began politicizing it to directly challenge negative stereotypes. The language of "the closet" and "coming out"—developed in gay rights activism—offered an analogy for what she was doing and linked fat acceptance to another, more established, progressive cause.

Disclosing Fat Pride

Because body size is hyper-visible, the idea that one can "come out" as fat initially seems like an oxymoron.[1] Granted, there are some contexts where one's fatness can be hidden—such as online, over the phone, or when one has undergone extreme weight loss but continues to identify as fat. Still, in most contexts fatness is hyper-visible. As writer Roxanne Gay, who writes about being very fat as the daughter of Haitian immigrants in her memoire *Hunger*, explains: "Fat, much like skin color, is something you cannot hide no matter how dark the clothing you wear nor how diligently you avoid horizontal stripes."[2] Working from this same insight, comedian Wanda Sykes wrote a whole skit about the impossibility of "coming out Black," based on the idea that coming out means revealing a hidden identity.[3] Explaining why "it is harder being gay than being Black," she tells the audience to uproarious laughter, "I didn't have to come out Black. I didn't have to sit my parents down and tell them about my blackness. I didn't have to sit them down: 'Mom, Dad, I gotta tell y'all somethin.' I hope you still love me. I'm just gonna say it. 'Mom, Dad, I'm Black.'" She then parodies her mother's hypothetical response: "No! Not Black! Anything but Black, Lord!" And yet, while Sykes treats "come out black" as a joke, fat-identified women *do* talk of coming out as fat. So what do they mean?

When a woman who weighs over 250 pounds talks about when she first "came out" as fat, she is not referring to the day that she shocked and surprised her friends or family with the news that she was fat. Yet coming out as fat is still disclosing something to others. It is revealing that a person identifies—not as a "thin person trapped in a fat body"—but as someone who is and will remain fat. As Roxanne Gay wittily puts it, "I ate that thin woman, and she was delicious but unsatisfying."[4]

Part of the transformation that occurs when individuals politicize body weight is that they come to think of their fatness as a central part of their own identity. Fat acceptance activists talk about coming to identify as fat—rather than thinking of themselves as, in the words of one, "a thin person who just needs to lose twenty pounds." Fatness thus becomes a non-negotiable aspect of self, not a temporary state to be remedied through weight loss. The subtitle of Marilyn Wann's book, "Because You Don't Have to Apologize for Your Size," speaks to this.[5] Revealing an affirmative attitude about fatness is radical in a society in which anti-fat sentiment is so pervasive as to be taken for granted.

Fat rights activists explain that using the word *fat*—as opposed to, say, *overweight, curvy,* or *Rubenesque*—to describe themselves is a key component of coming out. As Marilyn Wann says, "It's the unabashed use of the *fat* word." Other fat rights activists similarly argue that, in the words of one, "if there is marker for me, when I would say I came out as a fat person, it's when I first reclaimed the word *fat*." Marilyn Wann further argues that, after using the term *fat* to self-identify, the next step is to "get [other] people to use the F word. There is nothing inherently bad about the F word. I don't use euphemisms because these reinforce the concept that there is something wrong with fat." The fat acceptance zine "Bogeywomen zine" suggests responding to the statement "You're not fat" by saying "I am fat, honey. Don't assume I'm as terrified of the word and the concept as you are."[6] Similarly, Lisa Tealer—a (biracial) African American plus-size model, plus-size aerobics consultant, diversity consultant, and writer—says that when she meets someone for the first time, she describes herself as a "fat black woman."

When they express surprise, she says she responds by saying "Fat is not a four-letter word. I'm very comfortable with the word *fat*, so feel free to use it. Fabulous And Thick. That's what it stands for." Tealer integrates the word *thick*—commonly used among American blacks to appreciatively denote fleshiness—into the word fat, creatively arguing that FAT is an acronym for Fabulous And Thick.

In the case of fatness, disclosure to others works differently from what Harvey Milk envisioned. It is not that people suddenly realize that they have fat friends. It is that they realize they have *unapologetic* fat friends, who are unwilling to accept second-class citizenship due to their bodily difference. By reclaiming their fatness as their own, people are refusing to be humiliated, shamed, or silenced by their weight. For instance, when a woman tries to cut in front of her in line and calls her a "fat ass" when she protests, Michelle says she "just smiled and said, 'Yes, I've got a fat ass, but you cut in line and I'm first.'" Michelle explains that the woman who cut in front "could not handle the fact that I was absolutely unashamed to be called fat, that that was okay by me because it's just an adjective like thin, tall, short, you know, brown, green, young, old." In most offline contexts, people cannot hide their body size, and many large people live in fear that someone will mention it. They try to be inconspicuous—even allowing someone to cut in front of them—so that people will leave them alone. Because Michelle accepts her fatness, others are unable to use it to silence and oppress her. As she put it, "If someone else can't make me feel bad about myself for being fat, then they can't control me with that."

Lisa Tealer—quoted above—recounts an incident with a new gynecologist, which she also shares in corporate workshops about weight-based discrimination, that speaks to how fat acceptance can be empowering. At the start of the appointment, after the doctor tried to engage her in a conversation about her weight, Tealer informed her that she was part of the "size diversity community" and that her weight "was not up for discussion." She told the doctor, "I'm very happy with who I am, and what I look like." Tealer recounts that the doctor "waited until she got me into the stirrups and decided to lecture me about my weight." She describes the scene:

> She waited 'til she puts the speculum in and decided to start telling me about, you know, estrogen levels and, you know, obesity leads to diabetes. And, I'm like, okay, now, I just told this woman that my weight is not up for discussion, I'm sitting here on the table, what am I gonna do?

Tealer says she "kind of went somewhere else" and took a month to write a letter of complaint because she was so traumatized. But she did ultimately write to the director of the clinic and reported the doctor to the state. The doctor was no longer working there at the time of our interview. Tealer attributes her ability to stand up for herself to her involvement in the fat acceptance movement.

In unapologetically coming out as fat, people reject cultural attitudes that fatness is unhealthy, immoral, ugly, or otherwise undesirable. They claim the right to define the meaning of their own bodies and to stake out new cultural meanings and practices around body size. Queer theorists have similarly challenged meanings of disability. For instance, Robert McRuer argued that asking deaf people: "Wouldn't you rather be hearing?" reinforces "compulsory able-bodiedness." In response, McRuer called for "coming out crip," where crip (short for crippled) functions as an appropriation of a derogatory term for disabled.[7] As with fat, coming out in this context means affirming and valorizing a stigmatized and highly visible trait.

Stigma and Visibility

Fat rights activists are innovating by using *the closet* and *come out* in a novel way. Rather than revealing to others that they are fat, they use *coming out* as fat to mean rejecting the negative stigma and shame commonly associated with fatness. They mean refusing to apologize, refusing to be shamed.

Yet we should not exaggerate the extent to which coming out as fat is an exception. In fact, this case can help query the role visibility plays in coming out more generally. We typically speak of coming out as gay or lesbian to refer to revealing to family and friends (or others) that one is gay. This is what Harvey Milk had in mind when he urged people to come out. Yet many people—particularly those who are gender nonconforming—may be assumed, rightly or wrongly, to be gay or lesbian. Effeminate men, for instance, are often assumed to be gay, while masculine-presenting women may be presumed to be lesbian. Queer theorist Eve Sedgwick uses the term "glass closet" to refer to people whose gender nonconformity makes them visibly gay, despite failed attempts to conceal their sexual orientation.[8]

Men in feminized professions, such as nursing or hair styling are often (correctly or incorrectly) assumed to be gay,[9] while women in male-dominated trades such as construction are presumed to be lesbian.[10]

Moreover, what counts as effeminate or masculine varies by social context. The situational comedy *Seinfeld* riffed on this in an episode in which Jerry Seinfeld begins to carry a "carryall"—a handbag for men. His friends and neighbors tease him for carrying a "purse," calling him a "dandy." "It's not a purse!" he protests, "It's European!" My husband—who is French—moved to the United States and was surprised to learn that wearing salmon-colored shirts and paisley ties marked him as effeminate, rather than fashionable, in corporate America. In other words, gender and sexuality are "read" differently across national contexts.

More to the point, coming out has never been *only* about revealing a hidden identity. It is about *proudly* reclaiming this identity. Remember Kendell—the young black man working as an activist and aspiring to law school we met in Chapter 2—and how he defines coming out. He describes it as "basically presenting yourself as a member of the LGBT community unabashedly." Thus community and pride—and not just disclosure—are an integral part of coming out.

Fat Community

As with people coming to identify as gay or lesbian, community plays a crucial role in this shift of perspective. Socializing with other fat people allows fat rights activists to embrace their own fatness. Michelle—who, as we learned above, told a woman at the post office that she did have a fat ass but was still before her in line—says she was not always able to assert herself like this. Before she joined NAAFA she says she felt she would not find love or professional success as long as she was fat. Her involvement in NAAFA allowed her to "free the shackles with all the other personal restraints that I put in my life." After joining NAAFA, Michelle got a steady boyfriend, completed her BA, and was considering getting a higher degree.

Sherry—a fat-identified woman and physical trainer at an exercise program tailored for heavy women—describes showing up for an NAAFA national convention meeting for the first time as her own *coming out*:

> The idea of walking into a NAAFA convention is really scary, and so I think even walking into one is kind of empowering because you're admitting you're fat out loud. Even though you may look fat, it's hard to admit it. As we talk about it in NAAFA, it's coming out as a fat person. I've had that

conversation with more than one person, and they understood what I was talking about.

Sherry joined NAAFA on the recommendation of the founder of an exercise program for large women, who had previously recruited and trained her to work as a trainer. Until getting involved with the fitness center and then joining NAAFA, Sherry did not have fat friends. She explained that, alone, as a fat person, she had hoped that she might "disappear" but that in groups of two or more "you're definitely going to be made fun of." But the great thing about having fat friends, she said, is that "they can actually give me clothes."

"Fat-pride community," is, however, in the words of Marilyn Wann, "very grassroots and small. It's not even a lawn. It's a few blades of grass." In spring 2018, NAAFA was no longer holding its annual convention and had announced on its website that it would "not be hosting a conference/convention in the near future," because "the expenses associated with coordinating and guaranteeing a physical event have increased to the point that they are more than the organization can afford at present."[11] In June 2019, however, it held a 50th anniversary conference in Las Vegas.

In the absence of physical communities, fat-pride community has formed online—on list servers, blogs, and websites. Before that, books provided an outlet and conduit for fat acceptance. Joy Nash, a millennial actress and comedian, was attending the University of Southern California (USC) where she completed a BA in sociolinguistics when she produced the short film *Fat Rant* for a film class; the film went viral on YouTube. Nash said that before making her film, she had never been to a fat acceptance meeting. Yet she had read classic fat acceptance books such as the anthology *Shadow on a Tightrope* and Marilyn Wann's *FAT!SO?* As a result, she said she "knew that [she] wasn't alone."[12] This knowledge helped embolden her to produce her *Fat Rant*, in which she declared that at 5'8" and 250 pounds, she was "fat": "I'm fat and it's OK. It doesn't mean that I'm stupid or ugly or selfish or lazy. I'm fat . . . F-A-T. It's three little letters. What are you so afraid of?" Other fat acceptance activists similarly spoke of feeling part of a virtual community.

Yet the lack of offline community may contribute to the reasons the fat acceptance movement has not yet developed a strong counterculture. Marilyn Wann addressed this in a 2009 email to me, saying that "fat people have yet to find a point of anger that would mean no turning back. Fat people still go along with blaming ourselves—rather than blaming the prejudice against us—when we're treated as second-class or untouchable." For instance, Marilyn shared a story about how—at a NAAFA convention—she joked about "how Slim-Fast is self-hatred in a can, and [later learned that] a woman sitting nearby leaned over to another NAAFA member and confided, 'I've drunk a Slim-Fast every morning since I've been here.'" I heard similar stories from other fat acceptance activists, who said they knew many NAAFA members who claim to embrace fat acceptance while continuing to diet.

Just as many fat people, including members of fat acceptance associations, would rather be thin, prefer thin mates, and hope to have thin children, blind people—who also do not have a common culture, history, or language—tend to shun the company of other blind people, seek sighted mates, and do not wish to transmit their blindness to their children.[13] In contrast, members of the deaf world—who have a vibrant culture, their own language, and pride in their deafness—prefer to socialize with and marry other deaf people and often hope to have deaf children.[14]

Wann and others describe the contemporary fat-acceptance movement as "pre-Stonewall," implying that it is early in its development and that it will—over time—become more radical. Yet, as we saw in the previous chapter, there was a lively gay community prior to the riots in Stonewall. Indeed, the Stonewall Inn was one of many offline places where gay men, butch lesbians, drag queens, and transgender people congregated. It is unclear how the fat-acceptance movement will become more radical given its continued failure to create a vibrant offline community. Dieting groups, such as Weight Watchers or Overeaters Anonymous, could—in theory—provide constituents for such a movement, in that they bring together large numbers of women who see themselves as fat. Yet many of these women have average—or somewhat higher than average—weight. Moreover, they come to these groups because they are committed to exiting the category of fat, undermining their capacity to develop fat pride.

Positive Self-Identification

People are unlikely to learn fat pride at home, even—or especially—if they have fat parents. Gay, lesbian, or bisexual youth often learn homophobia or simply *heteronormativity*—the idea that heterosexuality is normal—from a young age from their heterosexual parents. They not only risk rejection from their family if and when they come out as gay, but they also are likely to in-ternalize shame around their sexual desires. In contrast, fat kids often have fat parents, due to the strong genetic component for body size.[15] Yet given the ubiquitous nature of anti-fat sentiment, they are extremely *unlikely* to have fat-*accepting* parents. They thus often learn fat hatred from parents who themselves struggle with internalized fat shame.

Indeed, I heard horror stories about chubby children being put on weight-loss diets from a tender age. During an interview in a Manhattan park on a beautiful sunny fall day, Sherry—the physical trainer we met above—said that she was put on a diet when she was three months old. She laughed nervously and explained: "My mother hates when I mention that. 'Well mom, all I have to do is tell people how old I was when you first put me on a diet.' [My mom] says, 'But the doctor said [to do it].' Yeah, they said that I was gaining weight too fast." Based on the doctor's recommendation, Sherry's mother fed her watered-down infant formula. That was the first of many childhood weight-loss diets imposed by Sherry's mother, with the encouragement of the family pediatrician. Sherry explained, through tears, that her earliest memories were of being ravenously hungry and of her mother denying her the sustenance she craved, setting her up for a lifetime of disordered eating, a deep sense of deprivation of maternal love, and difficulty advocating for herself.

It thus makes sense that, as in the case of being gay, coming out as fat requires overcoming internalized shame and affirming one's own right to love, food, and happiness. Several fat rights activists argued that they needed to develop positive self-esteem before they could integrate and accept their fatness. It was also a prerequisite for political activism. That is, before you can be an activist, you have to be individually empowered.

Political Strategies and Social Networks

Ironically, fat women did not found the largest national fat acceptance association—NAAFA. Rather, the founder was Bill Fabrey, a white, heterosexual man of average body size. Bill Fabrey's connection to this issue is that he identifies as a "fat admirer" or "FA," a man romantically attracted to very large women.

I met Fabrey—a retired engineer—at the same 2001 NAAFA convention in Cherry Hill, New Jersey, where I met Marilyn Wann. Fabrey was working at a stand at the "Trade Sale" with his (second) wife Nancy Summer. We chatted a bit at the stand before sitting down to do a formal interview. He told me how he unfairly gets more credit than his wife for whatever project—such as writing a column—he and his wife jointly undertake because he "has a penis." Even when she does things on her own—such as making a NAAFA workbook—people assume he did it.

Fabrey recounted to me the story of when he first realized he was an FA, his narrative closely resembling the coming out stories of gay men and lesbians. He said that he "had always felt that way" as a child. He told me that "coming out was difficult, but I did it at the age of twelve." When he shared his feelings with his mother, she told him, "after she got over her shock," that he was simply "going through a phase," echoing how parents respond to children who come out as gay. He said it took his parents 20 years to come to terms with his—he hesitates, searching for the right word, and then says—"taste."

Given the similarities between coming out as gay and coming out as an FA—both of which involve disclosing a stigmatized form of sexual desire—I initially thought fat admirers may have been the conduit by which talk of coming out traveled between gay rights activism and fat rights activism. However, it turned out that the influence ran the other way. Bill Fabrey said that he only started talking about his "coming out experience" after hearing "fat feminists" and specifically lesbian and queer feminists talk of coming out as fat: "I never thought of it until they used it," he says.

Indeed, lesbians, queer women, and gender-queer people have been disproportionately involved in fat rights activism, so that gay liberation rhetoric was woven into the history of fat liberation from the start.[16] In the early 1970s, feminist lesbians founded the radical feminist fat rights group, the Feminist Underground (FU)[17] and, in the 1980s, the Fat Feminism Caucus of NAAFA.[18] Since then, lesbians and bisexual women have organized and supported scores of San Francisco-based fat activist groups, including performance groups such as the Fat Lip Readers Theater, Big Burlesque, Fat Bottom Revue, Bod Squad, Big Moves, the Padded Lilies, the Fat Women's Swim, *Radiance* magazine, and the Fat Girl zine.[19] There have also been queer cultural and fat positive events, such as Fat Girl Speaks—organized in Portland in the late 1990s and early 2000s—and the National Association for Lesbians of SizE (NOLOSE).

A 1983 anthology, *Shadow on a Tightrope: Writings by Women on Fat Oppression*, included several essays that were part of a literature package developed by the Fat Underground in the 1970s as well as others written more recently.[20] One of the essays from this volume is titled "Coming Out: Notes on Fat Lesbian Pride." In the essay, "thunder" offers a "personal narrative" of "the process of coming out as a fat woman."[21] She writes about "coming out as a lesbian" and calling herself "a radical dyke with pride" but that "coming out as a fat woman acknowledging my size, accepting it, feeling proud and gaining strength has been a longer journey, and in many ways a lonelier one.[22] Thunder writes about how her siblings called her "ali baba and the forty chins" and how her mother disavowed thunder's weight gain as a teenager by refusing to buy her larger-sized clothes, while encouraging her to join Weight Watchers and, when that failed, see a diet doctor. Thunder writes about how her mother's effort to change her made her feel ashamed and angry but that she ultimately was able to overcome her shame to go "from *being* a fat woman to *coming out* as a fat woman."[23] Thunder concludes her essay: "We must first overcome our own self-hate, and then develop an analysis of fat that takes into consideration women's power and societal attitudes about that power."[24]

In contrast to thunder's tale of overcoming shame, NAAFA founder Bill Fabrey recounted how fortunate he was that his parents were always extremely supportive, telling him he could accomplish anything to which he set his mind—despite disapproving of his taste in women. Fabrey credited this loving support—which he says most fat women never get—to the fact that he was able to found NAAFA. Fabrey said that the precipitating event that led him to found NAAFA in 1969 was the *New York Times'* refusal to publish the announcement of his marriage to his first wife, who weighed 350 pounds. He said that the prestigious newspaper had published announcements of couples with similar social backgrounds; he was convinced that the only reason it declined his wedding announcement was because of his wife's weight. To protest the weight-based discrimination faced by women such as his wife and the courtesy stigma that FAs suffer due to their association with very fat women, Fabrey founded NAAFA, originally called the National Association to Aid Fat Americans.[25]

While Bill Fabrey initially envisioned NAAFA as a civil rights organization, modeled after the National Association for the Advancement of Colored People (NAACP), the organization quickly responded to more social needs. For instance, at the NAAFA conference in August 2001, I was hard-pressed to find a panel on political activism. There was a panel on commercial flying and fat rights, but it was more about learning your rights as a consumer—when, for instance, you cannot fit into a standard seat in an airplane—than about becoming an activist yourself on this issue. There was also a round-table on chapter leadership and a panel called "shout it from the rooftops" about "how to talk with the people around you about size acceptance and the impact NAAFA has made on your life," according to the NAAFA conference program. This is arguably personal politics but not traditional lobbying.

Instead, most panels were social in nature. There were several sessions on self-esteem or "body esteem" and a session on self-empowerment called "worth your weight." There was a session on "how to build a successful on-line business," a session discussing the medical risks of weight-loss surgery, and a session on "fitness at any size." There were also various exercise classes offered throughout the long weekend, including a chair dancing class and a water aerobics class. In the evening, from 8:00 to 10:00 PM, various "affinity groups" met to discuss topics including chat rooms, using the internet, and "putting a face to a name—meeting folks from the NAAFA discussion board." At 10:00 PM, there was a pool party, followed by late night parties in the hospitality suite. There was also an auction and a fashion show, in which fat women strutted across the catwalk, sporting clothes sold by vendors at the conference. The people I met there told me that most people who join NAAFA or attend a conference come to find romance, friendship, and self-esteem. They generally do not intend to become activists.

Indeed, there were several sessions focused specifically on romance—many implicitly assuming heterosexual romance. A session entitled "Healthy Relationships 101" was open to anyone, but several sessions—presumably for people interested in opposite-sex relationships—were closed to either men or to women. A session on dating for "BBW" (Big Beautiful Women) was closed to men, and a session for FAs called "guide to supersize care" was closed to women.

Bill Fabrey explained to me by email in December 2009 that "there has always been a disconnect between NAAFA leadership and its members." While NAAFA leaders have generally been, in his view, politically liberal in general and supportive of sexual minorities specifically, "rank-and-file NAAFA members have always been people who are not intellectuals, are not particularly liberal in their politics (although there are variations throughout the political spectrum), and have trouble dealing with controversy or more than one minority issue at a time."

Bill Fabrey further explained that in the early years of the movement, NAAFA leaders avoided talk of "coming out" as fat precisely because the term was associated with members of sexual minorities, and they did not want to alienate rank-and-file members. Over time, however, NAAFA leaders—including Fabrey—have been more willing to link their cause to that of the gay rights movement. Like other NAAFA leaders, Bill Fabrey said he has always been "supportive of gays and lesbians." He attributed this to his "own minority sexual preference of being an FA, and realizing the similarities [of his own experiences] to what [members of sexual minorities] faced in society and their families." He proudly recounted how his second wife, her lesbian romantic partner, and a few other lesbian friends named him an "honorary lesbian." Among early usages of the term "coming out" in NAAFA newsletters was an article without a byline, but which Bill Fabrey said he wrote. It described how "the first NAAFA office was located in Fabrey's spare bathroom, and the membership file was maintained in their walk-in closet . . . (Talk about fat people and their admirers coming out of the closet!)."[26]

Like Bill Fabrey, those who eventually started talking about coming out as fat or as fat admirers were typically socially connected—in some way—to people who identified as gay, lesbian, or queer. The earliest mention I found—with Fabrey's help—to "coming out" in old NAAFA newsletters was in the spring/summer of 1981. There, Kimm Bonner—then chair of the New England chapter of NAAFA—explained: "Personally—what I've gotten out of this [joining NAAFA] is to come out of the closet—I feel really good about who I am. I've been able to tell everyone in my life—family, friends, people at work that 'Hey—this is me—if I like it, you should accept it too.' "[27] Kimm Bonner says that her motivation "must have come from the gay movement" and that she has "several friends who are gay."

The next reference I found, in NAAFA newsletters, to coming out as fat was in 1988. In this newsletter, then-executive director Sally E. Smith wrote, "In my first year at NAAFA, I came out of the closet on size acceptance issues."[28] When I asked how she came to talk of "coming out as fat," Sally Smith explained that she worked for LIFE (Lobby for Individual Freedom and Equality), an umbrella group of primarily gay and lesbian organizations whose mission was to lobby for responsible AIDS legislation. She said that she was "sure that being immersed in (what was at the time) a gay rights issue provided a prism with which to view my experience."[29]

As more fat rights activists spoke of coming out as fat and talk of "coming out" began to be integrated into US culture more broadly, people without direct ties to queer politics also began framing their experiences in this way. Barbara Altman Bruno spoke of coming out as fat in both the 1993 and 1995 NAAFA newsletters. In 1993, she wrote that "it takes most people a period of time before they will 'come out' as fat people, and join NAAFA."[30] In 1995, she wrote: "Your 'coming out' process [as fat people] may have taken many years, perhaps decades."[31] Bruno, who described herself as straight and "happily married for 32 years" at the time of the interview, says that she may have picked it up from one or several NAAFA board members who were living in San Francisco, where "*coming out* was a common term."[32] Indeed, fat acceptance activism has been especially active in San Francisco, the capital of gay rights activism.[33]

In 2006, Kathy Barron wrote about coming to realize that many fat people are " 'in the closet' in terms of acknowledging themselves as fat," and urged "all NAAFA members to come out as proud fat people and fat activists."[34] She attributes her use of the expression to the fact that she "used to hang out a lot in Hank's Gab Café (on Marilyn [Wann's] FAT!SO? website)," saying, "I'm sure that Marilyn had something to do with it—she has been a huge inspiration to me and a driving force in much of my fat activism."[35] Marilyn Wann, in turn, says that her website and earlier zine was inspired by her gay male friends in Queer Nation, who took her to "politicized/punk drag shows and other gay community stuff."[36] She said she drew inspiration from queer zines being produced in San Francisco at the time, including Diseased Pariah News and Hothead Paisan: Homicidal Lesbian Terrorist. Marilyn Wann noted that when she began printing FAT!SO? in July of 1994, she used the "fat dyke community as a major support for [her] work."[37] "Even now," said Wann, "when I think of local fat activist community, most of the people I turn to are fat and queer women or gender-queer people."[38] The fact that certain types of people—specifically those connected to gay rights activism—have been on the forefront of talking of coming out as fat points to how different kinds of identity politics are interconnected and how political strategies move across social networks.

The case of fat rights activism shows the power in the idea that someone can come out of the closet as a specific kind of person, thereby refusing to be shamed or silenced. As we will see in Chapter 4, the idea of coming out as a particular kind of person is also being used to mobilize undocumented youth, who have a lot to lose by revealing their undocumented status.

4

Overcoming Fear

People identifying as queer, lesbian, or gay have made legal gains that offer some measure of safety to those coming out as a member of a sexual minority. In contrast, overcoming the fear associated with disclosing one's undocumented status remains a huge hurdle for coming out as undocumented. Undocumented youth recognize that by revealing their immigration status to others, they risk their own—and potentially their undocumented family members'—deportation.[1] These deportation fears compose one distinct aspect of their immigration status.[2] While always a risk, deportation threats have become particularly salient over the past two decades, as deportation rates have risen in part due to the proliferation of partnerships between local police and immigration enforcement officials.[3] Undocumented immigrants and their family members have responded by adapting their everyday activities to avoid police or immigration enforcement officials and by keeping their immigration status a secret.[4] This fear has constituted a major obstacle in organizing undocumented immigrant youth.

Facing these challenges, the undocumented immigrant youth movement has used the concept of coming out as undocumented to help embolden undocumented immigrant youth to disclose their status and mobilize for inclusive policies. This movement has largely revolved around advocacy for the federal DREAM Act. First introduced in 2001, the federal DREAM Act aims to create a pathway to legalization for undocumented youth to come to the United States as children. Most versions would allow undocumented young adults under the age of 35 years to legalize their immigration status if they entered the United States before the age of 16 years, have lived in the United States for at least five years, obtained a high school diploma or equivalent, and spent at least two years in higher education or in the military. In 2017, the DREAM Act would have made approximately 2 million undocumented youth eligible to legalize their immigration status.[5]

The federal DREAM Act and other integrative laws, such as state laws that increased the access of undocumented young people to higher education, have been inspired by the stories of undocumented youth.[6] Tereza Lee, an

Come Out, Come Out, Whoever You Are. Abigail C. Saguy, Oxford University Press (2020).
© Oxford University Press.
DOI: 10.1093/oso/9780190931650.001.0001

undocumented high school student and piano prodigy trying to figure out how to attend college without a social security number, inspired the original Senate version of the federal DREAM Act. Senator Dick Durbin prepared to introduce a private immigration bill that would have granted her legal status; this morphed into what is now known as the DREAM Act. She remembers, "Some other undocumented students heard about this [private] bill and they would approach him in the parking lot secretly and tell him they're also undocumented, 'Can you write a bill for [us] too?' and Sen. Durbin realized he needed to redraft the bill into a larger bill and that became the DREAM Act."[7]

Eighteen years later, the federal DREAM Act is still not law. But it has fueled the emergence of the undocumented immigrant youth movement. The fight has dragged on as immigration has become an increasingly divisive topic of public debate. In January 2018, a Democratic move to attach the DREAM Act to a spending bill led to a three-day government shutdown.[8] Even if there has not (yet) been success in passing the DREAM Act, the undocumented immigrant youth movement has shifted cultural understandings of undocumented immigrant youth. Gallup polls show increasing support for the key points of the DREAM Act, ranging from 54 percent in 2010 to 65 percent in 2015 to 84 percent in 2016.[9] Immigrant youth have achieved this by offering an alternative image of "illegal immigrants" sneaking across the border—that of educated and talented "DREAMers."[10] Even as the DREAM Act remains elusive, reframing the nature and character of undocumented immigrants has important material consequences.

Before examining how the undocumented immigrant youth movement has used the concept of coming out to overcome fear and mobilize constituents, let us take a closer look at how undocumented immigrant youth internalize fear of disclosure.

Learning to Hide and Seek

Undocumented immigrant youth learn early about the risks of disclosure. Just as parents teach their children not to run into the street, parents of undocumented children teach them to hide their undocumented status. Karla, whose family migrated to the United States when she was 14 years old, speaks to this. Her dad traveled back and forth between Mexico and the United States several times in search of economic opportunities to support his family. Unlike many undocumented young adults who migrated at younger ages, Karla remembers helping influence the family decision to move to the United States so that they could be together. She knew that she would be undocumented but says she thought that she would still have more opportunities in this country. Talking to Laura E. Enriquez in 2008 at a Starbucks in Los Angeles, Karla discusses learning early to hide her immigration status:

> One thing that my parents made sure to tell me was, to be good, a good kid in school, not get into any trouble because I wasn't the same as everyone else. And I know they were trying to do it to protect me, [reasoning] "I don't want my kid to get detained and be deported." But that was sort of like a fear that I had for a long time. All I remember was my parents telling me, "Don't tell anyone that you were born in Mexico. If anyone asks, you were born here, but you were taken to Mexico and then now you're back."

Karla's parents were keenly aware of the dangers of Karla disclosing her undocumented status, namely, that she or her family members could be deported, a risk that does not exist for the other groups discussed in this book. Throughout high school, Karla struggled to balance hiding this secret with her need to find support to pursue her studies. Karla recalls spending her first week of high school crying alone because she could not speak English. As she gained mastery of the English language and advanced in her high school classes, Karla dreamed of attending college. This near-impossible feat became more achievable in 2002, when she graduated from high school and California Assembly Bill 540 went into effect, allowing her to pay more affordable in-state tuition rates.

Karla enrolled in community college and remembers learning about the federal DREAM Act during her first year. A student from her political science class approached her on the bus and asked her to sign a petition: "She explained to me, oh this is the DREAM Act, what we do, you should support." Karla signed and asked for more copies. She remembers going to a copy center to make more "because I was just like, I gotta do something." Her peer was taken aback when Karla handed over 300 signed copies a few days later. Karla remembers, "And that's when I told her [I was undocumented]. Because she opened up to me and she was like, 'I'm undocumented so this will help me.' And I said, 'okay it will help me too.'" This student was the first person Karla had told at her community college. Telling the student about her status felt important because the student had trusted Karla but also because this newly proposed legislation had the potential to help Karla find

social and legal support. Looking back, Karla suspects this was "the beginning of figuring out who I am."

Soon after this, Karla got involved with a budding undocumented student
organization at the community college and worked with them to campaign
for the DREAM Act. She slowly began to be "open about my situation" to
professors. These supportive interactions made it easier to set aside prior
messages to conceal her immigration status. After she transferred, Karla
helped establish an undocumented student organization at her new university, sharing her story to raise awareness on her campus and beginning to
collaborate with undocumented youth at other universities.

Around the time Karla was organizing her fellow undocumented
students at a California state university, undocumented students at the
University of California-Los Angeles (UCLA) became some of the first
to publicly share their stories. While fear kept most silent, a few brave
souls began to reveal their immigration status as they sought support—
emotional support from their undocumented peers, substantive support
from professors and their university administration, and legislative support from their elected officials. Some were featured in a 2006 *Los Angeles
Times* article, "The Invisibles." Protected by pseudonyms, they talked
about their migration journeys, their work to create IDEAS (Improving
Dreams Equality Access and Success, a club established in 2007 to advocate for undocumented students on campus), their struggles to pay for
and finish their education, their future dreams, and their desperate need
for the federal DREAM Act to create a pathway to legalization.[11] Stark
photographs—college scenes with cut out human figures—accompanied
their stories. Their work continued with actions on campus, including a
mock graduation in which undocumented and allied students rallied to
raise awareness and foster support for the federal DREAM Act.

Within the context of a UCLA course on undocumented students, students
authored an 84-page book entitled, *Underground Undergrads: UCLA
Undocumented Immigrant Students Speak Out.*[12] The volume—developed
from 2006 to 2008—featured profiles of undocumented students sharing
their migration journeys, their struggle to pursue higher education, and
the importance of creating a pathway to legalization. The students were
bold but not without caution. The cover featured a student's profile in full
shadow, backlit by spotlights illuminating a UCLA building in the background. All entries about currently undocumented students featured an in-
troductory line, "A pseudonym has been used to protect the identity of the

person profiled." Their photos were always from behind or showing them as children.

One of the final entries featured the testimony of Tam Tran, "a courageous undocumented student who had testified twice before Congress." Tam Tran shared her unique migration journey. An American-raised Vietnamese refugee born in Germany, she had been ordered deported, but with no country to be deported to, she would be forever undocumented without the federal DREAM Act. Despite being afraid and uncomfortable testifying, Tam Tran agreed to represent her friends, who, due to deportation fears, "could only be here today through a blurred face in a video."

Tam Tran's inspiring and poetic testimony was followed by newspaper articles in the *Los Angeles Times* and *USA Today*—"Three days after a 24-year-old college graduate spoke out on her immigration plight . . . , U.S. agents arrested her family." When Tam arrived home from her trip to Washington, she learned that her father, mother, and brother had all been taken into immigration custody. In the coverage, US Representative Zoe Lofgren, who invited Tam to speak, accused immigration officials of "witness intimidation." Tam Tran's family was released a few days later, but the message was clear—there are real reasons to be afraid to speak out. While their book was in production, the students' hopes were dashed when Congress failed to pass the DREAM Act, yet again.

Still, their efforts began to transform the landscape that undocumented students face on campus. Daniel—a Korean undocumented student who started at UCLA in 2007—remembers finding out that he was undocumented during his senior year in high school:

> When I was applying to UCLA, . . . for my social security number I didn't know what to write. So I asked my dad what it was, and obviously he didn't have [an] answer for me except just to tell me that I didn't have one. . . . He brought out this paper from the USCIS, and it pretty much said that our family's visa had expired.

Daniel learned that his family's visas were revoked after nine years because their sponsor had mismanaged their paperwork. He kept this to himself. He said, "For about a year or two I never wanted to speak out, you know? I was always doing the marching band things. I was always into school, but I didn't want to tell others about my status." He explains that after his parents told him he was undocumented, "They told me to not tell anybody. You know, don't rock the boat." He categorizes this as "very typical." Though later than Karla, Daniel also learned to hide.

This changed one fateful day when, as a UCLA sophomore, Daniel saw an announcement in the school newspaper—IDEAS was offering a scholarship for undocumented students. He applied and was awarded one. He joined IDEAS so that he could be part of the group and "do something about it." It was spring of 2009 and the federal DREAM Act had been reintroduced in Congress. He recalls, "I didn't want to tell others about my status until I got involved with IDEAS. Students in IDEAS, they were very comfortable about their statuses. They were out there at marches, rallies. They were giving speeches in public. And so when I saw them, I thought . . . maybe I can do it too."

Daniel soon began telling others about his immigration status to garner support for the DREAM Act. He gave his testimony at his marching band fraternity meeting: "a lot of people were shocked. But at the same time very supportive." Underscoring the power of coming out, his fraternity brothers signed 40 postcards asking Congress to pass the DREAM Act. A member of IDEAS recruited Daniel to speak at a legislative visit with a local congressman who had yet to commit to voting for the DREAM Act. After the visit, another undocumented student in attendance asked him if he would like to speak at a dream graduation rally and press conference that would be held at Los Angeles City Hall.

Daniel remembers being "kind of hesitant, because, you know, I was scared." He worried about what could happen if things went badly. But he ultimately agreed, telling himself, "I've got to do it. Especially with the lack of involvement with the Asian community, I felt it was my obligation to step up and help out in any way." He and other activists saw his participation as particularly important in highlighting the diversity of undocumented experiences. People needed to know it is not just a Latino issue, they reasoned. Asian and Pacific Islander experiences and voices also needed to be included. It was in this context that Daniel decided to put his body on the line to ensure that his community was represented. Still, he was fearful: "The night before I was really thinking about it. And I actually even wrote a little will, like a little note and kept it on my desk. Just in case I get deported or whatever. That's how I felt. What if shit goes down! I wrote some things, just in case something happens."

The rally was powerful. Over a hundred people—mostly college students from across southern California—stood packed together on the steps of the city hall. Many wore graduation caps and gowns and held signs: "Our dreams can't wait," "We are human," "My dream the American dream," "Citizenship Yes! Deportation No!" Speakers stepped up to a small podium to give their testimonies from behind a yellow poster board, "PASS THE DREAM ACT NOW" (see Figure 4.1). There were over a dozen news cameras trained on them. The speakers were mostly students like Daniel who passionately recounted their achievements and the doors that have been slammed shut in their faces. In front, a line of students dressed in caps and gowns held individual letters: "NOW WHAT?" Others held mock diplomas or certificates declaring future careers. The press conference ended, and the group marched around the area, chanting. Some of the leaders and featured speakers, including Daniel, talked with the press. The scene foreshadowed what was to occur at future coming out rallies.

As Daniel became more public, his parents continued to caution him, saying, "Why do you have to go out there and at rallies when you know you're putting us in danger and [creating] the possibility of facing deportation? Don't do it." Daniel suggests that this reaction was "very typical . . . coming from an Asian family." He explains, "Still, 'til this day, you don't have that many Asian undocumented students out in public. There's always that stigma in our community." While Daniel spoke out, fear and stigma keep many

Figure 4.1. Undocumented students protest for passage of the Dream Act.

others quiet. People talked about the students and families targeted by immigration enforcement after publicly sharing their stories. Though a few years had passed, Los Angeles networks still buzzed with memories of Tam's family's detention.

Still, Karla and Daniel—along with a growing group of immigrant youth leaders—cautiously shared their stories. This happened slowly, as they met other undocumented students, formed undocumented student organizations, sought institutional support, and waded into legislative advocacy. They became admired as brave and inspiring leaders who set aside fear-driven messages to hide their immigration status because their lives depend on it.

It's Time to Come Out

Their advocacy pushed legislators to reintroduce the federal Dream Act in spring 2009. Immigrant youth activists dreamed of new methods to draw out more undocumented youth and bring in new supporters. Immigrant youth-led organizations began to coordinate nationally. In January 2010, four immigrant youth from Florida—Felipe Matos, Gaby Pacheco, Carlos Roa, and Juan Rodriguez—started off on the Trail of Dreams, trekking four months and 1,500 miles from Miami to Washington, D.C. on foot. Their goal: "challenging the distorted depiction of immigrants in this country . . . [and] dispel[ing] the myths by talking to the average American."[13] Sometimes their conversations changed the minds of virulent anti-immigrants or inspired the immigrant community members to join them for a few miles of their journey. Other times they were not so lucky. But still, Gaby Pacheco remembered it as "creating change one step at a time."

David, a leader from Chicago's Immigrant Youth Justice League (IYJL), recalls how the Trail of Dreams inspired him and other undocumented students and youth: "We were talking about the Trail of Dreams and we were trying to think of things we could do in Chicago that would be similar to the Trail of Dreams, something that would inspire people to join us." They decided to hold a rally. Within a few months this idea morphed into a nationwide campaign to mobilize undocumented youth to "Come Out of the Shadows."

IYJL had formed just a few months before, in late 2009, organized "by a group of undocumented students who came together to stop the deportation of the organization's co-founder."[14] Undocumented youth gathered to hold rallies, speak to the media, and fight to stop the deportation of one of their peers. Unlike in California, most states at this time had not passed laws to facilitate undocumented students' access to higher education and so there were no established undocumented student organizations. This was the first time that many of these Chicago undocumented students found themselves in spaces with other undocumented youth. Lulu, another one of IYJL's co-founders, recalls early meetings where there was almost a craving to talk about one's undocumented status:

> Most of the people there had never had a space to share their stories as un-documented [youth], and a lot of people actually came out as being un-documented [there]. . . . That was supposed to be the first 15 minutes, you know, the introduction portion of . . . the agenda. And it turned into like a two-hour conversation of . . . just being able to share stories of each other. And it was a really, really intense first meeting.

This led to subsequent "Shout it Out" events with the express purpose of sto-rytelling among undocumented youth and a decision to "organize just some-thing bigger."

Activists latched onto the idea of having a public rally on March 10, 2010. They remembered the immigrant rights rallies that had been held on that day in 2006 to oppose the proposed Sensenbrenner bill (H.R. 4437), which crim-inalized undocumented immigrants and their communities, by criminal-izing the violation of immigration law, expanding immigration enforcement, and making it a crime to provide assistance to undocumented immigrants. Chicago's march on March 10, 2006, was followed by the mass mobiliza-tion of immigrant communities leading up to nationwide marches on May 1, 2006.

IYJL leaders decided to "reclaim that day" but were unsure what exactly they would do. One leader, Uriel, recalls:

> We had a lot of discussions amongst ourselves. And really a lot of it was shaped from Harvey Milk, a former city council member of San Francisco who has given this speech and really was a big advocate for the LGBT com-munity to come out and organize, and participate in the public life and the political life. . . . If you don't come out nobody's gonna know that you're there. . . . They're gonna say or do whatever they want because nobody's standing up, and you're not standing up for yourself.

They drew inspiration from Harvey Milk's famous speech, reviewed in Chapter 2, in which he exhorts gay men and lesbians to come out to their parents and friends, and fellow workers to "break down the myth and destroy the lies and distortions. For your sake, for their sake. For the sake of all the youngsters who've been scared." Harvey Milk's use of the plural imperative in "let's break down the myth and destroy the lies and distortions" promises to supplant isolation with solidarity, not only with other undocumented youth—and with the earlier LGBTQ movement—but also with the broader US civil sphere. Citing this quote in their call to action, leaders urged their peers to "come out" with the hope of empowering undocumented youth to overcome their fears and actively participate in the movement. As Lulu summarizes, they hoped "to give a face to this issue that exists, instead of just dealing with numbers."

Just as fat queer women helped diffuse coming out politics from gay rights to fat rights, so undocumented queer people—who have taken up the moniker "undocuqueer"—sparked talk of coming out as undocumented.[15] Lulu remembers, "Coincidentally a lot of the folks that brought this idea of coming out also identify as queer or part of the LGBT community, and so that was an idea that was borrowed from the queer community." There are an estimated 267,000 LGBT-identified people among the adult undocumented immigrant population, representing approximately 2.7 percent of undocumented adults in the United States.[16] LGBT-identified people, however, are disproportionately represented among leaders of the undocumented youth movement.[17]

Speaking to how the idea of coming out resonates for undocumented immigrant youth leaders, IYJL leader Ulysses explains: "It seemed very similar to the immigrant community in which a lot of people feel isolated, . . . [feel] threatened, either physically, verbally, mentally at the workplace, at school, in their homes [and] in their communities [by immigration agents]." In face of such fear, the imperative to "come out" requires courage and openness and is juxtaposed with the "myth," "lies," and "distortions" that need to be "destroyed." Of course, no analogies are perfect. Whereas the discussion in Milk's speech about feeling scared resonated with undocumented immigrant youth, presumably urging their coming out to parents—who know about and often share their undocumented status—did not. Still, the undocumented immigrant youth movement has productively used the concept of coming out to help mobilize fearful constituents.

The IYJL leadership amplified the resonance of *coming out* by pairing it with the preexisting notion of undocumented immigrants living "in the shadows," a term media outlets have used since the late 1980s. Whereas "the closet" evokes a small and private place where a single person might hide out of shame, "the shadows" conjures an image of a large area that hides a population estimated to number 11.2 million in 2010[18]—capturing undocumented immigrants' sense of communal fear. IYJL leader Roberto explains how the IYJL leadership strategically harnessed the power of these two preexisting cultural narratives by pairing them:

> That messaging of living in the shadows . . . is used by the media, used by a lot of people. . . . [We] basically took the immigrants in the shadows, the coming out, and being inspired by the civil rights movement of direct action [to] take that next step [and] breaking that fear.

Roberto emphasizes how this particular mode of transformation was a strategic move to engage with the media while also more accurately reflecting the lived experiences of undocumented immigrants.

Thus, on March 10, 2010, IYJL hosted a "coming out of the shadows" rally.[19] They marched to Federal Plaza where they set up a stage and held a rally outside the immigration enforcement offices there. David, another IJYL leader, explains that the goals were twofold:

> Internally, we wanted to empower undocumented young people. . . . You have agency here. You don't have to feel afraid to talk about your status, you shouldn't be afraid. We wanted to empower undocumented people living in the United States to become politically active. And outwardly, we wanted to bring attention to us. . . . We wanted mainstream media to be talking about us.

The rally itself was not that different from the one in Los Angeles where Daniel had spoken almost a year earlier. But it was clear that the audience was no longer making only an external call for legislative action but also an internal call to activate undocumented youth. Speakers no longer shared just stories of struggle and perseverance but also unabashed statements of their immigration status—"I stand here to tell you I am no longer afraid to come out of the shadows. My name is Nico. I'm undocumented." Leaders called into bullhorns—"Undocumented"— and the crowd responded, "and unafraid." Others chanted, "No papers." "No fear!"

As they were planning their inaugural event, IYJL leaders brought the concept of "coming out of the shadows" to a nationwide meeting of un-documented youth organizers—including those from United We Dream and dreamactivist.org[20]—to consider instituting this strategy nationally. Building on the planned rally in Chicago, immigrant youth leaders from across the country declared March 15–21, 2010, National Coming Out of the Shadows week. Citing and building on the quote from Harvey Milk's famous speech, a dreamactivist.org email urged readers: "No longer will we let ourselves be intimidated, scared and ashamed." Leaders sought to activate youth to join a broader political movement: "We are empowering ourselves to seek a better future, a future in which we are respected, in which our families live with dignity, in which our American Dream is possible."

In Los Angeles, Dream Team Los Angeles held a partner event on March 18, 2010, in a small public park in the middle of downtown Los Angeles. An email announcing the event urged members to "come out and share their stories of being undocumented with strangers walking around" because, as it explained, "It's time to come out and claim our place in society, and be-cause living in the shadows is way too cold!" The event started with a small press conference where two leaders "came out," detailing their struggles and accomplishments as undocumented young adults and calling for the passage of the federal DREAM Act. Wearing newly designed "I am Undocumented" T-shirts, attendees fanned out to "come out" to anyone who would stop and talk to them on the bustling sidewalk. They asked strangers to sign postcards stating that they support the DREAM Act; these were later delivered to elected officials as part of a strategic plan to show how much support exists for this legislation.

Having helped organize this early "Coming Out of the Shadows" event in Los Angeles, Karla says she hoped to help other undocumented youth accept their undocumented status and learn that "there's other people like them.... [And] let [citizen] people know, we're no different from you guys." A year later, Karla continued to be active in re-imagining what it could mean to come out of the shadows. She explains:

> March 10 has actually been designated as the national coming out as un-documented day. So the idea is for young people who have never shared their stories publicly, who have never come out to their friends or their teachers or anyone, as being undocumented to do that. To take that step on

that day or that week. So I mean it could be like a very public event, which is what they do in Chicago. . . . [But] there's different levels of coming out. So for someone who never told her teacher or best friends, or boyfriend that they're undocumented, that's sort of like the day . . . that could be the first step to come out. Tell a very close person that you've never told about your status, share with them your story and come out. . . . Write about your story, and put it on a website. Make a video. Or speak in front of hundreds of people at a rally. . . . Take a picture with a poster that says "I'm undocumented" or something and post it online.

Recognizing the giant leap from absolute silence to coming out at a public rally, national leaders envisioned ways to build feelings of empowerment among undocumented youth. For instance, for the second annual "Coming Out of the Shadows Day" in 2011, the National Immigrant Youth Alliance (NIYA) released a how-to guide, detailing five levels of coming out ranked by level of difficulty and risk: (1) one-on-one to someone you know well, (2) at a meeting of other undocumented youth or allies, (3) at a press conference, (4) at a rally, and (5) through a direct action or civil disobedience.[21] The organization provided helpful hints and information about how to safely engage at these levels. Despite attempts to broadly define what it means to come out, however, it has since become largely synonymous with these public "Coming Out of the Shadows" rallies.[22] As IYJL leader Uriel notes, coming out is "almost branded to be used for these types of actions."

Learning to Be Unafraid

Just as the NIYA how-to-guide suggests, coming out as undocumented is a process that builds over time. It is not just that the levels build from safest to most risky; but they are also presented as sequential steps. For example, the description of Level 1 walks readers through possible scenarios in which they could come out to someone they know well—"friends, family that doesn't know, a teacher maybe." There are even checkboxes to record that you completed Level 1 if you have shared your story with at least one person. Discussion of Level 1 concludes with a question: "Want to take it to the next level? Read the next section and see if you are up for it." Each level continues in the same way, expanding the number of people told, building a growing list of identified supporters, and garnering media attention. Budding activists are essentially encouraged to cross each level as they build the courage to share their story with a wider audience.

Participating in lower levels helps many undocumented youth 'learn to become "Undocumented and Unafraid." Lulu, one of the IJYL leaders, speaks about building up the courage to speak at IYJL's second "Coming Out of the Shadows" rally in 2011. She recalls the first time she came out: it was to a high school counselor and "a really scary moment." She reflects on why: "Cause I [was] raised with—this fear of sharing this part of [myself] with other people. And so coming out was a very intense, very frightening experience." The more she did it, however, "the less frightening that was and the more empowering I realized [it was in] sharing my story . . . or staking my claim or just letting people know that this is a really important issue for me." She found encouragement in hearing other undocumented youth share their stories and was bolstered by the idea that a "growing community of people [are] coming out and people [are] becoming allies to this movement."

As undocumented youth work through these levels, they often de- velop more political motives and take part in public rallies and actions to build awareness of and support for policy changes. These "Coming Out of the Shadows" rallies became a common advocacy tool for this polit- ical purpose and a formula developed. Take the example of one such rally in October 2011 at a university campus in southern California.[23] About 20 students gather outside the campus library, wearing bright green T- shirts with bold letters declaring "I AM UNDOCUMENTED." A poster hanging from a table declares "Undocumented and Unafraid," while another states "We are . . ." under which are various words filled in by participants, including "DREAMers," "future leaders," and "students." As the lead organizer sorts out logistics among the student speakers, a second student begins to direct the others to march in a small circle. The chant changes every minute or so, but often returns to a sing-songy declaration of "Undocumented and Unafraid." As classes let out, a steady stream of students passes by, encouraging the protestors to get louder. Through the chanting and with their T-shirts and signs, these student activists perform coming out as undocumented and unafraid. They build community as they raise their voices in unison—bringing themselves together and gar- nering support from peers and professors.

Simply attending the event requires students to shed some of their fear. Several have signed up to speak, actively "come out" by publicly sharing their struggles—emotional turmoil after family members were deported, being turned away from a program because of lacking a social security number, or having to postpone academic terms to save up for tuition. Students are nervous. One is called up and takes the microphone with hesitation. She pauses and breathes deeply. The audience claps and a leader urges, "Come on Amalia! You have all our support. We're here for you." She begins, "I'm a little bit nervous so I wrote my story yesterday as I was thinking about whether I was going to come up here or not. And I'm so nervous right now. My heart's just going bum-bum-bum." Holding the paper tight in both her hands, she reads the words quickly, telling the audience about her journey to the United States at the age of four, being reunited with her dad, and starting school. In high school, she says, "the reality hit me. I was not going to receive any financial aid nor loans nor any type of government support because to them I don't exist. And if I wanted to continue going to school I'd have to pay tuition on my own." She talks about struggling to pay for college, working all weekend every weekend to save money. She concludes, "I am undocumented but that doesn't make me any different. I still have a soul and a heart. . . . I am educated and I'm being educated. I want to make a difference in this place I call home. And I am unafraid."

Amalia's claim to being unafraid is clearly aspirational rather than an accurate description of her emotions. After all, she just admitted that her heart was racing, a physical symptom of fear. Moreover, the group's fragile claim to being unafraid quickly breaks down in response to open expression of anti-immigrant sentiment when a bystander interrupts another student a few speeches later. He has been shaking his head as a student talks about his struggle to enroll in and afford college. Wrapping up, the speaker affirms, "We believe that we should get an education. We believe that we should be able to travel. We believe that we should be able to go anywhere we want without being scared." Seemingly pushed to the brink, the bystander bellows, "At taxpayers' expense?" The speaker retorts: "Not at taxpayer's expense. We pay taxes! That's just a myth. We pay tax with an ITIN [individual tax identification number]. . . . If you don't believe me—I-T-I-N—look it up!" Indeed, it is through ITINs, sales and excise taxes, and property taxes that undocumented immigrants contribute an estimated $11.64 billion a year.[24] The crowd cheers for the speaker and a few try to engage the dissenting bystander in conversation until he storms off. The lead organizer says, however, that this outburst intimidates some speakers who then refuse to speak and makes others—who have already spoken—fear potential repercussions.

While hostile reactions stoke the fear of some undocumented youth, they push others to further action. Karla explains how fear and stigma weighed on her: "Being undocumented is so heavy, it feels so heavy in your shoulders that unless you come to terms with that, it will be a constant weight that will be on your shoulders." It was this feeling that drove her to become a leader in the immigrant youth movement, to come out, and to try to inspire other youth to "come to terms with the idea of being undocumented." Her desire to build community and create change was stronger than the constant fear that has always been "in the back of [her mind]" and has haunted her ever since moving to the United States.

This is why Karla decided to escalate the tactics to campaign for the federal DREAM Act, coming out with other students by staging a sit-in that targeted a key elected official. She explains that participating in this action

> was a way to conquer that fear [of deportation] and get past that whole thing. And just reclaim my sense of humanity and my freedom, because I never felt more free in my life than [during] the six and a half hours . . . I was sitting in . . . and then after I was arrested. It was the most liberating thing ever.

Indeed, Karla says that it is precisely the risk she took by coming out and publicly demanding change that makes her action empowering to other undocumented youth. She says that if she were not undocumented, her participation in this movement "wouldn't have the same impact . . . because you're not risking everything."

Karla strove to help people realize that being undocumented is "not a handicap." She explains:

> It's actually something that's more empowering than our limitation. Actually I see my life, everything I've been able to do—and the people that I've worked with—[everything we] have been able to do and accomplish. With very little resources, with very little time. Juggling so many things. And that makes me feel more empowered. That makes me feel like I can do more if I have more resources.

Rather than be discouraged by the challenges she faces, Karla finds pride in overcoming so many obstacles.

Effecting Change

The "Coming Out of the Shadows" strategy was an integral part of a coordinated nationwide effort to pass the federal DREAM Act before the 111th congressional session adjourned in December 2010. "Coming Out" events helped politicize a base of undocumented young adults, change the narratives around undocumented immigrants and youth, and build up a substantial group of allies. Organizations like United We Dream identified congressional targets and coordinated national call-in campaigns. Local immigrant youth organizations told their stories and urged local entities—city governments, school boards, and university presidents—to signal support for the DREAM Act. The mayor of New York City and 18 powerful leaders of the New York business community even issued a public letter of support. Others went after heavy-hitting allies—the AFL-CIO, the American Federation of Teachers, Microsoft, and the US Hispanic Chamber of Commerce.[25]

Despite all of these efforts, the DREAM Act failed to pass, yet again. Leaders were successful in getting the DREAM Act incorporated into a must-pass National Defense Authorization Act, but it was dropped after a senate filibuster. On December 8, 2010, the House of Representatives passed a stand-alone DREAM Act bill. Ten days later, the Senate vote on the bill drew a majority but was five votes short of overcoming a filibuster.

While unsuccessful in effecting this particular policy change, the immigrant youth movement did bring about important cultural change within the immigrant community. Several immigrant youth leaders reflect on the DREAM Act's near passage in a *Colorlines* feature printed soon after.[26] The reporter cites movement leader Matias Ramos:

> In the past, many people maybe only used their middle names when talking to the press. . . . Or it was only people already facing deportation who came forward. I think it's this year that the story telling, the testimonies, have become the center and focus of the actions.

Ramos knew this secrecy well as he had before also used pseudonyms and blacked-out figures to hide his identity. While he and other students had previously found ways to tell their stories, it was clear that the coming out strategy paved the way to empower a large group of undocumented youth. It encouraged them to embrace their undocumented status and reclaim power for their community. This exponentially multiplied the number of immigrant youth willing to fight for themselves and their communities. There were now many more Karlas and Daniels to lead and inspire others. The battle was lost, but a stronger foundation had been laid for the next.

The movement also continued innovating to inspire undocumented youth to come out. Preparing for the second annual "National Coming out of the Shadows" week in March 2011, leaders added "unapologetic" to the rallying cry of "undocumented and unafraid." A post to the IYJL website in January 2011 notes that "we know that what we want to say is that we are still undocumented and unafraid, and this year are adding unapologetic." This addition was inspired by a speech made by one of their members, Alaa Mukahhal, the month before the DREAM Act failed to pass. The blog post provides an excerpt of her speech:

> I wonder what's it going to take to pass this act. What do I have to do to show you the urgency of the situation? . . . How many more families have to be separated, how many more futures suppressed and swept under the rug, how many more youth have to cut open their veins to show you that their blood flows thick with the American Spirit? Do I have to get arrested and beaten, do I have to get deported and defeated; tell me, what's it going to take?

Mukahhal determines that it is going to take action: youth voices, detained students, migrant workers, recent immigrants, and longtime citizens. She concludes, "We can no longer wait for our paths to be unblocked and for our futures to be handed back to us. The time is long overdue. *We are undocumented, unafraid, and unapologetic in our pursuit for equal opportunity, and we know exactly what it's going to take* (emphasis added)."[27]

"Undocumented, Unafraid, and Unapologetic" becomes the tagline for the 2011 "Coming Out of the Shadows Week." Facing a slump after their unsuccessful DREAM Act campaign, IYJL seeks to use "unapologetic" to re-energize undocumented youth and re- articulate why they still need to come out. A 2011 IYJL flyer prominently features the theme (see Figure 4.2). A promotional video from IYJL fosters the language of being unapologetic. It opens on a close-up of the face of a young Latina woman:

> My name is Cindy. I'm 21 years old. I'm undocumented. I'm unafraid. And I'm unapologetic. On March 10, 2011, we are going to have undocumented youth proclaim their undocumented status. They will tell everyone that

Figure 4.2. A 2011 IYJL flyer encourages undocumented youth to come out as undocumented, unafraid, and unapologetic.

they should not be sorry for being in the United States. That they should not apologize for getting an education, that they should not be sorry for their parents trying to make a living in the U.S. By coming out we share our stories. We put our face to this issue. We are human."[28]

Another IYJL leader is quoted in a news article: "We have to be unapologetic about our parents who brought us here. . . . As a matter of fact we are extremely thankful that they did."[29] They are no longer asking for forgiveness and goodwill but they are demanding the respect and opportunities that they and their families deserve.

In February 2011, DreamActivist.org sent out a nationwide email proclaiming: "The day on which we declare ourselves undocumented, unafraid, *and* unapologetic is almost upon us" (emphasis in original). It calls back to the first year of actions:

> Last year, hundreds of DREAMers across the country took the historic step of coming out as undocumented youth in schools, community centers, houses of worship and city halls. This step led us, undocumented youth, to become a force to be reckoned with, a movement that can never be forced back into the shadows.

It includes quotes from youth leaders across the country that epitomize what it means to be unapologetic. For instance, Angy from the New York State Youth Leadership Council declares, "Nobody, not even the Senate, can stop us. We're here and we're not leaving, be proud and be loud!" Reyna, from the Immigrant Youth Justice League, likewise declares: "This year, not only are we undocumented and unafraid, but we are also unapologetic. We are and we deserve to be a part of this country, and we won't let anyone tell us differently."

Being unapologetic is about loudly proclaiming one's undocumented status without shame and not apologizing for seeking a better life. It is about claiming space and demanding respect, for one's self, one's family, and one's community. It is a reaction to dehumanizing and criminalizing narratives.

"Coming Out" language and narratives have spread immigrant youth stories beyond these "Coming Out of the Shadows" events and into the public consciousness. For example, in June 2011, Pulitzer prize–winning journalist Jose Antonio Vargas published an editorial in the New York Times, "My Life as an Undocumented Immigrant." Like IJLY leaders, Vargas was inspired to speak out by the four immigrant youth who walked the Trail of Dreams. He recounted migrating from the Philippines when he was 12 and learning he was undocumented when he tried to apply for a driver's license. He remembers coming out as gay in high school. "Tough as it was, coming out about being gay seemed less daunting than coming out about my legal status. I kept my other secret mostly hidden." Vargas hid for over a decade, compartmentalizing the problem as he pursued journalism. Now 30, he is "done running." He says, "I'm exhausted. I don't want that life anymore. So I've decided to come forward, own up to what I've done, and tell my story to the best of my recollection." A year later, in 2012, *Time* magazine featured a cover story by Vargas. The cover declares, "We are Americans*" with him standing at the front of a crowd of undocumented youth. Below is the caveat, "*Just not legally" with the tagline, "We're some of the nearly 12 million undocumented immigrants living in the U.S. Why we're done hiding."[30]

In its retelling, Vargas's narrative is now sprinkled with talk of coming out. He recounts several conversations he has had since he "chose to come out publicly—very publicly—in the form of an essay for the *New York Times* last June." He explains that he is now "a walking conversation that most people are uncomfortable having." The questions they ask reveal just how confused and unaware people are of the US immigration system. He also notes,

> I've also been witness to a shift I believe will be a game changer for the debate: more people coming out. . . . At least 2,000 undocumented immigrants—most of them under 30—have contacted me and outed themselves in the past year. Others are coming out over social media or in person to their friends, their fellow students, their colleagues. . . . But each becomes another walking conversation. We love this country. We contribute to it. This is our home. What happens when even more of us step forward? How will the US government and American citizens react then?

At one point he declares, "We are living in the golden age of coming out. . . . As a group and as individuals, we are putting faces and names and stories on an issue that is often treated as an abstraction." Vargas acknowledges that there are risks but, like the immigrant youth leaders who first developed the strategy, also believes that coming out offers protection and community. He ends with recounting a conversation with an immigration official he contacted: "Are you planning on deporting me?" I asked. He learns that in some ways his fears of deportation as a consequence of coming out are effectively baseless: "I quickly found out that even though I publicly came out about my undocumented status, I still do not exist in the eyes of ICE. Like most undocumented immigrants, I've never been arrested. Therefore, I've never been in contact with ICE." While deportation risks are real, especially with the increasing criminalization of immigrant communities and communities of color, coming out may not be as dangerous as one might think. In fact, there may be more benefits than costs.

In June 2012, the same month the article appeared, that President Barack Obama announced the Deferred Action for Childhood Arrivals (DACA) program. DACA provides temporary protection from deportation and work authorization, renewable every two years, for people who meet eligibility criteria very similar to that laid out for the federal DREAM Act. An additional benefit is that having a valid social security number also allows recipients to obtain drivers' licenses, establish credit, and begin to freely navigate everyday life. Under the auspices of the DACA program, undocumented youth are able to build credit and purchase homes, complete higher education, launch careers, and open businesses.[31] DACA does not, however provide a path for citizenship or permanent residence. Moreover, as an executive order, rather than a law passed by Congress, it is also more vulnerable to being rescinded, as we are seeing at the time of this writing.

The establishment of DACA was a win for the immigrant youth movement. While it was not a pathway to legalization, it provided the basic protections that DREAM-act eligible youth needed to advance their lives in the United States. Concurrently, immigrant youth leaders began acknowledging the exclusivity of policies like DACA and the DREAM Act; it left out a large majority of the undocumented population, including their parents, who remained vulnerable. No longer unified around a single policy goal, the immigrant youth movement moved on to other, more disparate, advocacy goals. Indeed, March 2013 appears to have been the last coordinated "National Coming Out of the Shadows Month" and the messaging had already begun to shift away from undocumented youth and toward a broader focus on ending deportation and detention practices.[32]

Still, "Coming Out" narratives ultimately cultivated the emergence and growth of the next generation of immigrant youth leaders. They came of age and learned to be undocumented when their older peers were declaring that they should "come out of the shadows" and be "undocumented, unafraid, and unapologetic." Leticia, an active member of the undocumented student community at the University of California, was in her first year of high school when these narratives emerged in 2010. She began participating in local, state, and national organizing when she started college in the fall of 2013. The national movement was no longer actively centering "coming out," but remnants remained. Leticia and her peers still organized "Coming Out of the Shadows" events on their college campus. These had the same goal of empowering undocumented students to come to terms with their identity, but their external goal was now focused on institutional change and support for the growing undocumented student population. Leticia also learned the rallying cries and lessons behind being "Undocumented, Unafraid, and

Unapologetic." In a conversation with Laura E. Enriquez, she describes what it means to her:

> It is being open about my status. Unapologetic in claiming my identity—despite the shame and stigma associated with it. Unapologetic in calling out the very systemic institutions and actors that create and perpetuate my oppression because of my status. Unapologetic in taking up space and refusing to be treated as less than everyone else—and by extension potentially making others uncomfortable in doing so. Unapologetic in the decision that my parents made in migrating over in search of a better life for me.

The impact of three years of nationally coordinated Coming Out events and narratives reverberates through the outlooks of undocumented youth like Leticia, whether they know the history or not.

* * *

Storytelling has played in integral part in humanizing undocumented youth and their undocumented family and community members. Countless undocumented youth have raised their voices to challenge negative stereotypes and develop positive images about undocumented immigrants. These images are not without pitfalls. For instance, they risk marking youth as deserving of relief while contributing to the further criminalization of undocumented immigrants who appear to be less deserving. Recognizing this, undocumented youth have sought to develop more inclusive narratives.[33]

Still, calls to "come out of the shadows" have helped galvanize the storytelling of undocumented youth while fostering growing support of immigration relief for this group. Their narratives have filtered into the public consciousness and into political rhetoric. Consider the language used by President Barack Obama to announce the DACA program in June 2012:

> This is about young people who grew up in America—kids who study in our schools, young adults who are starting careers, patriots who pledge allegiance to our flag. These Dreamers are Americans in their hearts, in their minds, in every single way but one: on paper. They were brought to this country by their parents, sometimes even as infants. They may not know a country besides ours. They may not even know a language besides English.

They often have no idea they're undocumented until they apply for a job, or college, or a driver's license.

Note that the examples and logics that President Obama used were the exact same ones that undocumented youth—who had the courage to come out as undocumented and unafraid—had been using for over a decade. Indeed, by helping mobilize fearful undocumented youth, the concept of coming out— first developed in the gay rights movement—has helped change the national conversation about immigration.

5

Producing a Sense of Linked Fate

A poster advertising Season 12 of the reality television show *Sister Wives* features Kody Brown beaming in the center with his flowing dirty blond hair and beard (Figure 5.1). His arms are outstretched in an embrace of his four wives: two on each side. Each woman looks directly into the camera, smiling. They are dressed casually, in pants, sweaters, and cardigans that look like they could have been purchased at the Gap. They seem like unremarkable, typical Americans.

The reality show *Sister Wives* has provided the Brown family with an extremely public forum for coming out as polygamous or, as these families refer to themselves, members of "plural-marriage families."[1] The Brown family has reaped monetary benefits from starring in their own reality television show, but their participation is also driven by political goals. As Kody Brown explains: "When we open ourselves up, those stereotypes people have suddenly change when you meet us. . . . This is part of our reason for essentially 'coming out'—it's a story that needs to be told."[2]

For Mormon fundamentalist polygamists, coming out in this way forms part of a broader political strategy of likening polygamy to same-sex marriage, a strategy that has already paid off. For instance, in December 2013, in a federal district court in Utah, Kody Brown and his wives evoked *Lawrence v. Texas* 539 U.S. 558 (2003)—ruling that a private, consensual sexual act between two men is protected from state intrusion—to argue that Utah's anti-polygamy law was unconstitutional (*Brown et al. v. Buhman*, 2:11-cv-0652-CW, Utah 2013).[3] The court accepted the Browns' reasoning that because the state no longer prosecutes other forms of sexual cohabitation among consenting adults (e.g., married people cohabiting with someone other than their spouses pending a final divorce), singling out religious cohabitation for prosecution constitutes a violation of the First Amendment guarantee of free exercise of religion and constitutional due process (*Brown et al. v. Buhman*, 2:11-cv-0652-CW, Utah 2013). The court thus struck down the part of Utah's anti-polygamy law used, until then, to criminalize members of Mormon fundamentalist plural marriages.

Come Out, Come Out, Whoever You Are. Abigail C. Saguy, Oxford University Press (2020).
© Oxford University Press.
DOI: 10.1093/oso/9780190931650.001.0001

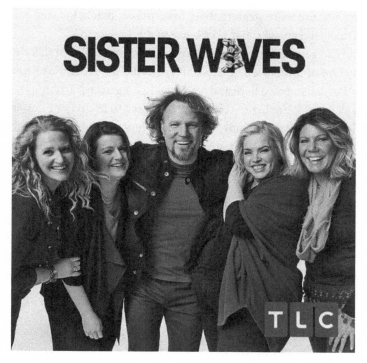

Figure 5.1. A poster promotes Season 12 of the reality television show "Sister Wives," featuring Kody Brown and his four wives.

As early as 2000, leaders of the plural-marriage family movement drew inspiration from the gay rights movement to frame their activism as coming out as polygamist. Mary Batchelor—one of the authors of the edited collection of pro-plural-marriage testimonials *Voices in Harmony: Contemporary Women Celebrate Plural Marriage*,[4] executive assistant at the Utah Domestic Violence Council, and former director of Principle Voices—explains that the news media first referred to her co-authors and her "coming out" as polygamists. An energetic blond woman in her 40s, Batchelor says she was initially surprised by this usage of the term as it has always been, for her, associated with coming out as gay, but ultimately it resonated with her. Batchelor explains: "I wrote a book, and I came out publicly as a polygamist, and I—yeah. And in some ways it's funny because I do use that terminology because I can resonate with it now. And so we actually do use that terminology." Batchelor said that she sometimes feels judged for using language so tightly associated with gay rights: "There are people that say, well, you're—you're just piggy-backing on [the gay rights movement]. . . . Like we're somehow cheating because we're stealing that." In response, Batchelor says: "and we're like, 'actually it resonates. It makes sense to me. I relate to it.'"

An article reporting on the edited volume, titled "Political Polygamists Coming Out of the Closet,"[5] quotes Mary Batchelor's co-author Anne Wilde saying "Polygamists are here and we are not going away," echoing the Queer Nation slogan, "We're here; we're queer; get used to it." In her interview with us, Wilde describes publishing *Voices in Harmony* as her coming out. In her 60s, she carries herself with strength and grace. She wears button-down blouses and pants, her auburn hair in a sensible bob. A convert to Mormon fundamentalism, Wilde spent 33 years in a plural marriage until the death of her husband and has spent much of her life studying her chosen religion. She is an avid fan of *Big Love*, a prize-winning Home Box Office (HBO) television show about plural marriage that ran from 2006 to 2011, and she is active in her religious and secular community. Wilde readily acknowledges that her chosen lifestyle is challenging and does not bring out the best in everyone, but passionately fights for the rights of Mormon fundamentalist plural-marriage families and the decriminalization of polygamy.

To this end, she co-founded the leading polygamy advocacy group Principle Voices and serves as a member of the Utah Attorney General's Safety Net Committee, an outreach organization created to work with po-lygamist families. Speaking in her mid-century home in a Salt Lake City suburb with a view of the surrounding mountains, Wilde says that her advocacy efforts have successfully increased the visibility of plural-marriage families, given them "credibility," and "been very helpful for [others] to learn more about us personally firsthand." She says, "We should have equal civil rights just like any other minority or any other alternative lifestyle. . . . I think eventually it will come to that, because there are so many alternative families out there, and we just want to be considered as one." As part of the research for her book, Wilde conducted a survey of plural-marriage families, finding 19,000 adult and children members of families living in plural-marriages in the western United States; Missouri; Bountiful, British Columbia (Canada); and in an Apostolic United Brethren (AUB) community in Mexico.

Diffusion of a Social Movement Tactic

The experience of plural-marriage family activists shows that being connected to gay rights activism by social networks or overlapping memberships—as is the case with both the fat rights movement and the undocumented movement—is not a prerequisite for adopting coming out politics. Not surprisingly, we did not meet any Mormon fundamentalist polygamists who self-identified as lesbian, gay, or queer. In fact, only Anne Wilde mentions a social tie with someone who was gay—a cousin whom she describes, along with herself, as one of the two "black sheep of the family."

As we have discussed, the term *coming out* is in the air. But this alone does not explain diffusion to the plural-marriage family movement. Rather, analogies drawn between same-sex marriage and polygamy have made the concept even more salient in the case of Mormon fundamentalist polygamists. For instance, a 2001 article in the *National Catholic Register* quotes the director of the Utah branch of the ACLU comparing the fight to decriminalize plural marriage with the fight for marriage equality: "The bigamy statute, like sodomy statutes and like other anachronistic moralistic legislation, goes to the core of what the Supreme Court identifies as important fundamental privacy rights."[6] The Utah branch of the ACLU thus provides a conduit for talk of coming out from the LGBTQ to the polygamist context, underscoring the central role of legal cases in making this connection.

Likewise, Charley—another convert to Mormon fundamentalism and husband of a prominent activist—cites the landmark Supreme Court case *Lawrence v. Texas*, 539 U.S. 558, 597-99 (2003), striking down sodomy laws as an infringement on the right to liberty, as an opportunity for plural-marriage-family activists:

> There's this other thread in our cause to try and bring about this sort of societal shift in what's going on in the judicial arena, because ultimately if we can win, we can get to the point where it can no longer be said that polygamists are committing a crime. . . . The homosexuals won that battle with Lawrence in 2003, when the Supreme Court said you no longer make any laws against homosexuals. So if we can get that affirmed in our context then I think that would be a big victory.

Indeed, the late Supreme Court Justice Antonin Scalia explicitly argued in his dissent in *Lawrence* that the *Lawrence* ruling would create a slippery slope that would—by logical extension—make anti-bigamy laws unconstitutional.

Just as Mormon fundamentalist polygamist activists recognized an opportunity in *Lawrence*, they also saw a threat in laws that would restrict same-sex marriage. Discussing California's Proposition 8—a California ballot proposition and state constitutional amendment passed in the November 2008 California state elections that banned same-sex marriage in the state of California—one activist explained:

> If [Proposition 8] goes through, that's not good for us as polygamists because then . . . marriage between a man and woman will be the only thing that is good and truthful in California or whatever, and that's not good for us. It's funny because we don't like to compare ourselves to gay people a lot because they do that out of personal sexual preference and we do it for a religious purpose, but our fight is similar because we are all fighting for what the definition of a family or a marriage is. And we as polygamists or gays would like it to be whatever you choose as long as its consenting adults and not abusive and all those things

While Mormon fundamentalist polygamists express anti-gay sentiments and do not like to compare themselves to members of sexual minorities, they also recognized that the marriage equality movement offered a political opportunity for the plural-marriage movement by challenging the idea that marriage could only be a union "between one man and woman."

As sociologist Judith Stacey pointed out in her 2011 book, "the slippery slope argument that links gay marriage to polygamy has borne some ironic fruit."[7] Perhaps most unlikely of these is Anne Wilde's adored TV show *Big Love*, which was written and produced by a gay male screenwriter couple Mark V. Olsen and Will Scheffer. As Stacey recounts, when Terry Gross of the popular National Public Radio (NPR) show *Fresh Air* interviewed the screenwriters in 2007, they credited the Republican campaign against marriage equality with inspiring the series. Taking offense at statements made in 2004 by former president George W. Bush about what makes a proper family and who can and cannot marry, they came up with the idea to explore such issues through the struggles of a fictional fundamentalist Mormon polygamist family.[8] Stacey indicates how the show's characters "frequently adopt the idiom of the closet to describe the family circumstances, and they draw analogies between social stigma and discrimination against polygamous and gay families."[9] Moreover, Stacey shows how the series inspired polygamy-rights groups to adopt these same rhetorical devices, arguing, for instance, that "polygamy rights is the next civil rights battle."[10] Stacey further shows how Christian conservatives have lumped gay marriage with polygamy because "they mistakenly associate both with promiscuity."[11]

Disclosure as a Political and Social Tactic

Charley originally converted to mainstream Mormonism after meeting a missionary. In the late 1980s, after having been married to his first wife for six years, he met with some Mormon fundamentalists with the goal of bringing them back to the mainstream Mormon Church. Charley's mission backfired, however, after the Mormon fundamentalists told him "things that [he] had never known that galled [him]." He learned that the mainstream church had concealed the fact that polygamy was central to Mormon founder Joseph Smith's early teachings, leading Charley to conclude that the mainstream church was "systematically lying" to him. He describes leaving "the [mainstream] LDS [Latter Day Saints] church with a gusto," moving to Utah, and becoming "zealous" about the fundamentalist Mormon cause. Later, Charley and his wife welcomed a second wife to their family, who later became a prominent plural-marriage activist. Charley's first wife eventually became unhappy with the living situation, however, and ultimately divorced Charley. At the time of the interview, Charley and his second wife were legally married and monogamous, while still supporting the idea of polygamy.

In a joint interview with his wife, during which she frequently corrected or contradicted him, Charley explicitly compares the treatment of polygamists to that of "black people and gay people" and compares the Brown family that stars in the reality show *Sister Wives* to civil rights leaders Rosa Parks and Martin Luther King Jr. and to comedian Ellen DeGeneres, who publicly came out as a lesbian in her groundbreaking 1990s sitcom:

> There was a lot of sensitivity before that, and then her show sort of came out, and now people aren't anywhere near as sensitive. And so there's definitely momentum in the gay and lesbian world. And we're seeing exactly the same thing. I mean, we have *Big Love, Sister Wives*. . . there are—there are just things that have happened that have kind of brought polygamy more into the sanity context where people don't think of it so more like we're, you know, green Martians with pointy ears.

For Charley, Rosa Parks, Martin Luther King Jr., Ellen DeGeneres, and the Brown family are all "people who kind of come out as the vanguard and [who are] trailblazers for the rest of the crowd." Using the concept of coming out helps ground Charley's claims within the history of gay rights.

Charley's wife gives presentations and trainings to police officers and caseworkers about plural-marriage families. Charley says these presentations offer a "three dimensional" view of fundamentalist Mormons that contrasts with the way caseworkers and senators see them before the trainings, "in a very two-dimensional way . . . like cartoon characters." He describes how his wife and a "handful of other women polygamists" enter a room

> and there'll be 60 people in the room, and they go into the meeting or the presentation with the two-dimensional cartoon in their head, and they come out of there with this three dimensional [understanding, concluding:] "OK, these people are completely normal."

Charley proudly recounts how people tell his wife after the presentation, "Oh my gosh! I'll never again think of you as these cartoons." He says this is a "significant payoff," as it means "there's one more person out of 6 billion people in the world who isn't going to throw rocks at us, or toilet paper our trees, or, you know, poke fun at our kids in school." Better yet, he says, some of these people are leaders, who work as reporters, social workers, in government, or in law enforcement, who will go on to advocate for Mormon fundamentalists.

Mormon fundamentalist polygamists also speak about the importance of being out as a plural-marriage family in the broader Mormon mainstream community for these same reasons. For instance, Becky—one of two wives who are also half-sisters married before the age of 20—explains that her entire family participates in Scouts, plays, school activities, and outings— "things that we didn't do when we were younger." Becky and her sister-wife Cindy speak about how, growing up, their parents lived in fear of the negative economic and social repercussions that would ensue if people knew they were polygamous. They recall houses spray-painted with epithets, driveways covered in eggs and fish, and neighborhood kids being forbidden to play with children from polygamist households.

Despite continued perceived risk, Becky, her sister-wife, and their husband describe—in a group interview—how they have intentionally been open with the current neighbors. When they arrived in their current neighborhood, they introduced themselves to their mainstream Mormon neighbors and told them about their lifestyle. They say their neighbors were receptive and, because they knew and liked their family, started questioning their negative stereotypes about polygamous families. The bishop of the local mainstream Mormon church even went so far as to invite the whole family to attend the mainstream Mormon church for a while before rescinding the invitation due to concerns from the broader church leadership. Becky says that such community engagement has paid off. As tangible evidence of this, she points to the time a third-grade teacher—in the context of lessons presenting polygamists as bad people—asked the students to take a picture or draw a picture of a polygamist house. Because they knew and liked Becky's family, mainstream Mormon parents objected to the assignment. Not only did the teacher retract it, but the principal also called the family to apologize. Becky attributes this victory to the fact that her family was "out," engaged, and well liked within the community. This provides additional evidence of the relevance of Harvey Milk's strategy—discussed in previous chapters.

Mormon fundamentalist polygamists struggle for integration and acceptance in mainstream Mormon communities, where they tend to live. This theme comes up in our interview with Isabelle, a fourth wife who lives in a huge house in the suburbs of Salt Lake City with her husband, three sister-wives, and about 20 children. They have a small farm in their backyard, with livestock and some crops. When Nicole Iturriaga arrives for an interview, the older boys of the family proudly show her how they use the roosters for cockfights, while younger children play with a chicken head in a mason jar and even smaller children draw pictures of the chickens losing their heads. The entire family regularly shares meals and—in the afternoon—the father holds "coffee hour" with his kids, during which the adults drink coffee and the kids drink hot cocoa. Before such communal gatherings, family members jump into action, pulling out long tables and rushing to complete chores.

Nicole Iturriaga interviews Isabelle in the front room—set off from the rest of the house and containing a sofa and a big white gun safe. Above the fireplace and mantel hangs a painting of Adam and his three wives. Isabelle's warm eyes shine brightly below elaborate braids—a variety of French braiding that she says is easy to do with enough practice. Isabelle is so kind and down-to-earth that she is disarming. Her conservative dress makes her easily recognizable in this region as Mormon fundamentalist, although she might be mistaken for Mennonite in Pennsylvania. She wears no makeup or jewelry. At the first interview, she is pregnant. At the second—two years later—she has two children in tow.

The official "house mom," Isabelle stays home with the children and does much of the domestic labor for the family. She tells Iturriaga how empowered she felt when the schoolteacher acknowledged her as a legitimate interlocutor on behalf of her co-wives' children. Isabelle describes how, when she attended a school meeting for a co-wife's daughter, the teacher initially assumed Isabelle was the child's biological mother. When she realized that she was not, the teacher said that she was "not supposed to be talking to you about her," to which Isabelle responded that she was "kind of her mother," having been responsible for the child's schooling up until that point. Isabelle recounts that the teacher accepted this account and, from then on, the school treated Isabelle as the go-to mom for all of the family's children. For Isabelle, being recognized as her co-wives' children's mother was "cool" and a form of "coming out." It is not only Isabelle's status (or identity) as a polygamist that was recognized but also what this implied about her relationships with her co-wives and their children.

Visibility and Disclosure

Experiences of coming out range from appearing on television to telling a teacher that you are raising your sister-wives' children. Experiences of coming out also vary based on how easily identifiable you are as Mormon fundamentalist polygamist. Some fundamentalist Mormon polygamist women—including the Brown women, other women who are "independent" or not affiliated with a specific church, and members of the Apostolic United Brethren (AUB) or the Allred Group—dress like other Americans and uphold many of the same values, including condemning underage marriage and supporting education for women. They embody assimilationist politics—they are just like other Americans except for their polygamous lifestyle. In contrast, the infamous Fundamentalist Latter Day Saints (FLDS) practice arranged and underage marriage, and the women wear prairie dresses with their long hair in intricate braids—making them more culturally marginal and easy to pick out of a crowd.[12]

But dress is not always aligned with ideology. For instance, members of the Davis County Co-op (also known as the Kingston Family) practice underage and intra-family marriage, but women members now wear modern fashion, thereby blending in more easily.[13] Inversely, members of The Work of Jesus Christ (also known as Centennial Park or "The Work")—like Isabelle— oppose underage marriage and support education for women and girls, but women members dress in long skirts and long-sleeved shirts and wear long, intricate braids. Whereas they might be seen as Mennonite or Orthodox Jews in other geographical regions, they are readily recognized as Mormon fundamentalist polygamists in southern Utah.

Mormon fundamentalist polygamists who dress in modern fashion can easily blend in. For them, coming out means, as it did for Mary Batchelor and Anne Wilde, proudly going public—in a book, on television, or on radio—about their polygamist lifestyle or, as it did for Becky and her family, openly taking part in mainstream Mormon community activities with their entire family. In contrast, for those who dress in long skirts and long-sleeved shirts and wear long, intricate braids, like Isabelle, coming out can mean being accepted as the mother of a sister-wife's child or—in some cases—even leaving the house. This has particular resonance among sects that have traditionally kept all but the first wife hidden. "We joke about it," says a member of The Work, "'Cause if sometimes we haven't seen our friends from other communities for a while [and then do], we'll say, 'Oh, I guess he let her out of the closet, huh?' It's just a joke to us." These examples show how the specific meaning of *coming out* can vary widely based on context, enhancing its versatility and resonance. .

As we have seen, a common theme is that coming out is a continual process; you cannot come out once and for all.[14] Mary Batchelor explains this idea is equally relevant in the context of polygamy:

> It's an ongoing process because there are people that—as public as I have been—there are people that don't have a clue, and they meet me for the first time and they don't know anything about my history. And I can assume they knew, and then months and months later some weird thing will come up . . . and then you go through the whole reaction again. . . . And so you make assumptions and you just assume you're safe, and then people find out, and suddenly you're not safe anymore, and you start to have a little bit of trauma, [and wonder:] "How is this person gonna react to me?"

Echoing this same idea, Charley speaks of coming out as a "habit" or practice, rather than something you do once and for all.

In the 21st century, use of social media is an increasingly important way in which people present themselves to others. The average person has five social media accounts and spends around 1 hour and 40 minutes browsing these networks every day.[15] Social media have transformed social interactions, as people's social lives are increasingly conducted online.[16] This is true for Christina, who is 22 years old at the time of the interview. She has long brown hair and wears jeans and a T-shirt. Just looking at her, you would never know that she is the daughter of a prominent plural-marriage activist who started a group of families living off the grid near Moab in a big rock formation. The community has blasted out caves in which they have built modern houses—almost all with satelite televisions. . Solar panels, a well, and a small farm allows the community—almost exclusively Independent Fundamentalist Morman in plural marriages or committed to the principle—to be almost completely self-sufficient.

Christina's mother is a medical doctor and a prominent plural-marriage family activist. At the time of the interview, Christina is about to become the second wife to a family living somewhere in the Midwest. The first wife is near her age and one of her close friends. Whereas Christina discloses her polygamous lifestyle in some contexts and to some people, she explains that she is not "out" to her Facebook friends. She says she chose "to leave my marriage out of my Facebook entirely." She explains:

> It starts getting complicated if [my friend and soon-to-be sister wife] says, you know, "I'm_____, this is my name, I'm married to this person," and I say, "this is my name, I'm married to this person." We've both got pictures of the same guy. Clearly, we're polygamists, but not everybody on my Facebook friends list knows that, and they really don't need to. So I was like, well . . . my close people will know that I'm married, and I don't need to put pictures up, and I don't need to post it on Facebook.

Rather than broadcasting her polygamous lifestyle to her entire Facebook feed, Christina decided to come out more selectively.

Post-Feminism and Free Choice

Plural-marriage family activists thus link their cause to same-sex marriage as part of a broader strategy of recasting polygyny as progressive. Yet, working against them are mainstream perceptions of polygyny as oppressive to women. As part of an effort to counter these attitudes, the burgeoning plural-marriage movement has propelled women into leadership roles, thereby demonstrating that they are freely choosing this family structure.[17] In addition, plural-marriage family activists explicitly claim the mantle of feminism, to counter widely held views of polygamy as patriarchal and sexist.[18] Mary Batchelor says she gets "greatly offended when somebody argues that my lifestyle, or my religious beliefs, or whatever, is inherently abusive to women." Mary Batchelor argues that the notion that polygyny is inherently oppressive to women is "patronizing and paternalistic" and the idea that she needs rescuing "totally contrary to feminism." Mary Batchelor thus builds on the post-feminist trope that feminism is about women being able to "choose" what feels right to them, whether it is working as a lawyer, exotic dancer, "opting out" of work, or choosing to be the fourth wife in a fundamentalist Mormon family.[19]

In contrast with talk about sexual orientation and body size being largely innate or undocumented immigrant youth being brought to this country as young children by their parents, plural marriage activists embrace the language of choice. They talk about choosing polygamy of their "own free-will," loving it, and having "to fight for it." They refute the idea that men have all the power in a plural-marriage family or make all the family decisions, describing women in plural marriages as "very strong" and opinionated." One likens the husband to "a president of a corporation" and the wives to "the council." Most of the time, the man and women "sit and they talk, and they hash things out," she says. It is only when "there's a dispute where they can't agree" that the man will say "This is how it's gonna be." This allusion to a board meeting, where all the members have a voice, dispels the notion that iron-fisted patriarchs rule over voiceless wives. Yet, the image of the husband as the president, rather than a common member of the council, suggests a clear gender hierarchy.

Another woman in a plural marriage says, "If the women will just com-municate with each other, be open with each other, [they] can accomplish so much more." The "if" makes clear that this is not always the case and implies that divided, individual women have little power. As one woman acknowledges: "He is still the man of the house. We do very much live in a patriarchal society." The "we," could refer to Mormon fundamentalist society. Indeed, fundamentalist Mormon doctrine allows men to marry multiple women but not vice versa, and this constitutes a basic structural inequality, as does the fundamentalist Mormon belief that women can only enter heaven through their link with a male "priesthood holder" who holds the keys. While not disputing this, plural-marriage family activists emphasize how the broader society—and not just polygamist communities— is also patriarchal. Indeed, they repeatedly emphasize the deficiencies of mainstream American monogamous marriage to establish the superiority of plural marriage as an institution. For instance, one member of The Work—who cleans homes for monogamous women and has observed the conflict between these women and their husbands—concludes: "There's a lot of monogamous women that would probably be better in polygamy." She herself says that she would never want to be "an only wife."

Plural marriage family activists make three distinct arguments about why polygyny is superior to monogamy. First, they criticize "single guys," as immature or, in Christina's estimation, "super needy . . . constantly texting, calling, basically monopolizing my life." Becky expresses pity for her friends in monogamous relationships who "have to be there every night . . . doing all of the wifely things all the time." This echoes college women's critiques of serious relationships as greedy of their time and energy and their preference for the lower-cost hook-up.[20] For Mormon fundamentalists, polygamous marriage—in which, in Christina's words, "it's only every other night"—offers an alternative lower-cost form of sexual and emotional intimacy.

Second, Mormon fundamentalist women contend that plural marriages provide female companionship and support. Christina says her plural marriage "works a million times better" than her former relationship with her "super needy" ex-boyfriend because "I have a family, I have a husband, [and] I have my best friend, who's also married to him." Others similarly argued that marriage is easier emotionally when you have a sister wife with whom you can strategize, share domestic duties, and receive emotional support. In a world where everyone—men and women—"need a wife," plural marriage can seem attractive.[21]

Third, Mormon fundamentalist women argue that, compared to monogamy, polygyny provides more opportunity for leisure, education, and employment because sister wives help shoulder domestic responsibilities. As Anne Wilde puts it, a woman in a plural marriage can have "the best of both worlds," in that she can "have a family, have children, and then she can still decide to get a college degree, . . . [or] a career . . . and not have to take [her children] to a babysitter." As another woman put it, "You can say [to your sister wife], I'm gonna go play volleyball, so you take care of the household." The idea that a man might pick up the slack at home to allow a woman to pursue education, a career, or a volleyball match does not seem to occur to them any more than it occurs to the college students pursuing hook-ups in lieu of serious relationships. Rather, polygyny—like hook-ups—appears as a solution to the "stalled revolution" in men's entry into domestic work, while doing nothing the speed up the revolution.[22]

Creating a Sense of Linked Fate

While reluctantly likening themselves to black civil rights activists, gay rights activists, and feminists, plural-marriage family activists distance themselves from those Mormon fundamentalist sects—such as the notorious Fundamentalist Latter Day Saints— known to endorse coerced underage marriage and incest. This is especially true for members of The Work, which broke away from the FLDS in 1984 over disagreement about these issues and whose members continue to be confused with the FLDS members due to their conservative dress. Members of The Work say they feel they need to repeatedly correct employers and friends who assume they are part of FLDS. "No. That's not us," says one, "We're not like that. It's nothing like that."

Is the act of distancing, on one hand, or linking their cause to those of other groups, on the other, driven by or generating a sense of linked fate? Linked fate refers to the idea that an individual person's well-being is inextricable from the well-being of a larger group of which that person is a part. It is used most commonly to discuss African Americans' sense of linked fate with other African Americans.[23]

On one hand, the efforts of plural-marriage family activists to distance themselves from the FLDS seem to be driven by the concern that when fringe groups engage in coerced underage marriage or incest, this "hurts the rest of us because we're all painted with the same brush," as one high-profile leader and independent put it. To manage the risk of being lumped together with the FLDS, plural-marriage family activists who were independent or in sects that oppose underage marriage counter that sexual abuse is not limited to polygyny and does not characterize plural marriage as a whole.[24]

On the other hand, some Mormon fundamentalist polygamists may be coming to see their fate as linked to that of gay men and lesbians, and not only to those of others in plural marriages. For most, this is purely strategic. While they condemn the "gay lifestyle," they argue that the government should not regulate people's private lives, mostly because of the implications this has for them and their lifestyle. As one said, "I don't like the idea of gays but they have really helped our movement." On this issue, Mormon fundamentalist polygamists have taken a position radically different from that of the mainstream Mormon Church of the Latter Day Saints. The church had been among the most strident and organized opponents of gay rights for decades until April 2019, when it reversed its controversial 2015 policy classifying people in same-sex marriages as "apostates."[25]

A small handful of the more prominent activists, however, expressed support for the LGBTQ community because they can relate to being stigmatized due to their romantic choices and family structure. For instance, Mary Batchelor says she relates to the "freedom of association movement, which is largely where the gay movement comes from, because I am very much a freedom-loving person." In sum, while being socially conservative in other ways, our respondents generally support same-sex marriage and LGBTQ rights for strategic reasons, which—in a few cases—seem to be generating deeper empathy and solidarity. Likewise, the fact that some of these women identify as feminists may make them more supportive of other feminist causes, such as opposition to sexual violence—a topic that is itself increasingly coming out into public awareness for reasons examined in the next chapter.

6

Airing Dirty Laundry
and Squealing on Pigs

The MeToo movement that went viral in late 2017 underscores the trans-
formative power of (and resistance to) coming out and outing. African
American activist Tarana Burke founded the original MeToo movement in
2007 to let sex abuse survivors—especially girls and women of color—know
that they were not alone. She recounts that the impetus for the movement
came a decade earlier, in 1997, when a 13-year-old girl confided in Burke
that she had been sexually abused and Burke did not know how to respond.
"I didn't have a response or a way to help her in that moment, and I couldn't
even say 'me too,'" Burke said.[1] In 2007, Burke created Just Be Inc., a non-
profit organization that helps victims of sexual harassment and assault. She
sought out the resources that she had not found readily available a decade
earlier and committed herself to being there for people who had been abused.
She named her movement Me Too.[2]

This movement went viral a decade after that, in late 2017, after over three
dozen women accused Hollywood producer Harvey Weinstein of sexual harassment, assault, or rape. Initially unaware of Burke's use of the term "Me
Too" but publicly crediting Burke for the MeToo campaign when she learned
of it, actress Alyssa Milano posted "Me Too" on Twitter, Snapchat, Facebook,
and other social media platforms, and urged others to do the same.[3] Millions
of women followed Milano's lead, effectively coming out as victims of sexual
harassment, assault, or rape. Several people have bitterly noted that it was
not until famous white women spoke about being victimized that the public
took notice, whereas abuse of ordinary girls and women of color has elicited
public indifference for years. For her part, Burke has argued that Hollywood
actresses—precisely because of their high profile and influence—are ideal
allies for this movement. "I understand why people are frustrated that it took
celebrities for this to take off because in a perfect world, people would just
care and would want to see this situation elevated to a public issue, but that's
just not the reality that we live in," said Burke. She explains:

Come Out, Come Out, Whoever You Are. Abigail C. Saguy, Oxford University Press (2020).
© Oxford University Press.
DOI: 10.1093/oso/9780190931650.001.0001

We are a society that thrives off of celebrity culture, so it always takes something to break the ice, and if it takes celebrities coming forward, for me, I don't have time to be annoyed that it didn't happen in a different way. I'm just happy that it happened. I just think that it's worth acknowledging that it took celebrities to make it happen, but I'm a realist—so how else would it happen to spark a national movement? I'm not mad and I'm not surprised.[4]

If celebrities could draw attention to the problem of sexual abuse—including of girls and women of color—that was all for the good.

And draw attention to the problem, they did. Following Milano's post, millions of people followed suit. Some posted "#MeToo" to social media without further commentary. Many of my own Facebook friends copied and pasted a message forwarded by Milano: "Me, too. If all the women who have been sexually harassed or assaulted wrote 'Me too' as a status, we might give people a sense of the magnitude of the problem."[5] Others posted an edited version of the original post that broadened the category of women to also include "femme, trans, and genderqueer folks." Milano expressed the hope that the social media campaign would shift the focus from Weinstein to victims and "give people a sense of the magnitude of the problem."[6] Whether or not she acknowledged it, this strategy followed that of Harvey Milk and other gay rights activists who encouraged people to come out as gay so that other people would realize that they already knew and liked people who were homosexual.

One of my Facebook friends posted simply but poignantly, "#metoo . . . and I believed it was my fault." Another posted, "#metoo all the fucking time. Why is this even required? If you don't know that it is all the women all the time then you are not paying attention." A French Facebook friend expressed strikingly similar sentiments, saying (my translation): "#metoo. Of course me too, also her, also them, I don't know a woman who has not been attacked: exhibitionism, insults, harassment, unwanted touching, forced kisses, groping, rape." The posts kept coming. Soon, my Facebook feed—and the Facebook feeds of others—was full of these posts. Indeed, this itself became the object of commentary on Facebook. For instance, one post in my Facebook feed said:

There are at least a thousand #Metoo on my timeline. These stories don't come in the singular. Some of violence and rape; others of avoidance or concession for survival or safety. All of it makes me nauseous and furious; mind blown that we are still here doing what we do. #metoo

Hashtag MeToo was tweeted nearly a million times in 48 hours, according to Twitter. In the United States, Facebook reports that 45 percent of users have had friends who posted "Me Too." Worldwide, there were more than 12 million Facebook posts, comments, and reactions in less than 24 hours, by 4.7 million users around the world, according to the company.[7]

Whereas visibility was the dominant theme in talk of coming out, being heard (speaking up, having a voice, etc.) was a common theme in the MeToo movement. Consistent with this, the December issue of *Time* magazine chose "the silence breakers" as the "person of the year. The magazine put five of these silence breakers on the cover, including celebrities Taylor Swift and Ashley Judd; Susan Fowler—whose 3,000-word blog post on sexual harassment at Uber led to the ouster of CEO Travis Kalanick and drew attention to the problem of sexual harassment in Silicon Valley; lobbyist and activist Adama Iwu—who organized more than 147 women to expose sexual harassment in California government after experiencing harassment herself; and Isabel Pascual (pseudonym)—who shared her story about the sexual harassment, stalking, and threats to her family she experienced as a strawberry picker in California. Tarana Burke, while acknowledged in the article itself, was not on the cover—a fact that many saw as indicative of how African American women's contributions continue to be minimized or overlooked.[8]

The online movement was global, with similar media campaigns erupting across the world. Some of my French Facebook friends used the #metoo hashtag. Others used the French hashtag "balance ton porc," which can be translated as "out your pig"—even closer to the imagery of coming out and outing—or "squeal on your pig," which again emphasizes being heard.[9] The French #balancetonporc became popular the day *before* Milano launched #metoo.[10] In India, the tipping point for a "mostly social media-led holistic movement that combines women's freedom with a wider call for social justice for minority men and women" occurred even earlier, in 2012, following the fatal gang rape of a 23-year-old medical student in Delhi.[11]

In China, despite state censorship that prevented a viral social media campaign, feminist university professors and students for the first time started signing petitions, with their real names, about sexual harassment in universities.[12] In February 2018, one of South Korea's most prominent theater directors in this deeply patriarchal society apologized for sexually abusing actresses, five days after a Facebook post by a former actress set off a cascade of abuse accusations against him.[13] In Russia, in late March 2018, several news media outlets vowed to curtail their coverage of the State Duma, the lower chamber of the Russian Parliament and widely viewed as a rubber stamp for the Kremlin, a day after its ethics commission exonerated a lawmaker accused of sexual harassment by several women journalists.[14] By coming out about having endured sexual abuse and outing the perpetrators, women worldwide have challenged the status quo.[15] Of course, the precise way these movements would unfold would vary cross-nationally based on different legal contexts, including differences in laws governing such things as human rights, worker rights, and defamation.[16]

Sharing Stories

Just how much one needs to share emerged as a topic of some debate within the MeToo movement. Alyssa Milano herself did not provide details about her own experiences with sexual harassment or assault and did not pressure other women to do so. Indeed, she contended that this is what #MeToo is about: "You don't have to tell your story. You just have to say 'me too.'"[17] But many people did share stories, recounting specific details about workplace sexual harassment endured over the years. For instance, a fellow university professor shared her account of sexual harassment and sexism within academia:

> #MeToo. Yep!! More than once!! When I was an assistant professor, a man with authority over me explained that no one complained about sexual harassment at this university because everyone was somewhat guilty. This, as a threat . . . , and a silencing strategy and by way of explaining to me the culture of the place, in case I didn't want to "get it." This pitiful character also routinely imposed his sexual jokes to everyone around including the female staff. That was before Anita Hill, before I learned that sexual harassment was about demonstrating power and putting our nose in it. Many senior colleagues were witness to this and worse, but this behavior was normalized and the man was celebrated publicly again and again. I certainly felt let down.

Being a university professor myself, I have many Facebook friends who are also in academia. I read many accounts on my Facebook feed of senior faculty using their position of authority as gatekeepers to fellowships, conferences, or other professional opportunities to pressure women into having sexual relations with them. One of the people who recounted a senior faculty member using his position of authority to try to pressure her into having sexual relations with him also wrote that she "quit [her] job as an assistant professor . . . largely because of unaddressed and widespread sexual predation." She expressed regret that as an older faculty member, she cannot do more to protect her graduate students from "inappropriate male sexual behavior" that goes "completely unpunished in the work place—kept as a secret that everyone knows about."

I read accounts, however, that spanned professions and industries. People wrote about being "smacked on the butt and fondled" in a restaurant job, being told to learn to take a joke or to get tougher skin when they reported incidents, and being ostracized for reporting incidents. Some wrote that they quietly endured the abuse, while others retold how they responded with physical force. Regardless, many said they quit their jobs in response to the treatment. Even when women were able to put an end to this sort of behavior and stay at their jobs, they wrote about feeling demeaned and told how their jobs were made more difficult. In telling their stories, they were—like others who have come out as gay, fat, undocumented, or Mormon fundamentalist polygamist—raising awareness.

As with the movements we have examined in the preceding chapters, there are different levels of visibility within the #MeToo movement. On one level, there is a sense in which all victims of sexual assault and harassment have been invisible, due to the shame that leads many to censor themselves and the efforts of abusers—through non-disclosure agreements and other mechanism—to silence them.[18] On another level, it is powerful white women—including movie stars like Ashley Judd, Gwyneth Paltrow, and Uma Thurman—who initially dominated media coverage of this issue. Yet women of color are especially vulnerable to sexual assault and harassment and experience being objectified in specific ways, even as they are less likely to be believed when they speak out. In an article about how the #MeToo movement "looks different for women of color," Mai Nguyen, a consultant, recounts how she is called "China doll" and how there is even "more of an expectation for Asians to act ladylike and timid and not have an opinion."[19] Public relations firm founder Emerald-Jane Hunter says that

> being a woman in the workplace has its challenges. Then being a black woman doubles those challenges. And then when you're thick or curvy, your curves felt like a curse. When black men see you, that's the first thing they see. You're objectified, you're thick, you're curvy, you have that phat ass, with a p-h. They think that's a compliment. You don't think you're being seen in any other way.[20]

Moreover, she says that black women are less likely to speak up: "We lack the empowerment to come forward from a deeper place—it's more than being a woman and more than shame. It's not being raised to know there is power in speaking up. We're conditioned to think power never cycles to us."[21] It can be even more difficult for African American women to speak up when the offender is a black man. As professor and writer Shanita Hubbard explains, "We have this mindset like we have to protect our black men. They suffer themselves from unchecked power in the hands of police. But we prioritize that like we don't suffer the same abuse, and our pain is not prioritized."[22]

Sexual abuse is, of course, not limited to workplaces. The #Metoo movement has sought to highlight the pervasiveness of sexism, sexual harassment, and assault. People share experiences of being catcalled and assaulted by strangers. A Facebook friend of a friend in India writes about

> that feeling of constantly being on the lookout to make sure you are safe. It's that random stranger in the park masturbating at you, that random man at the age of 13 brushing against your boob while passing you by in a not even remotely crowded market, it's that man punching your butt in one of the best clubs in Delhi, it's those lewd songs being sung on the way home in Bangalore.

Highlighting how sexual harassment and fat shaming intersect for heavy women, one woman writes about receiving both "compliments"—in the form of catcalls—and "insults" ("moos, oinks, and other weight-based bullying"). While she says she prefers "the positive comments to the negative," she notes that in both cases "it is just men thinking every woman on the street needs to know his opinion of her appearance—and we DON'T."

A theme that runs through many accounts of sexual assault is how "lucky" women are that the abuse they experienced was not worse. For instance, the woman quoted immediately above says she feels lucky that a man who grabbed her around the neck from behind and tried to drag her on to railroad land was not carrying a gun and that she was able to get away and call the cops, and that the attempted rapist spent a few weeks in jail. Another writes about feeling lucky that "it wasn't worse" after two boys kicked her and called her a bitch after she refused to give one of them her phone number. A third writes before beginning a list of sexual abuse suffered over the years, "I was never raped, so I consider myself very fortunate." That so many women feel lucky after having been insulted, assaulted (sexual or otherwise), nearly raped, and so on speaks volumes.

Artist Zahira Kelly-Cabrera argues that as an Afro-Latino Dominican woman, she is "hypersexed" and assumed to be a sex worker—due both to the fact that sex tourism is "huge on the island" and also to a long history of white men sexually exploiting African and Native women. As such, "people feel they can be more violent towards you or are entitled toward your body. That it's just what you deserve."[23] Professor and writer Shanita Hubbard explains how black women are loath to speak out against street harassment and assault in their neighborhoods out of fear of worsening the racism that black men face:

> Growing up with older guys from the hood, they grab your butt or physically assault you in some way. I didn't talk about it. I didn't see it being addressed. I saw it happen to a lot of young girls. But it would sound like I'm trying to play oppression Olympics. When I try to say that for young black girls, it's hard to come forward, it can be met with, "Do you think it's easy for young black guys from the hood?" I get that, and that's not what I'm saying.[24]

Black women may thus silence themselves—or remain closeted about the harassment and assault they experience at the hands of black men—not only out of shame but also as part of an attempt to protect black men.

On this point, in an interview with Trevor Noah on the *Daily Show*, Tarana Burke speaks about the need to hold "more than one truth" at the same time. She explains that there is a "true history of blacks being accused of rape and sexual violence in this country." But it is also true that in every community—with the exception of Native Americans—the people who commit sexual violence are, by and large, members of that community. By extension, given that we know that black women are sexually assaulted, "it happens, by and large, at the hands of black men." So, she urges, "we have to unravel this idea that we have to protect our men and we have to protect our community from this." We also need to "dismantle notions we have about womanhood and sexuality" whereby once a girl "develops and . . . gets a body" she becomes "solely responsible for protecting herself from perpetrators. It becomes her fault that she develops breasts and a behind and grown men find her attractive." We need to remember that "the adults are solely responsible" for keeping children safe, she explains.[25]

The MeToo hashtag accompanied many a story of sexual violence at the hands of a person the victim knew. Among these, accounts of attempted date rape were common. As one woman puts it "I ran out—a.k.a. escaped—from more than one man's apartment." Journalist Cindy Rodriguez says that, as a Latina, white men she dates sexualize her, assuming that "Latinas are these sexual bombshells walking around just waiting to have someone ravish us."[26]

People also write about sexual violence endured as children. The majority of these are from women writing about being molested or raped by men they trusted as young children or as teenagers. Having studied the topic of sexual harassment and sexual violence for over two decades, I know the statistics about how many people are affected by sexual harassment (30 percent of American women, according to one recent survey) and attempted or completed sexual assault or rape (one in six women, according to a recent estimate).[27] I, nonetheless, found myself moved by the sheer number of posts and the details in them.

Many men also write to express their solidarity for the women they know and to encourage other men to take note. One writes that he has "spoken to male friends to invite them to imagine what it is like to live in a world where every day when you leave your house you might be in fear for your safety." In this sense, they present themselves as allies.

Other men share their own personal experiences of being the target of sexual harassment, sometimes pointing out that women are more likely than men to be victims of sexual harassment and assault. One shares his experiences in order to "broaden the scope of this very real plague in our society." This man shares a horrific childhood experience of having been sexually assaulted at the age of 7 years by a male acquaintance of his mother's and then shamed and bullied for it—by his mother and her friend—when he was "caught in the act." He writes that his mother told him:

"I bet you loved it, you little faggot." My mother scowled at me along with her friend . . . as they were clearing out my bedroom of all of my possessions. "You won't need any toys since you like playing with dicks, you little cocksucker."

He writes that his mother made him write "I will not be a cocksucking faggot" 1,000 times, leading him to conclude that this was his mother's greatest concern. Unsurprisingly, this experience left lasting scars and underscores the potential intersection of sexual assault and homophobia.

Some object to the framing of sexual assault and harassment as a woman's issue in the first place. For instance, bisexual genderqueer writer Trav Mamone notes that while several trans women have come out with #MeToo stories, no trans and gender-nonconforming people were featured in *Time* magazine's profile of the #MeToo "Silence Breakers" as "Person of the Year" for 2017.[28] Moreover, Mamone argues that transgender people are at even greater risk of sexual assault than cisgender women, or women who were identified as girls at birth.[29] Mamone recounts how a non-binary friend, who was assigned female at birth, posted a MeToo status on Facebook until seeing "the word 'woman' being associated with it," after which the friend took it down. Mamone explains "that there was no hostility toward trans or gender nonconforming people but that the discourse centered around cis women so much that they felt like they were not welcomed."[30] Mamone suggests that "instead of framing the conversation as a cis men versus cis women struggle, it's more appropriate to frame it as a discussion on toxic masculinity and how it often preys on non-men and those considered not "manly" enough."

At stake in these debates are questions that we have seen in other instances of coming out: who gets to represent the movement? Who is invisible within a movement whose primary goal is to claim greater visibility?

Airing Dirty Laundry: The Clothesline Project

The #MeToo movement underscores the increasingly important role the internet—and specifically social media—is playing in the diffusion and evolution of coming out politics. The #MeToo movement is an excellent example of what sociologists Jennifer Earl and Katrina Kimport call e-movements—entire social movements that unfold online.[31]

While the viral nature of the #MeToo movement is new, efforts to draw public attention to the problem of sexual violence are not. Indeed, the #MeToo movement reminds me of a campus-based project that has been going on since the 1990s: the Clothesline Project. This project organizes students across college campuses to "Break the Silence of Violence" about incest, domestic violence, and sexual violence by publicly displaying in the center of college campuses clotheslines full of T-shirts that speak of such violence (see Figure 6.1). The shirts vary in size—based on the age and size of the woman or girl at the time of victimization—and by color, to represent the type of violence suffered. White represents those who have died because of violence. Yellow designates survivors of physical assault and domestic violence. Red, pink, and orange all represent survivors of rape or sexual assault, whereas blue and green signify survivors of incest or childhood sexual abuse. Purple stands for survivors of attacks due to a perceived sexual orientation. Brown and gray both designate survivors of emotional, spiritual, or verbal abuse. Black stands for those who were either disabled because of an attacked or attacked because of a disability.

Figure 6.1. UCLA Clothesline Project (Credit Dotan Saguy).

Walking across a campus quad, one sees clotheslines full of different colored T-shirts with handwritten messages. A yellow T-shirt declares in handwritten block print:

> I forgive you, but of course I will not forget. My mother, sibblings [sic], and I have become strong. We are happy, successful and stand tall together. Where are you? I hope you've gotten the help you need. I AM A SURVIVOR! I AM STRONG! I AM LOVABLE! I AM CAPABLE! I AM BEAUTIFUL!

The term *survivor* recurs frequently in the messages on the shirts. It represents a concerted (but controversial) effort to reframe people as survivors instead of victims—the language of law enforcement. Proponents argue that *victim* suggests passivity and helplessness whereas *survivor* evokes strength and resilience. Others, however, bristle under what they perceive as efforts to force them to feel like survivors when they in fact feel more like victims.[32]

Still, many of the T-shirts speak about reclaiming power and renouncing a victim status. For instance, handwritten words printed on a red shirt declare:

> Sometimes I blame myself. I was drunk and had taken a large amount of ecstasy. I should have just gone home. I was gang raped. Those three nasty men took my virginity. I was so intoxicated, I don't even remember their faces. I wanted to lose my virginity in a special way. It changed me. I lost all self-respect. Now I am working on no longer being a victim. I am repowering myself.

A blue T-shirt calls out, by first name only, a school athletic coach who sexually assaulted multiple girls under his supervision—noting that no one believed the girls, not even the parents:

> Jack—This is the color of our team leotard. You were such a good coach that no one believed me—not even the parents. For 20 years I carried the burden even after you pled guilty. But you know what? You don't have power over me anymore. Think of the girls I protected from you by going to the police. I could say I hate you, I could say you've ruined me, but in truth you have my compassion, because I don't have to go through life fighting the temptation to voilate [sic] little girls. Instead, I FORGIVE YOU i [sic] forgive you.

The author of the words on the shirt tells the coach that he no longer has power over her. She takes charge and forgives her assaulter.

Another blue T-shirt is scrawled with the words, "You hurt me and said NEVER TELL. . . . But now I'm grown, you'll never touch me again." It is signed "Happy to be Free." An orange T-shirt denounces a "fucking rapist of a husband" who has since been divorced. Through these messages, a familiar narrative emerges in which a victim becomes a survivor; the powerless find their power.

Some T-shirts tell a different story. For instance, a purple one asks, "How am I still alive? Middle & High school was HELL. I never thought that I'd graduate. You all hurled whatever you could at me you put hate notes and gay porn in my bag and locker. You spread the worst rumors about me. You all told me that I was broken and unloved, a waste. MY LIFE WILL ALWAYS BE DIFFICULT." A black T-shirt is covered with childish scribbles and the words, "The Pain is gone But the scars and tears wount [sic] go away."

Together, by airing their "dirty laundry," participants in this project raise awareness about sexual violence. Likewise, since the 1970s, women have organized Take Back the Night marches on college campuses to draw attention to the issue of sexual violence. The marches serve both instrumental (that is, education and policy change) and emotional (empowerment, consciousness raising) goals. At these women-only nighttime events, marchers chant "No Means No and Yes Means Yes" and "Hey Ho, Patriarchy Has Got to Go." Unlike the Clothesline Project, in which both victims and perpetrators are shielded with anonymity, during the Take Back the Night marches, some women share their personal stories with the hope that this will also empower others to do so.[33]

In another dramatic college-based protest against sexual assault, in 2014–15, Columbia student Emma Sulkowicz, who uses gender-neutral pronouns, outed themself and their rapist.[34] Sulkowitz carried a dorm room mattress everywhere—as both an act of protest against Columbia University for its inaction in response to the report of sexual assault by fellow student Paul Nungesser and a work of performance art, titled "Mattress Performance (Carry that Weight)" (see Figure 6.2). The performance represents the painful burden rape victims carry.[35]

Social movement scholar Nancy Whittier argues that student protests against university responses (or lack thereof) to sexual assault on campus are among the things—along with "slutwalks"—that make the #metoo

Figure 6.2. Emma Sulkowicz's Mattress Project (Carry That Weight).

movement possible.[36] The impetus for the first slutwalk came in 2011 when a Toronto police officer told an audience of university students that "women should avoid dressing as sluts in order not to be victimized."[37] Angered by the statement, a small group of women organized the first "slutwalk," a march involving an estimated 3,000 to 4,000 people—representing more than 50 organizations and businesses.[38] They intentionally and self-consciously reclaimed the word *slut* to reject the view that women who engage in and enjoy sex on their own terms are shameful or deserving of victimization. They denounced *sexual profiling* (akin to *racial profiling*, in which people are judged guilty based on appearance), and *slut shaming* (that is, negatively labeling women for being sexually active).[39] After the first march in Toronto, "slutwalks" went viral and global.

The slutwalks—like the Clothesline Project, Take Back the Night marches, and Mattress Project—drew attention to the problem of sexual assault, but they varied in the extent to which they involved either women coming out as victims/survivors or the outing of perpetrators. The Clothesline Project does neither, while the Mattress Project did both. The #MeToo movement often involves women sharing their own stories without outing their abusers and, in this form, is the least socially controversial. When women name those who harassed, assaulted, or raped them, the event becomes more controversial and also has greater impact. The hashtag MeToo captures the first impulse while the French hashtag BalanceTonPorc, or OutYourPig, captures the second.

Outing Pigs

Whether the #MeToo movement was about simply saying "me too," sharing your own story of being harassed, or publicly naming and shaming your harasser, it quickly became a topic of debate and controversy. In the days following the first posts, *Guardian* columnist Jessica Valenti argued that it was time to name the perpetrators of sexual harassment and violence and not just the victims. She conceded that "telling our stories can help—it can help victims not feel quite so alone and make others understand the breadth and depth of the problem," but argued that "nothing will really change in a lasting way until the social consequences for men are too great for them to risk hurting us." She asked, "Why have a list of victims when a list of perpetrators could be so much more useful?"[40]

Of course, women have long recognized the utility of sharing the names of perpetrators among each other, to warn each other about men who are known to harass, assault, or rape women. This is known as a "whisper network." Journalist Alana Massey writes about how such a whisper network protected her when she was 14 years old:

> While serving as a bridesmaid in my cousin's wedding at the age of 14, I was relieved that the groomsman I was matched with was especially friendly with me. I had anticipated not knowing anyone at the wedding, seeing as they were all 25 and older and mostly from Arkansas, 3,000 miles away from me. "You're really mature for 14," he told me, touching my forearm, just as an older woman I'd never met or seen approached us both and they greeted each other warmly. "Now Alana, you be careful with this one, he's trouble!" she said jovially in her thick but charming Southern accent, and they both laughed. He went to get a drink, and the woman's smile suddenly dropped. She pulled me close to her and said, "Sweetheart, you stay close by

your mama and sister. If he asks you to go anywhere with him, don't." She let go of my arm and walked away. Two hours later, the groomsman asked me if I'd ever driven before and whether I'd like to drive his truck around. I declined his offer, and to this day, I wish I had found and properly thanked that wedding guest who had warned me away from God knows what.[41]

Some industries have whisper networks through which women share information about the people with whom you don't want to find yourself alone. Such whisper networks are, however, private by definition. Moreover, some of the most vulnerable women—including women of color, young women, and women who are not well connected—are less likely than better-connected women to have access to these networks.[42] Jenna Wortham writes about how women of color like herself are not "invited to the happy hours or chats or email threads where such information is presumably shared." Instead of being warned, as a young business reporter, about "the New York investor known for luring women out to meals under the guise of work," she "found out the hard way."[43]

The fact that some of the most vulnerable women are not part of the whisper network was a large part of writer Moira Donegan's motivation for publicly sharing—in October 2017—the "shitty media men" list, which collected a range of rumors and allegations of sexual misconduct, much of it violent, by men in magazines and publishing.[44] As Donegan explains, "The anonymous, crowd-sourced document was a first attempt at solving what has seemed like an intractable problem: how women can protect ourselves from sexual harassment and assault."[45] Jenna Wortham writes about being "in a van with a half dozen other women of color, riding through the desert on our way to a writing retreat" a few days after the list appeared and realizing both "the extent to which harassment polluted [their] industry" and the extent to which white women in their industry had not included them in their whispering. She writes that "despite my working in New York media for 10 years, it was my first 'whisper' of any kind, a realization that felt almost as hurtful as reading the acts described on the list itself." Once the list became public and men learned about it, it was effectively shut down. Before then, however, "when it still felt secret, for women only," Wortham says she "moved through the world differently. The energy in the air felt charged, like after the siren goes off in the 'Purge' movies." She says she "wanted every single man put on notice, to know that they, too, were vulnerable because women were talking."[46]

Not everyone was pleased about the list, however. Some criticized the document itself—even when kept within a relatively small circle—as "reckless, malicious, or puritanically anti-sex."[47] Donegan explains:

> Many called the document irresponsible, emphasizing that since it was anonymous, false accusations could be added without consequence. Others said that it ignored established channels in favor of what they thought was vigilantism and that they felt uncomfortable that it contained allegations both of violent assaults and inappropriate messages. Still other people just saw it as catty and mean, something like the "Burn Book" from *Mean Girls*. Because the document circulated among writers and journalists, many of the people assigned to write about it had received it from friends. Some faced the difficult experience of seeing other, male friends named. Many commentators expressed sympathy with the aims of the document—women warning women, trying to help one another—but thought that its technique was too radical. They objected to the anonymity, or to the digital format, or to writing these allegations down at all.

In other words, people criticized women's use of the spreadsheet to try to keep each other safe, not just the fact that the spreadsheet was ultimately leaked to the news media.

The list's creator herself says she never meant for the document to go public.[48] She initially merely hoped "to create a place for women to share their stories of harassment and assault without being needlessly discredited or judged . . . to create an alternate avenue to report this kind of behavior and warn others without fear of retaliation." This occurred in a context in which established mechanisms for reporting such behavior were biased against the victims. In her own words:

> The police are notoriously inept at handling sexual-assault cases. Human-resources departments, in offices that have them, are tasked not with protecting employees but with shielding the company from liability—meaning that in the frequent occasion that the offender is a member of management and the victim is not, HR's priorities lie with the accused. When a reporting channel has enforcement power, like an HR department or the police, it also has an obligation to presume innocence.[49]

Many of the women who used the spreadsheet—like Donegan herself—were especially vulnerable—young, new to the industry, and not yet influential. For them, "the risks of using any of the established means of reporting were especially high and the chance for justice especially slim." Donegan envisioned the spreadsheet as circumventing the challenges of traditional avenues:

> Anonymous, it would protect its users from retaliation: No one could be fired, harassed, or publicly smeared for telling her story when that story was not attached to her name. Open-sourced, it would theoretically be accessible to women who didn't have the professional or social cachet required for admittance into whisper networks. The spreadsheet did not ask how women responded to men's inappropriate behavior; it did not ask what you were wearing or whether you'd had anything to drink. Instead, the spreadsheet made a presumption that is still seen as radical: That it is men, not women, who are responsible for men's sexual misconduct."[50]

This represented a radical shift—albeit one that Tarana Burke and others had been advocating for decades—with the potential of upending relations of power. No wonder it made people uneasy.

This is not to say there were no issues with the document. Donegan herself recognized that there were "pitfalls." For one, the document was vulnerable to false accusations. As a result, Donegan added a disclaimer to the top of the spreadsheet: "This document is only a collection of misconduct allegations and rumors. Take everything with a grain of salt." She envisioned the spreadsheet as informing women of allegations and trusting them "to judge the quality of that information for themselves and to make their own choices accordingly." The spreadsheet distinguished between different types of behaviors and included notes to contextualize incidents, although the premise was "that all of these behaviors were things that might make someone uncomfortable and that individuals should be able to choose for themselves what behavior they could tolerate and what they would rather avoid." Once more than one woman accused a man of physical sexual assault, his name was highlighted in red.[51]

Donegan envisioned the document as a way to warn other women about "the behavior of a few men," and was shocked to realize how badly the list was needed, "how much more common the experience of sexual harassment or assault is than the opportunity to speak about it." Women anonymously recounted "being beaten, drugged, and raped." They reported "being followed into bathrooms or threatened with weapons." They told of being groped at work or shown a colleague's penis. Donegan says, "There was the sense that the capacity for honesty, long suppressed, had finally been unleashed. This solidarity was thrilling, but the stories were devastating."[52]

The spreadsheet began to take on a life of its own and escape the control of its maker, however. In the 12 hours between the time the list went live and Donegan took it down, it grew to include the names of more than 70 men—including 14 accused of physical sexual violence by multiple women—along with brief descriptions of their alleged misconduct. Donegan worried that managing the document would eventually put her in the uncomfortable position of having to decide which stories to include and which to exclude. She fretted that she might lose her job and her career. At the same time, she saw how cathartic it was for women to be able to tell their stories and support one another. Many of these women lacked the privileges—including whiteness, health, education, and social class—that Donegan had. And what if the document itself could be used to stop assaults before they happened?[53]

Reluctantly, Donegan took the list down, after getting a text message that Buzzfeed was planning an article on it[54] but before the document itself was posted on Reddit. Donegan initially thought that she could create this document because she did not think that people with authority "care about what we had to say there." But Donegan created her list one week after the news broke about Harvey Weinstein's systematic harassment and assault of women in Hollywood.[55] It was a new moment and people in authority did care. While the document is no longer live, it lives on in the form of downloaded PDFs and screenshots. While its creator did not mean for it to be used for disciplinary purposes, it has been put to that use. Media organizations including BuzzFeed, *Mother Jones*, the *New York Times*, and Riverhead Books—each of which had more than one current or former employee on the list—initiated investigations.[56] Of the men on the list, seven ended up losing their jobs or having significant professional setbacks before the end of the year.[57] Others said the list negatively affected their professional and personal lives even if it did not lead to their suspension or firing. Still others lost their jobs as the result of separate complaints and investigations into sexual misconduct.[58]

In contrast to the #MeToo campaign on social media, where many women came out about their own experiences as the targets of sexual violence without necessarily "outing" the perpetrators of the violence, the Shitty Media List outed the perpetrators while shielding the identities of the targets of violence. Just as some critics, in the 1990s, likened to McCarthyism the outing of politicians who supported anti-gay politics while privately engaging in same-sex sexuality, so some likened the Shitty Media Men List to McCarthyism.[59] The analogy is even more strained, however, in this case than it was in the 1990s outings. First, Donegan created the list as a semi-private document to be shared with other women in her industry to help them protect themselves. The list was not designed with the goal of purging categories of people from public employment, even if it ultimately had employment implications for many. And the powerful white men on the list did not constitute an oppressed minority. They were not being named for their political sympathies or sexual orientation but for preying on vulnerable colleagues.

When word first got out that writer Katie Roiphe was planning to name the still unknown author of the document in an article she was writing for *Harper's*, this created controversy of its own. Some people warned that the author would be threatened, raped, or even killed.[60] Ultimately, Donegan decided to out herself on her own terms before Roiphe or someone else did. She did this in an article published in *The Cut*, from which I quote above.[61] Donegan wrote there that in the weeks after the spreadsheet was exposed, but not her identity, her life "changed dramatically." She lost friends—both those who thought she had been overzealous and those who thought she had not been zealous enough. She lost her job. She writes, "The fear of being exposed, and of the harassment that will inevitably follow, has dominated my life since. I've learned that protecting women is a position that comes with few protections itself." She writes, "I still don't know what kind of future awaits me now that I've stopped hiding."

Meanwhile, a separate group of women working in advertising created an anonymous Instagram account—@DietMadisonAvenue—dedicated to exposing sexual harassment on Madison Avenue. Created in October 2017, it had over 19,000 followers by March 2018. It published names of alleged harassers along with details of accusations against them through Instagram Stories that disappeared after 24 hours. By March 2018, it had shared 17 names and had collected an additional 158 to be vetted. An operator of the account, communicating to a *New York Times* journalist through private messages on Instagram, said that it vets allegations before making them public by verifying work histories and obtaining supporting documents like nondisclosure agreements. An operator of the account estimated that eight men have been fired after being named on @ DietMadisonAvenue.[62]

This Instagram account received some of the same critiques that were leveled at the Shitty Media Men list. An open letter from a group of women working in advertising said, "It is not acceptable to use an anonymous social media account to accuse people, pass judgment, and use other bullying techniques to help the victims."[63] One of the women who signed the letter—a freelance executive producer—says that by reporting allegations to the account instead of to their companies, it "becomes this trial by social media and men just don't have a chance to respond or defend themselves."[64]

Others praised the account for providing women with a new way to warn each other about certain men in the industry and to hold those men accountable. The women operating @DietMadisonAve say they can connect accusers with investigative reporters and with lawyers specializing in sexual harassment litigation, as well as provide information on whistle-blower laws, complaining to human resources departments, and finding mental health counselors. [65] Kat Gordon, founder of the 3 percent Movement, which promotes the role of women in creative leadership at advertising companies, says she was conflicted about the account's approach but understood the frustration of women "who didn't feel like they had justice." She says, she was "sad" that the account exists but that the fact it exists "is emblematic of something that's really broken. Sometimes you need a grenade."

Just as the streets of New York City provided a backdrop for many of Queer Nation's outings of gay politicians and celebrities in the 1990s, so New York City became an epicenter for the outing of perpetrators of sexual assault and harassment in 2018. In the former case, the outings aimed to reveal hypocrisy and bring about greater acceptance of homosexuality. In the latter, they serve to reveal the pervasiveness of unlawful behavior—sexual assault and rape—and incite outrage.

And, of course, outing is not limited to New York City. One woman rented a month's worth of advertising space on three 50-foot-wide digital billboards—in Albany, New York; Fairfield, Connecticut; and Springfield, Massachusetts—to draw attention to an unprosecuted rape case. This case concerned a former teacher who allegedly sexually abused and raped her when she was a student at Emma Willard School in Troy, New York, in the 1990s. While the teacher was fired for the abuse, he was also given letters of recommendation to teach elsewhere and was still teaching when the bill-board went up. The original billboard design included the alleged rapist's name and face, but the billboard company would not allow that, fearing a lawsuit. Instead, the billboards pointed viewers to the victim's website, where they could learn the alleged rapist's name and read about the need for New York state to pass the Child Victims Act, which would make it easier for molestation victims to seek criminal charges or file lawsuits against their abusers. [66]

Shifting Tectonic Plates

Rape, sexual assault, and sexual harassment are illegal and have been for some time. Yet implementation of these laws is undermined by the trivializa-tion of sexual violence and disbelief in women's accounts. This is true world-wide and not only in the United States. Claire Saas, a French legal scholar, told me that most French judges do not take sexual harassment seriously. They may think a sexual harasser "went a bit far," but they are not truly shocked. This comes through, says Saas, in the euphemisms used to describe the harassment—a "stolen kiss," "caress," or a "(misplaced) gesture of tender-ness." A French sexual harassment lawyer who works in both criminal and labor courts told me of a case of an older female judge who responded to the account that her client's boss had put his hands on her buttocks, touched her breast, and incessantly commented on her buttocks by asking: "Don't you like it?" French legal scholar and feminist activist Catherine Le Magueresse told me that defense lawyers still openly suggest that women who wear cer-tain clothes are asking to be sexual harassed or assaulted. Colleagues often say, "She showed cleavage, she was seductive, she wore short skirts, she was a tease." Even young girls are sometimes said to have welcomed or invited sexual assault. Judges and jurors often assume that women are lying about having been assaulted, and even when they believe the accusers, "it has to go very far before it is considered sexual harassment," in the words of one French sexual harassment lawyer.[67]

Things shifted somewhat, however, in the wake of a French sexual ha-rassment scandal that predated Harvey Weinstein by over six years. On May 15, 2011, the New York Police Department (NYPD) arrested French presidential hopeful Dominique Strauss Kahn (DSK) on charges of sex-ually assaulting a maid at the Sofitel Hotel. The initial French public response was to deny that the assault occurred, attributing the arrest to a mix of political conspiracy and American "Puritanism."[68] Several leftist public intellectuals defended DSK, describing him as a charmer, seducer, and "friend of women," but not a rapist,[69] and they expressed indignation that one of their nation's elite men was being paraded handcuffed before cameras like a common criminal.[70] Journalist Jean-Francois Kahn, trivialized the assault, saying that there was no "violent rape attempt" but merely a *"troussage de domestique"*—literally lifting a female servant's skirts to have forced sex with her.[71] This initial reaction to DSK's arrest, however, ultimately offered France a long-awaited teaching moment on sexual violence and sexism. French journalists and the general public started to ask themselves and others: What is sexual consent? What constitutes force? Some French commentators denounced the implication of Jean-Francois Kahn's remarks—that wealthy men should have sexual access to poor women employed in their service.[72]

Activists, legal scholars, and lawyers specializing in sexual violence have told me that media reporting following the DSK arrest led to a tangible shift in how sexual violence victims are now received. In the words of a lawyer who represents sexual harassment victims in France's labor courts, since the DSK scandal, "we don't feel like we are automatically assumed to be crazy." The scandal created, she says, "a kind of upheaval in French society," where people are better able to openly consider sexual harassment accusations. "That doesn't mean we always win our cases" or that "it will be easy to win them" but "it is possible to hear what is going on," she says. Other lawyers similarly say that the charges brought against DSK helped raise awareness that powerful men can also harass, assault, and rape, and that, in Le Magueresse's words, "even if you are very powerful . . . you can get caught."

By extension, we might expect that the tsunami of accusations against Weinstein and others—as well as the way the media and employers have taken these accusations seriously—would lead US judges and lawyers to be more open to the idea that people who claim to have been sexually abused are telling the truth. Indeed, Catharine MacKinnon—who first conceptualized sexual harassment as a form of sex discrimination in employment and is largely responsible for how the Equal Employment Opportunity Commission (EEOC) and US case law define sexual harassment[73]—made this argument in February 2018. Specifically, she argued that the MeToo movement "has made untenable the assumption that the one who reports sexual abuse is a lying slut." She writes,

"Sexual harassment law prepared the ground, but it is today's movement that is shifting gender hierarchy's tectonic plates."[74]

Larry Nassar and Bill Cosby

The trials of Dr. Larry Nassar and actor Bill Cosby provide a glimpse of what this new landscape might look like. In January 2018, a sentencing trial was held for Dr. Larry Nassar for sexual abuse of over 150 girl athletes entrusted to his care. According to a 2016 lawsuit, Larry Nassar had been abusing girls with impunity for almost 25 years.[75] This was consistent with the message of the MeToo movement—and the Clothesline Project before it—that highlighted how common sexual abuse against girls is and how seldom it is prosecuted. Nassar was appointed national medical co-ordinator for USA Gymnastics in 1996 and in 1997, and then became a team physician and assistant professor at Michigan State University (MSU). The following year, according to court records, Nassar began sex-ually abusing a 6-year-old daughter of a family friend, who later told po-lice that Nassar "penetrated her vagina with his fingers 'every other week for five years.'"[76]

That same year a student-athlete at MSU reported concerns about Nassar to trainers and coaches, but the university "failed to take any action," ac-cording to a lawsuit.[77] A second MSU student-athlete reported concerns about Nassar to trainers or coaches in 2000 but again, the university failed to take any action, and Nassar attended the Olympic Games in Sydney, Australia with the US gymnastics teams. Also in 2000, Nassar sexually abused Rachael Denhollander during treatments for lower back pain when she was 15 years old, according to her criminal complaint.[78] In the years that followed, Nassar continued to treat Olympic gymnasts and MSU student-athletes. Victims continued to tell trusted adults—including parents and coaches—about the abuse they were enduring, but the adults did not report the abuse to the po-lice or take university action. Indeed, in 2014, MSU cleared Nassar of any wrongdoing following an investigation of a complaint from a recent MSU graduate.[79]

Sadly, Nassar was not an exception but—as we began to learn—indicative of a larger problem in USA Gymnastics. The truth began to come out in August 2016, when the *Indianapolis Star* published a lengthy investigation into USA Gymnastics and its handling of sexual abuse complaints over the

decades.[80] It reported that "top executives at one of America's most prominent Olympic organizations failed to alert authorities to many allegations
of sexual abuse by coaches—relying on a policy that enabled predators to
abuse gymnasts long after USA Gymnastics had received warnings."[81] It cited
several examples of children being abused after USA Gymnastics dismissed
warning signs about the sex offender and revealed that two former USA
Gymnastics officials admitted under oath that the organization "routinely
dismissed sexual abuse allegations as hearsay unless they came directly from
a victim or victim's parent,"[82] whereas best practices require reporting all
allegations to authorities. The *IndyStar* article reported that the organization
had compiled complaint dossiers for more than 50 coaches but that, despite
this, "SA Gymnastics . . . did not initiate a report to authorities."[83]

Within the context of its larger investigative reporting, *IndyStar* detailed—
for the first time on September 12, 2016—allegations that Nassar had abused
girls under his care. The report included claims from two former gymnasts
who independently came forward following *IndyStar*'s August 4 story.
Following these claims, USA Gymnastics announced—on November 4,
2016—that it had hired former federal prosecutor Deborah J. Daniels to review the organization's handling of sexual misconduct cases.[84] Meanwhile,
in December 2016, *IndyStar* revealed that "at least 368 gymnasts had alleged some form of sexual abuse at the hands of their coaches, gym owners
and other adults working in gymnastics" over a 20-year period.[85] It detailed
how its "lax oversight" allowed sexual predators to move from gym to gym,
while a culture of secrecy allowed sexual predators to continue coaching.
USA Gymnastics CEO Steve Penny resigned in March 2017 in response to
pressure from the US Olympic Committee. Later that month, after hearing
testimony from a US Olympic Committee official about USA Gymnastics'
missed opportunities to detect sexual abuse by its members and failure to
report allegations to authorities, US lawmakers voted to advance federal legislation requiring sports officials to be more aggressive in reporting and combating sexual abuse.[86]

The fact that few gymnasts pressed charges is typical of victims of sexual
assault and rape in general.[87] This is, in large part, because they rightly
fear being victimized a second time in the courtroom, as their testimony
is questioned and doubted and lawyers and judges cast aspersions on their
character. Further, they may lose their case despite telling the truth since the
criminal system requires that the accused be proven guilty beyond a rea-
sonable doubt, a standard that can be hard to prove. Internalizing cultural

messages that women and girls bring sexual assault upon themselves by the way they dress or act, many victims blame themselves. Very few publicly come out having been victimized. In this context, it is amazing that 150 women and teenagers came forward to share the testimony during a seven-day sentencing hearing in Ingham County Circuit Court in January 2018. Before the hearing, Nassar had already received a 60-year federal sentence for a child pornography conviction and had pleaded guilty to several state sexual assault charges. The purpose of the sentencing hearing was to determine a sentence in light of "victim impact statements."

During the sentencing hearing, Judge Rosemarie E. Aquilina, who locally had a reputation for blunt talk and wearing cowboy boots under her robes, struck an unusual tone for a court trial—blending justice with therapy and personal politics. Aquilina opened her courtroom to any victims, as well as their coaches and parents, to speak for as long as they like. "Leave your pain here," Judge Aquilina told one young woman, "and go out and do your magnificent things."[88] Her vow to let every victim speak unexpectedly turned the hearing into a "cathartic forum" emboldening dozens of women who had remained silent until then to come forward with accounts of abuse by Dr. Nassar.[89] While court officials initially expected 88 young women to speak, the number had risen to 150 by the conclusion of the proceedings.[90]

One young woman, Mattie Larson, spoke directly to Nassar, telling him, "Your priority should have been my health, yet your priority was solely to molest me." After her statement, Judge Aquilina told Larson: "You are so strong and brave, and you are not broken. You are glued back together perfectly. . . . Thank you for being part of the sister survivors. Your voice means everything."[91] Another young woman, Brianne Randall, likewise addressed her words—through tears—directly to Nassar: "You used my vulnerability at the time to sexually abuse me. I reported you to police immediately, and you had the audacity to tell them that I had misunderstood [inaudible] because I was not comfortable with my body. How dare you."[92] After testimony from each of the 150 women, Judge Aquila expressed her admiration and support for their bravery. She assured them that she was listening and that "the whole world" was listening too.[93] Among the people watching were other victims who had not yet decided to come forward with their stories but who felt empowered by what was happening at the court and subsequently told of their own experiences.[94]

In contrast, Judge Aquila responded to Nassar's letter, in which he complained about his emotional distress at a having to listen to hours of women's testimony, with a withering attack: "Spending four or five days listening to them is significantly minor considering the hours of pleasure you had at their expense and ruining their lives."[95] At the end of the hearing, Judge Aquila sentenced Nassar to 40 to 175 years in prison, in addition to the 60-year sentence he had already received for a conviction related to federal child pornography charges and to the separate sentence for at least another 40 years that he would receive from Judge Janice Cunningham in Eaton County, Michigan, where he pleaded guilty to three counts of criminal sexual misconduct.[96] After announcing the sentence, Judge Aquila told Nassar with evident relish, "I just signed your death warrant."[97]

Judge Aquila's trial of Dr. Larry Nassar offered affirmation and catharsis—typical of a clinical or confessional space—within an adversarial justice system procedure. It could be read as an adversarial justice system's version of restorative justice.[98] Restorative justice "expands the circle of stakeholders to those with a stake or standing in the event or the case beyond just the government and the offender to also include victims and community members."[99] It addresses victims' needs, including their need for information about the offense, why it happened, and what has happened since; their need to tell their story and receive public acknowledgment; their need to regain a sense of empowerment; and their need for restitution and vindication. Consistent with this, Aquila's trial provided all of these things including, most dramatically, a platform for Nassar's victims to recount their experiences and to know that the public had heard them. Restorative justice also encourages offenders to face up to what they have done, understand the impact of their behavior, and take steps to put things right as much as possible.[100] Aquila's efforts to make Nassar listen to his victims' accounts and grapple with what they say were consistent with that. Also consistent with restorative justice, Judge Aquila and several of the victims also focused on holding accountable the institutions named as co-defendants—including Michigan State, USA Gymnastics, the United States Olympic Committee, and Twistars Gymnastics Club—that were negligent in preventing Nassar's abuse for over two decades.[101] On May 16, 2018, Michigan State University announced that it had settled with 332 victims of sexual abuse by Larry Nassar for a total of $425 million.[102]

Stated somewhat differently, Judge Aquila's trial of Dr. Larry Nassar was both a legal procedure and a dramatic and cathartic coming out ritual as sexual assault victim/survivor for over 150 young women. As Amy Preston, the mother of a 19-year-old sexual abuse victim, told John Geddert—the owner of the gym where Nassar worked—in court: "John, you tried to teach our girls to be quiet and obey. We now stand before them and say, 'Speak.'"[103] Note again, the reference to being heard here. Given popular aphorisms about how children should be "seen but not heard" or about how women should "shut up and look pretty," telling girls and women to speak out against men's sexual abuse powerfully challenges the status quo. Women and girls are coming out and being heard.

Arguably, an even better natural experiment for the impact that the #MeToo movement has had on how we address rape in the United States were the two trials for sexual assault—one before and one after the eruption of the #MeToo movement—leveled by Andrea Constand against comedian Bill Cosby.[104] In the first trial in the spring of 2017, the jury, after six days of deliberation, was unable to agree about whether Cosby had drugged and sexually assaulted Constand, setting the stage for a retrial. In the second, after less than two days of deliberation, the jury found Cosby guilty on all counts.[105] After the first Cosby trial, a male juror—quoted anonymously by the *Philadelphia Inquirer*—said: "Let's face it: She went up to his house with a bare midriff and incense and bath salts. What the heck?"[106] Between the two trials, however, the stories of some very famous women accusing Harvey Weinstein of sexual misconduct and the voices of many other women have—some have argued—"made it plain how powerful men have been able to get away with such criminal behavior and shed light on the many reasons victims might choose to remain silent, including both explicit and implicit threats to their careers and reputations."[107] While legal experts caution against generalizing about the effects of the #MeToo movement based on the Cosby trials, they do suggest that the conviction is a mark of progress.[108]

* * *

As we have seen, there are many factors that bring us to the moment when so many young accusers can speak about the abuse they suffered at the hands of a powerful man and be heard. The MeToo moment is not an overnight occurrence, even if it may initially appear that way. Besides Tarana Burke's paving the way for the online "Me Too" movement with her offline movement beginning in 2007, a host of earlier actions—including Take Back the Night marches, the Clothesline Project, the Mattress Performance, and slutwalks— had laid the groundwork for the deluge of MeToo stories in late 2017. The news media also played a crucial role in drawing attention to the issue of sexual assault. Notably, in the case of Weinstein and Nassar, journalists and editors brought these stories to light, prompting the legal proceedings that would follow. This reinforces the point, made in Chapter 2, that, to be successful, the political tactic of outing requires the active participation of the mainstream media.[109]

7

Conclusion

Coming out provides language, concepts, and tactics for people who have been invisible or in hiding to become visible. The preceding pages have shown how this act can transform not only individual people's experiences in the world but also politics and social structure. Thus, when gay men and lesbians came out beginning in the 1970s, they not only changed laws but they also changed minds. People who thought that homosexuals were scary and strange realized that, unbeknownst to them until now, they already had colleagues and friends who are gay. They thereby came to see gay men and lesbians as like them, as worthy of rights.

As we have seen, *coming out* was first used to speak of one's social debut within the gay culture. The gay rights movement subsequently used a different concept of coming out—as revealing one's sexual orientation beyond the "gay world"—as a political tool to change hearts, minds, and laws. Originally, referred to simply as the "gay rights movement," in which *gay* was intended to encompass both men and women, it was expanded to the "gay and lesbian" and then "lesbian and gay" movement in response to arguments that lesbians and their concerns were being subordinated within the movement. Later the name was further extended to include bisexuals and transgender people, becoming the LGBT movement, thereby linking as a single cause homophobia and transphobia. More recently, the collection of letters has been broadened to LGBTQ+ to include people who identify as queer, questioning, intersex, asexual, within the Native American category of two-spirited, and so on. While connected in this way, there are important differences both across these letters and within each letter. For instance, the right to marry—a central issue of the movement during the first decade and a half of the 21st century—arguably is primarily a concern of lesbians and gay men in long-term monogamous relationships.

Bisexual people face specific prejudice both from heterosexuals and from lesbians and gay men, including that they are more likely to cheat on their romantic partners or are confused about their sexuality.[1] Bisexuals are also more likely than gay men or lesbians to be in the closet, with just 28 percent

Come Out, Come Out, Whoever You Are. Abigail C. Saguy, Oxford University Press (2020).
© Oxford University Press.
DOI: 10.1093/oso/9780190931650.001.0001

reporting that "all or most of the important people in their life" know about their orientation.[2] Some (but not all) transgender people face different struggles, including paying for costly medical treatment for sex reassignment procedures, which health insurance companies often do not cover and which the LGBTQ+ community as a whole has prioritized less than other issues— including prevention and treatment of HIV and AIDS, adoption rights, and marriage equality.[3]

Under the Obama administration, the LGBTQ+ movement increasingly expanded their focus to address transgender issues. As Mara Keisling— founder and executive director of the National Center for Transgender Equality (NCTE)—told my colleague Juliet A. Williams and me in an interview in April 2018, when she founded NCTE in 2003, she wanted "to make the gay rights movement an LGBT movement and to make sure that the LGBT groups were responsibly representing trans people instead of this slipshod irresponsible way they were doing it before." She also wanted to create "a separate trans movement." Sitting in her office in Washington, DC, Keisling explained, "The one gives us more power quickly. The other gives us a little more control." Mara Keisling is a tall and broad-shouldered 58-year-old trans woman with a warm, generous, and friendly manner. She wears shoulder-length hair, no makeup—the world would be a better place without it, she says, although she supports other people's right to wear it—and a button-down blouse. She graciously thanks us for coming, says she is happy to have the opportunity to talk to us, and seems to genuinely mean it.

Pointing to important legislative achievements of the Obama administration, Keisling notes the addition of gender identity to both the Employment Non-Discrimination Act and the Federal Hate Crimes Act. The former, which—at the time of this writing—is still under consideration by Congress, would prohibit discrimination in hiring and employment on the basis of sexual orientation or gender identity by employers with at least 15 employees. The act was expanded to include gender identity in 2009, when Congress passed and Obama signed into law the Matthew Shepard and James Byrd Jr. Hate Crimes Prevention Act. When asked how the transgender rights movement was able to make such progress during the Obama administration, Keisling points to the fact that transgender people within the administration were out as such.[4] Because they were visible within the administration, she says, their needs and well-being could not easily be ignored.

Coming out is about claiming the right to be seen, the right to recognition, the right to belong. It is about saying, "we're here" already, among you. This is how we are. Make space for us. In many ways, in his campaign and as US president, Donald Trump represents a narrowing of who belongs and who deserves dignity and rights. Specifically, at the time of this writing, the Trump administration is actively working to erode the gains the LGBTQ+ movement made under President Obama. For instance, in March 2018, the Trump White House issued an order under which transgender people who required or had already undergone "gender transition" would not be allowed to join or remain in the military.[5] By contrast, transgender people without a history or diagnosis of gender dysphoria—required for sex reassignment treatment— would be welcome to serve "in their biological sex."[6] Transgender troops, who would be grandfathered in under an Obama administration policy that allowed them to serve, could be discharged if they challenge the recommendation in court. Because the order essentially allows transgender people to serve as long as they do not act to bring their gender identity in line with their public persona or advocate for transgender rights, it has been likened to the earlier military policy "Don't Ask, Don't Tell." Under that rule, issued by President Bill Clinton, gay men and women could serve as long as they did not publicly acknowledge their homosexuality. While President Clinton hoped Don't Ask, Don't Tell would improve conditions for gay men and lesbians in the military when he issued it in 1993, it worsened them and was repealed in 2011. Transgender people first received their right to defend their nation as equals in 2016, under President Barack Obama, who made gender identity a protected category in the Pentagon's equal opportunity policy.[7]

While President Trump has not—at the time of this writing—tried to reinstate the Don't Ask, Don't Tell policy for gay men and lesbians, his administration is attempting to undo other safeguards against anti-gay discrimination. For instance, in 2017, the Justice Department filed court papers in a discrimination case before the Supreme Court, siding with a baker who refused to provide a wedding cake to a same-sex couple.[8] Also that year the department issued a brief in a workplace discrimination case in New York, arguing that Title VII of the Civil Rights Act of 1964, which prohibits discrimination "on the basis of sex," does not protect workers from discrimination based on sexual orientation.[9] The brief ran counter to a report from the Equal Employment Opportunity Commission, holding that discrimination on the basis of sexual orientation constitutes discrimination on the basis of sex and is therefore prohibited by Title VII.[10]

These kinds of actions create a hostile climate for LGBTQ+ people. Still, the gains made since the 1970s cannot be reversed overnight. The

LGBTQ+-rights movement has gained power and influence since those early days, and public opinion has shifted in ways that are not easily or quickly reversed. Having felt the relief and joy of exiting the closet, people are not willing to return so easily.

Indeed, the Trump presidency seems to be galvanizing the left. When my colleague Juliet A. Williams and I interviewed over 20 thought leaders and activists in the feminist and LGBTQ+ movements during the spring of 2018, a common theme was that the Trump administration has fired up the left and made it less complacent. Rather than forcing people back into the closet or into hiding, it seems to have convinced people of the need to come out.

For instance, when a proposed "bathroom bill"—which would have required that people use the sex-segregated restroom that corresponds to the "biological sex" on their birth certificate—came to the Texas legislature in 2017, this brought together a huge coalition of people from the LGBTQ+ community who formed and deepened friendships and networks. One person who first came out publicly as transgender at this time is Danielle Skidmore, a 46-year-old white engineer. When Juliet A. Williams and I interviewed her, in April 2018, she was running for Austin City Council. Skidmore is tall and thin with shoulder-length straight brown hair. When we interviewed her, she was wearing skinny blue jeans, a form-fitting sleeveless white T-shirt, and heels. She explained that it was not until she learned of the bathroom bill that she got involved in activism, through the Human Rights Campaign (HRC) and Equality Texas. She spoke about how powerful it was that the proposed bathroom bill brought "all these people to Austin," the state capital and her home:

> All these people [whom] I knew about online were now coming to Austin.
> So I became friends with all of these people and started to be more visible.
> So I have this experience now where people I don't know will send me a
> friend request from all over. [They tell me] "I see you. And I'm proud of
> what you're doing, inspired by it."

The LGBTQ+ movement's show of force ultimately helped defeat the bathroom bill. Legislative debates over the bill, in turn, played a crucial role in making transgender people visible in a way that they were not before. This then transformed them into a political force. As Skidmore explains: "The reality is everyone in Texas knows what being transgender is now, and that wasn't true in January of 2017. And many people now in Texas can say, 'Yeah,

I've met a transgender person.'" Skidmore herself admitted that she did not personally know another transgender woman even three years earlier. She argued that making transgender people visible and thereby normalizing them is essential for increasing tolerance and support.

Danielle Skidmore's campaign manager, Alicia Weigel, also came out during the legislative hearings over the bathroom bill, although not as transgender. At the time of our interview Alicia Weigel was 27 years old, tall and blond with blue eyes. During the joint interview with Danielle Skidmore, she was casually dressed, explaining that she does not care much for makeup or even brushing her hair. She does not really care, she says, as long as she can "get the sort of partners" that she wants, which for most of her life has not been a problem for her. She recognizes that this is a form of privilege. Yet, like most of us, Weigel also manages hidden stigma.

While Weigel appears to be a cisgender (that is, not transgender) white woman, the reality is more complicated. In her words, "I used to have balls!" This is because she was born with an intersex condition known as Complete Androgen Insensitivity Syndrome (CAIS). People with CAIS have an X and a Y chromosome. During gestation, the Y chromosome causes the undifferentiated gonads to develop into testes, which subsequently produce testosterone. So far, this is the typical developmental pathway for human males. The pathway diverges at this point, however, for people like Weigel who have CAIS, as they have a genetic mutation that prevents their body from processing testosterone. While their testes release testosterone in utero, the body cannot detect it. As a result, the testes never descend—remaining in the abdomen. Moreover, the external genitalia develop along the feminine pathway. Thus, the undifferentiated phallus grows into a clitoris—not a penis—and people with CAIS develop labia and a vaginal canal that ends "blindly" in a pouch. During puberty, the testes again release large amounts of testosterone. The body, however, converts the testosterone to the chemically similar hormone estrogen, causing the hips to widen and the breasts to develop. People with CAIS thus typically look and feel like ordinary women despite having internal testes and no ovaries, fallopian tubes, cervix, or uterus.[11]

People with intersex conditions, including CAIS, are rarely out as such. This, in turn, limits others' awareness of their existence or understanding of their needs. As Alicia Weigel explains, "No one knows we exist yet." One consequence of that is that "we don't have health care that can address our needs" since doctors know nothing about intersex conditions: "You'd be shocked how many times I'm in the stirrups at the gynecologist and they've never heard of an intersex person. So I'm sitting there with my hoo-ha out and having to explain to them who I am as a human. It's like a joke." In a follow-up email exchange, Weigel clarified that these sorts of interactions with doctors are "very triggering." She explains:

> When you've undergone many research "examinations" (under anesthesia, or worse, not) for medical experimentation as a kid, it's already triggering to be in a doctor's office . . . and then when the medical community consistently ogles your privates and has no idea how to treat you—you feel overexposed, under-treated, like you're in a zoo for others' education and not in a clinical setting to ensure your well-being.

The fact that Weigel's testicles were removed when she was a child requires her to be on hormone therapy for the rest of her life, whereas she would not otherwise have to. Yet no one knows exactly what those hormone levels should be, and Weigel recently discovered that her hormone levels are likely out of balance for healthy bone density—putting her at a high risk for osteoporosis. The medical risks related to such surgeries is an important reason the United Nations Committee against Torture, the World Health Organization, and lawyers working at the American Civil Liberties Union (ACLU), among others, have condemned medical or surgical treatments of intersex people without their informed consent.[12]

Bringing visibility to intersex is one of Alicia Weigel's main goals as an activist. A second goal is, in her words, "using [her] privilege as a cis-passing white woman to lift up other communities." Thus, she does a lot of activism for both the Black Lives Matter movement and for transgender rights.

Indeed, it was in order to advance transgender rights by defeating the Texas bathroom bill that Weigel first came out publicly as intersex, pointing to how political attacks on LGBTQ+ rights have galvanized the left. Given the argument on the right that "we need to go back to biological sex because that's cut and dried," Weigel says she thought her "voice might be worthwhile in the conversation" since her own body was proof that biological sex is *not* cut and dried. So she decided to come out. She was not yet integrated in the broader LGBTQIA+ community in Austin and explains that even since coming out, she knows only one other intersex person in Austin because "we're still so far behind the trans movement in terms of visibility and . . . people feeling comfortable sharing who they are."[13] So Weigel did not know to whom to turn. She had only met Danielle Skidmore a couple days earlier but sent her a late-night text saying that she planned to speak out against the bill. Skidmore, who saw Weigel—in her own words—as a "straight, white girl," said, "Great, we need all the allies we can get." To that, Weigel replied, "I think I'm going to do it as an intersex person" and then called to continue the discussion by phone. At that point, only Weigel's parents and one other person knew she was intersex. The next day, she came out publicly during the hearings.

Alicia Weigel says she is proud of having had the courage to come out as intersex and of how her voice helped defeat what she sees as a hateful and harmful bill. That said, her visibility has come at a personal cost. She explains:

> In the past, it was like, I would date someone, we would fall in love, and eventually I would tell them when it got to the point of like, "well, do we want to have kids?" I'm like "well, I can't have kids." And that's how it came out. And even then, it wasn't like, "I can't have kids because I have XY chromosomes and used to have balls." It was, "I have this genetic condition where I'm not able to have kids." And now it's just like out there in the netherworld, and so that I've found that I've just given up on dating apps because where frankly I used to blow up left and right on these dating apps and go on multiple dates a week, now people start talking to me and I can tell they Google me, and it just goes cold. Or like, even certain guys, even if we do start an intimate relationship, they'll ask me questions in bed. [That makes me wonder:] "Are we having sex or is this an interview?" It's just really weird and kind of kills the mood.

Offsetting these costs, however, is the fact that Alicia Weigel says she feels she is able to be more authentically herself, so that "[whomever] I do find, the love is going to be that much stronger because they know who I am beforehand. And they're able to fall in love with me, who I am." As we have seen in the previous chapters, the desire to be authentically oneself continues to provide a motivation—along with changing hearts, minds, and policy—for coming out.

Refusing to Go Back into the Shadows

Lack of adequate healthcare, triggering experiences with medical professionals, and challenges to finding a romantic partner are a significant cost to pay for being out. That said, Alicia Weigel did not talk about fearing for her safety. In contrast, undocumented immigrant youth have to over-come fear of their own or their family members' deportation before they are able to be visible as undocumented immigrants and have a political im-pact. The concept of coming out has helped the movement mobilize fearful constituents despite considerable risk and fear.

Since Laura E. Enriquez conducted the interviews with undocumented immigrant youth for this book, President Barack Obama finished his second presidential term and Donald Trump became the 45th president of the United States. Trump's presidential campaign increased pressure on undo-cumented immigrants, an effort that his administration is continuing. As candidate for the Republican nomination for president, for instance, Donald Trump told an audience at Trump Tower Atrium on June 16, 2015, "When Mexico sends its people, they're not sending their best. . . . They're bringing drugs. They're bringing crime. They're rapists."[14] As a presidential candi-date, in August 2016, Trump vowed to "immediately terminate" the Deferred Action for Childhood Arrivals (DACA) executive order that President Obama signed in June 2012 after the Congress repeatedly failed to pass the Dream Act. DACA deferred deportation for "Dreamers" who meet certain criteria on a two-year renewable basis.[15]

It is no wonder then that Trump's election, in November 2016, raised con-cern among the undocumented immigrant youth movement. Yet, despite the increased risks of coming out as undocumented under the Trump admin-istration, the undocumented immigrant movement continues to encourage it as a strategy to garner sympathy and support. A few days after the pres-idential election, *Nation* published an article by author and immigrant re-form activist Cesar Vargas, titled "Undocumented and Unafraid in the Face of Trump's Presidency," in which he wrote "Trump can try to take DACA away from us. But he won't take away our spirit to fight for our families." He concluded his article promising to show "that we are undocumented and unafraid."[16]

For a while, it seemed that the undocumented immigrant youth move-ment might even have been able to change President Trump's view of them, supplanting (or at least supplementing) the popular representation of "il-legal aliens" with a sympathetic image of young, ambitious, and talented "Dreamers." Trump himself gave voice to this perspective when he described undocumented immigrant youth, in a *Time* magazine interview in November 2016, as "good students" with "wonderful jobs" who were "brought here at a very young age" and who were stuck in "never-never land because they don't know what's going to happen."[17] These remarks speak directly to the power of coming out as undocumented, in which young immigrants provide a sympathetic face to this social issue by sharing their personal stories. In this interview, Trump told *Time* magazine that he wanted to work out something for Dreamers that would make people "happy and proud."[18] At a press conference in February 2017, he said that DACA was "a very, very difficult subject" for him and that he wanted to "deal with DACA with heart."[19]

Not known for consistency, however, President Trump rescinded DACA in September 2017, effective as of January 2018, although held up in litigation at the time of this writing. In response, undocumented immigrant youth activists again refused to be frightened into going back into the shadows. "We need to not be afraid. We need to not let cops and Congress terrorize us," said UCLA student Yael—a native of Mexico brought to the United States at the age of 4—in a *Los Angeles Times* article published after the presidential announcement about DACA. "This is the time to hit the streets and organize. DACA does not define us. Our success doesn't depend on legislation. We are human beings who deserve dignity, peace and justice above all."[20] The article concluded with Yael saying, "Our resilience and determination will not let this fear-mongering stop us." Below the article, however, was the following note, "Yael's last name has been removed from a previous version of this story after reports received of threats against her," inadvertently underscoring the limits of full disclosure and performing being unafraid in a social context of real and present danger.

In January 2018, a federal judge ordered, pending final judgment, that the US government keep DACA on the same terms and conditions that were in effect before the September rescission.[21] The Trump team appealed directly to the Supreme Court, which denied the request to bypass the Ninth Circuit court, meaning that the case would return to the lower courts and that the Ninth Circuit Court would hear appeals.[22] Meanwhile undocumented immigrant youth continued to come out as undocumented and unafraid. For instance, in early March 2018, nearly 200 protesters marched through the streets of Newark, New Jersey, to the offices of federal immigration officials, chanting "no papers, no fear!"[23]

On March 29, 2018, a federal judge in Brooklyn—citing Trump's "racially charged language" as a candidate and from the White House to prove that he rescinded DACA due to racial animus toward Latinos—ruled that a lawsuit seeking to preserve DACA should continue.[24] The judge specifically mentioned Trump's comment about Mexico sending "criminals" and "rapists" to the United States. In a separate prong of the ruling, the judge further stated that the decision to rescind DACA violated the Administrative Procedure Act, or APA, a federal law that bars the government from repealing policies arbitrarily, capriciously, or without a rational basis.[25] In the face of continued uncertainty about the future of DACA, the undocumented immigrant youth movement has continued to call on its members to come out as undocumented and unafraid, in the hopes that this will continue to change hearts and minds.

Combating Fat Phobia and Sexism

While the undocumented youth movement persists *despite* the Trump administration, other groups seem to be coming out *in response* to what the Trump administration represents. Trump has said many things—before and since becoming US president—that suggest women are only valuable if they are thin, young, and conventionally beautiful. For instance, during the Republican primary, candidate Trump suggested that Republican candidate Carly Fiorina was unelectable as US president, saying, "Look at that face; would anyone vote for that?"[26] He likewise tweeted that comedian Rosie O'Donnell, was "disgusting, both inside and out," calling her "a slob" and asking how she got on television.[27] He tweeted that Huffington Post editor and co-founder Ariana Huffington was "unattractive both inside and out,"[28] as if life—for women—is one big beauty contest. Such rhetoric has neither the intent nor the effect of making the world a more accepting or accommodating place for women who are heavy or otherwise do not conform to narrow ideals of beauty. Yet by making fat phobia and sexism visible, it seems to have energized political resistance.

It is unclear what effect, if any, the Trump presidency is having specifically on the fat acceptance movement, but there is abundant evidence that Trump's election has fueled the #MeToo movement discussed in the previous chapter. As readers may remember, during the presidential campaign, a recording of a conversation between Donald Trump and then-*Access Hollywood* host Billy Bush was leaked to the media. In what became known as the "Access Hollywood tape," Donald Trump bragged about how he sexually assaults women: "You know, I'm automatically attracted to beautiful [women]—I just start kissing them. It's like a magnet. Just kiss. I don't even wait. And when you're a star, they let you do it. You can do anything. . . . Grab 'em by the pussy.

You can do anything." In other words, while he directs disdain and humiliation to women he does *not* deem attractive, Donald Trump's own words suggest that he sexually assaults those women he *does* find attractive.

Initially, when these tapes were leaked, people speculated that they would bring Trump's bid for US president to a disgraceful end. CNN reported that the tapes "will surely doom any hope the GOP nominee has of improving his standing among women voters, especially highly educated, suburban women in swing states like Colorado and Pennsylvania," quoting a Republican Party staffer saying, "This is bad. I think this thing is over."[29] Initially, this led other women to come out—or talk openly—about their experiences with sexual assault. Canadian author and social media blogger Kelly Oxford, who has 745,000 followers on Twitter, shared five of her own experiences with sexual assault under the hashtag Not Okay and asked others to do the same. Oxford said that soon after, she was receiving about two stories per second and that, by the next day, Oxford had nearly 10 million Twitter interactions under this hashtag. Four days later, women across the United States and Canada and other parts of the world were still sharing stories of sexual assault.[30] The 3-million-strong private Facebook group Pantsuit Nation, founded just before Election Day 2016 in support of presidential candidate Hillary Clinton and in anticipated celebration of the first female US president, also witnessed hundreds of thousands of women breaking their silence about gender-based violence, among other topics.[31]

Yet, despite all of this, Trump won a majority of electoral college votes—becoming the 45th president of the United States.[32] And while about 94 percent of black women voted for Clinton, over half of white women voted for Trump.[33] The fact that Trump paid no political cost for such egregious misogyny triggered outrage among many women who had been victims of sexual harassment and, some argue, ultimately set the stage for the #MeToo movement, discussed in the previous chapter.

Maia Ermasons—a young woman who publicly accused famous playwright Israel Horovitz of sexual assault, leading several theater companies to cancel production of his plays—is a good example of how Trump's election fueled the #MeToo movement. Ermasons had known Horovitz since she was 11 years old, having performed in his theater as a child, and viewed him "like a grandfather"—both fun and protective.[34] Horovitz invited Ermasons's family and her to Boxing Day and she talks about feeling "very close to him."[35] Ermasons remained close with him as she got older, appreciating how Horovitz responded quickly to her emails and made her feel "valued and respected." Horovitz wrote recommendations for Ermasons and gave her monologues for auditions. He even spoke, upon her request, at graduation for her middle school, PPAS, the Professional Performing Arts School.[36]

So when, a decade later, Ermasons was going through a hard time and feeling lost and Horovitz offered to help, Ermasons accepted. Horovitz told Ermasons he would give her "as many of my short plays as you want, and you're going to produce them, and that's going to be your project. That's what's going to focus you."[37] Ermasons recruited another actor interested in producing and the two of them got to work changing language that felt outdated and working on casting. When Ermasons felt she had enough progress to show him, Ermasons contacted Horovitz to set up a meeting. During that meeting, Horovitz forcibly kissed Ermasons and touched her breasts. Ermasons resisted Horovitz's advances, and he eventually left, but Ermasons was furious. After doing some research, Ermasons discovered earlier news reporting on similar incidents of sexual assault involving Horovitz and other women. Ermasons contacted a prominent theater where Horovitz worked but the director did not call her back. Then—after seeing a celebratory Instagram post of Horovitz in rehearsal, Ermansons's fury was reignited and she wrote about her experience on Facebook *without naming the playwright*.

It might have stopped there, if it were not for the election of Donald Trump. When Trump was elected US president, however, Ermasons snapped. She returned to her original post and named the playwright: "I reposted the original thing—the original bit, the piece that I wrote. And I just put something at the top saying that in light of the election, I'm ready to say the name. It was the playwright Israel Horovitz."[38] Using Facebook, Twitter, and Google, Ermasons then tracked down other women who suffered similar abuse at the hands of the same man, many of whom also came forward. Ermasons also contacted the *New York Times*, which ran an article in November 2017 detailing the stories of nine women who publicly accused Israel Horovitz of harassment and abuse. Theater companies then canceled the production of Horovitz's plays, and the Gloucester State Company severed ties with him.[39] While Horovitz—like many of the other men outed by the #MeToo movement—was a powerful man, he was not untouchable, as "the ultimate unpunished sexual predator" seemed to be.[40] Maia Ermasons is just one example of how women have named their harassers and assaulters because, faced with a feeling of powerlessness before the US president, it "feels important to topple those perpetrators within reach."[41]

Coming Forward as Women

The #MeToo movement is part of a larger surge in political activism—led by women—that followed in the wake of Trump's election, in which people came out to affirm various identities and claim rights. Immediately after Donald Trump's inauguration, on January 21, 2017, a group of activists organized a "women's march," emphasizing the issue of sexual assault, with pink knitted "pussy hats" and slogans like "pussy grabs back" (see Figure 7.1). The march's title and the pink pussy hats enacted coming out as women,

Figure 7.1. A demonstrator holds a sign that says "pussy grabs back"—a reference to presidential candidate Donald Trump's comment about how he grabs women—at the Women's March in 2017.

affirming women's political power and visibility following the election of a man who was openly misogynistic. This march was the largest single-day globally coordinated public gathering in world history.[42] A crowd scientist estimated that half a million people marched in Washington, DC,, and it has been estimated that between 3.6 million and 4.6 million people demonstrated across the United States. Additional protests took place in cities across the globe, including Nairobi, Oslo, and Bangkok.[43]

This march was followed by many more, as well as by a surge of women running for public office—aided by new organizations like Flippable, founded in the wake of the election to turn state legislatures blue by targeting vulnerable seats, and Indivisible, which organizes progressives to protest Republican policy and is overwhelmingly led by women.[44] Sociologist Theda Skocpol, who co-authored a book about the Tea Party and has studied Indivisible, says the anti-Trump progressive uprising already has more local groups than the Tea Party did at its height. While the Tea Party had roughly 900 local groups and some 250,000 core activists at its strongest, Skocpol says, "Almost all the [Indivisible] chapters I've seen are generating people who are planning to run for office. I think it's at least as great and probably greater than the Tea Party popular upsurge."[45] The seats for which women have competed have included some liberated by men who resigned in response to allegations of sexual harassment.[46] Indeed, some argue that a fierce outrage about the election of President Donald Trump is the "single thread" running through the MeToo movement, the Women's March, and the spike in the number of women running for political office.[47]

Public protests led by women continue to flourish. In March 2018, public schoolteachers in West Virginia participated in strikes for nine days, despite the fact that teacher strikes are unlawful in the state and that teacher unions lack collective bargaining power.[48] The teachers refused to return to work until lawmakers gave them a 5 percent pay raise and agreed to address their rapidly rising health insurance premiums.[49] *New York Times* journalist Michelle Goldberg has argued that the strike is "part of a nationwide upsurge in intense civic engagement by women." Goldberg quotes an elementary school teacher: "As a profession, we're largely made up of women. There are a bunch of men sitting in an office right now telling us that we don't deserve anything better." The teacher describes the anti-Trump Women's March and the explosion of local political organizing that followed it, as a "catalyst" for teachers: "You have women now taking leadership roles in unionizing, in standing up, in leading initiatives for fairness and equality and justice for everyone."[50] Goldberg quotes the same teacher saying that "In the wake of Donald Trump's election, women across the country are standing up to say: 'No. We're equal here.'"[51] Following the West Virginia strike, thousands of teachers walked off the job in Oklahoma and Kentucky, leading one teacher to call the trend a "wildfire."[52] In April 2018, thousands of teachers walked out of their classrooms in Arizona to demand more funding for public schools.[53] "Rebellion, it seems, is contagious," notes Goldberg.[54]

When, on June 22, 2018, Justice Anthony Kennedy announced his retirement effective July 31, 2018, progressives feared that President Trump would appoint a successor who would—along with the existing four conservative Supreme Court Justices—reverse *Roe v. Wade*, the Supreme Court decision that women have a constitutional right to have an abortion. Facing the possibility of losing this right to control one's own fertility, some people encouraged women to come out as having had abortions as part of a political strategy to gain greater social support for the practice.[55] One writer points out that one in four women have had an abortion by the age of 45, but that few talk about it.[56] This silence, she writes, has a price. For one, "It renders the women who make this choice anonymous and lets those who would deny us our freedom do so without looking us in the eye." Sounding much like Harvey Milk, she suggests that it would not be "quite so easy to demonize this common experience" if they were aware that people they knew and loved—their "sisters and mothers and friends"—had had an abortion.[57] Likewise, law professor Carol Sanger writes that "the willingness of women and others to talk about abortion will over time make an immense difference to its legislative fate" since "legislative lawmaking depends in part on what legislators know, and that depends on how and when and with whom the issue of abortion has been discussed, and not only from a policy perspective."[58] Sociological research lends further support to the idea that one reason attitudes toward abortion—unlike attitudes toward same-sex desire—have not become more acceptable over time is because people who have had abortions are unlikely to disclose this fact to anyone whom they suspect will be disapproving.[59]

Coming Out on the Right

Mormon fundamentalist polygamists, discussed in Chapter 5, are different from the other groups covered in this book in that they tend to be on the political right. Yet, while they typically vote Republican, they also recognize how their struggle for acceptance is linked to other people's struggles for acceptance and inclusion and frequently compare their movement to the civil rights and gay rights movement.

In contrast, political conservatives have co-opted the concept of coming out to parody the LGBTQ+ movement and progressive politics in general. They organize a Conservative Coming Out Day, "a twist on LGBT coming-out celebrations, when conservatives proudly announce their presence to the campus.[60] "I'm sure you can figure out what that's a parody of," a young conservative explained to sociologists Amy Binder and Kate Wood. "People would say, 'Oh, I always knew there was something different about me, and, 'I would sneak into my dad's car and listen to Rush Limbaugh when no one was watching.'"

Likewise, white nationals—who have been emboldened by Trump's presidency to "come out of the woodwork"[61]—see their movement as diametrically opposed to identity movements on the left. They seem to feel vindicated by Trump's denunciation of "political correctness," in which one is expected to be sensitive to people's identities and experiences of discrimination. Whereas prior to Trump's election, people may have refrained from expressing racist views out of a sense that such expression would be met with social disapproval, the election of Donald Trump seems to have made the expression of racism more acceptable.[62] Psychologist Chris Crandall, known for his theory of how perceptions of what is socially desirable lead people to either express or suppress prejudice, has argued that "it was most likely the election itself—the public endorsement of Trump by the American people—that changed perceptions. Supporters of Trump and Clinton alike saw increased approval for expression of the prejudices that characterized the Trump campaign."[63] Crandall and colleagues reasoned that when the acceptability of a prejudice is contested as it is with racism, people are particularly reliant on social norms about when to express or when to suppress their feelings.[64] Because these norms play a central role in suppressing the expression of prejudice, changing them has a large effect on how people behave. Indeed, a 2019 poll by the Pew Research Center suggests that expression of racism has increased since Trump's election.[65] The Southern Poverty Law Center has likewise reported that the United States had more hate groups in 2018 than at any other point in at least the past two decades.[66]

Members of the extreme right speak of feeling liberated to express their true opinions after spending so long hiding them out of fear of public condemnation. As a *Chicago Tribune* article comments in the month following Donald Trump's election:

> Promoters of white nationalism—or the "alt-right," as some call it—are coming out of the woodwork now. They say they have been emboldened by Donald Trump's various calls to ban Muslim immigration in this country and deport millions of undocumented Latin Americans.[67]

Pairing *coming out* with *the woodwork*—where vermin reside—expresses this journalist's low regard for the alt-right while simultaneously acknowledging commonalities with *coming out of the closet*. Like the groups discussed in the previous chapters, the alt-right speak of feeling marginalized before Trump's election. As researcher and far-right expert Peter Montgomery explained to a *LA Times* reporter: "The idea that [Trump] is taking a wrecking ball to "political correctness" excites them. They've been marginalized in our discourse, but he's really made space for them."[68] This *LA Times* reporter, in turn, talks about how Trump's campaign has "opened the door for white nationalist groups to come out of the shadows," using the same language used to describe undocumented immigrant youth.[69] Like some of the other groups discussed in this book, white nationalists speak of having to hide their views and the relief that comes from being able to talk openly of their opinions. Yet the white nationalist agenda differs in that it is about excluding others from rights and resources, whereas these other groups are about achieving rights and resources without taking them away from others.

The anti-immigrant group FAIR (Federation for American Immigration Reform) has also tried to appropriate the expression "come out of the shadows" to reaffirm the idea of "illegal aliens" sneaking across the border and stealing jobs and educational opportunities from Americans. In a 30-second video clip, posted in September 2017, the president of (FAIR) said:

> We hear a lot about bringing illegal aliens out of the shadows, giving them driver's licenses, welfare benefits, health care, at American taxpayer expense. Here's a better idea: bring Americans out of the shadows, the millions who've lost jobs to foreign workers, the victims of crimes thanks to broken borders, the American kids whose places in college were taken by illegal aliens. It's time for Americans to come out of the shadows and speak up at FAIRUS.org [70]

Whereas the undocumented immigrant youth movement suggests that integrating undocumented immigrants would be a win-win, producing a stronger economy for everyone, FAIR suggests that the US economy is a zero-sum game, in which undocumented immigrants' gains are legal residents' losses. The undocumented immigrant movement's vision is consistent with other identity movements on the left, which typically strive to flatten social hierarchies and give all people equal rights. In contrast, white nationalism and anti-immigrant groups are about reinstating a hierarchy. For white nationalists, it is a hierarchy in which white heterosexual men are on top and women and people of color are subordinated.[71] Likewise, for anti-immigrant groups, it is one where legal residents are prioritized over undocumented immigrants. Yet, despite differences between progressive and reactionary groups, all of these movements engages in coming out to ground their movement in a moral project that is both deeply personal and national in scope. As such, they are arguably—at this historical juncture—quintessentially American.[72]

Bridging Breaches and Coming Together

While progressive movements ostensibly strive to bring everyone up and to celebrate diversity, the left often divides along lines of identity. This was on full display around the Women's March on Washington and across the country. Organized as a protest against President Trump's misogyny, racism, and xenophobia, the march—and its organizers and participants—quickly came under attack for privileging the experiences and perspectives of white cisgender women, while paying insufficient attention to the priorities of women of color and transgender women.[73]

Teresa Shook, a retired attorney living in Hawaii, first came up with the idea for the march, making a Facebook event page for what began as the Million Woman March but was renamed the Women's March out of recognition that "Million Woman March" was the name of a 1997 protest of black women. Tamika Mallory, Carmen Perez, and Linda Sarsour—three veteran New York City activists and Black, Latina, and Muslim, respectively—signed on as co-chairs.[74] Some of the most visible speakers at the marches in the United States were women of color—including America Ferrera, a Honduran American actress; Aisha Tyler, an African American talk show host, actor, comedian, author, producer, writer, and director; and Jessica Williams, an

African American actor and comedian. Janet Mock—an African American writer, TV host, and transgender movement activist—was one of the more high profile transgender women of color who spoke at the march. [75]

Nonetheless, there were several news reports about transgender women's complaints. The pink pussy hats—as well as posters featuring female genitalia—received particular ire for implying that only people with female genitalia are women. The *New York Times* article quoted above observed:

> Vagina plushies abounded, as did drawings of vulva and birth canals, and legs spread exuberantly wide. As rallying cries, these were initially thrilling to see, but they began to feel exclusionary as the day wore on. Equating vaginas with feminism with gender equality felt outdated, given that there were a number of trans women who showed up to support the cause.

While the above news excerpt was from the *New York Times,* right-wing media seemed to delight in and add to the discord. A Gender Studies graduate student teaching assistant first brought to my attention complaints about the march from transgender rights activists. She forwarded me an article and, as I read it, I realized it was published in the far-right publication *Breitbart News,* which gained visibility after the election of Trump. [76] The article, which defined transgender women as "a man trying to live as a transgender woman" and cisgender as "normal behavior, such as men living as men and women living as women," did not support transgender rights or even the validity of transgender identity. Its motivation in disseminating such complaints seemed solely to discredit the march.

Several women of color wrote articles about why they would not be marching or found the march objectionable. Part of the criticism was aimed at the apparent hypocrisy of white women who, as a group, voted for Trump and yet took up disproportionate space at the march. [77] A photo that circulated widely in the days after the march and was featured in an article published in the *New York Times* captured this beautifully. [78] The *New York Times* article describes the photo as follows:

> [It] features a Black woman named Angela Peoples (taken by her friend Kevin Banatte) holding a sign that reads, "Don't Forget: White Women Voted for Trump." In the photo, she stands nonchalantly, casually sucking on a lollipop with a jaded look in her eyes that suggests her familiarity with the ritual of protest, of demonstrating for civil liberties. Behind her stand

three white women, all wearing the pink knitted "pussyhats" that the march made famous. Two are on their phones, pleased grins beaming from their faces. One appears to be taking a triumphant selfie.

The fact that over half of white women voted for Trump surprised many and was widely interpreted to be indicative of white women's racism. It could also be taken as evidence of entrenched anti-feminism among white women. That should not be surprising; many of the leading anti-feminists—including Phyllis Schlafly, who founded the Eagle Forum and dedicated much of her life to combating the campaign to pass the Equal Rights Amendment (ERA), and members of the pro-life movement, which opposes women's right to control their fertility including through abortion—have been women.[79] While pro-choice activists advance the view that women and men are more similar than different and that women's lack of control of their fertility presents a barrier to social equality, the pro-life movement views women and men as naturally different. For pro-lifers, women should be mothers and men should be providers, and access to abortion makes each less likely to perform their given role.[80]

The poster seemed to imply that the white women at the march either voted for Trump or were responsible for the white women who voted for him. One article explained, "A vocal segment of women of color, especially black feminists . . . say [that white feminists] haven't worked hard enough to even win over a majority of their own ranks."[81] This split among white women reflects the extent to which Americans are divided not only by race but also by class, region, and values.

Women of color also objected to the fact that while the leaders of the march demonstrated a commitment to addressing racial inequality, many of the white women who showed up to the march did not. Having themselves shown up for a march they perceive as centering whiteness,[82] some women of color expressed frustration and anger that white women are not showing up en masse to Black Lives Matter marches. Actor and improvisation performer Amir Talai used humor to express this sentiment, with a sign reading, "I'll See You Nice White Ladies at the Next #BlackLivesMatter March, Right?"[83] Another African American protestor wrote about showing up with a poster that said, "NOT My President. Sincerely, A Nasty Woman and member of 'The African Americans,'" which she described as "a snarky reference to Trump's misogynistic and ignorant comments while on the campaign trail."[84] While several white women protesters cheered on the "nasty woman" part of the sign, she recounted that only black women commented on "The African Americans" part. Moreover, when she and a few girlfriends began chanting "Black Lives Matter," only 40 or 50 others joined in, "a comparatively pathetic response to the previous chorus given to the other chants." This, for her, epitomized "the continued neglect, dismissal and disregard of the issues affecting black women and other women of color."[85]

Indeed, given the unprecedented numbers of people who showed up to the Women's March, it was probably many participants' first march. Many white women were mobilized by the election of Donald Trump in a way they had not been by the murders of unarmed black Americans including Tanisha Anderson, Sandra Bland, Rekia Boyd, Philando Castille, Freddie Grey, Trayvon Martin, Alton Sterling, and others. This understandably fills many black women (and others) with sadness, disappointment, and rage. Yet, we can hope that the Women's March might be a "gateway" march that will lead to greater political mobilization not only around issues of gender but also around race.

This may sound utopic and unrealistic, but I have recently heard even more dramatic stories of political transformation. One of these stories emerged from ongoing research I am conducting with UCLA Gender Studies professor Juliet A. Williams. As part of our research on gender politics, we interviewed Kimberly Shappley, who was at the time a 47-year-old mother of seven who grew up in a socially conservative Christian family. In 2013, five years before we conducted our interview, Shappley had only a ninth grade education. Growing up in northeast Mississippi, Shappley had heard preachers using scripture to justify slavery and racism, the sinfulness of homosexuality, and the subordination of women to men. Shappley did not vote for Barack Obama, explaining, "Oh my God, I hated Obama! Oh good lord, why would anybody vote for a Muslim terrorist to lead our country? He wasn't even born in America. Right?" [Laughs] Shappley was "your typical Tea Party far-right ultraconservative person," the one "sending Christmas cards to the ACLU, like, 'sure hope you get to know Jesus better.'"

Then her sixth child, Kai—whom the doctors declared male at birth—began playing only with stereotypical girl toys and saying things like "girls like us, Mom." Kimberly Shippley's first reaction was to take Kai to see a deliverance ministry and begin conversion therapy. Upon the family's request, the school put away the "female-geared toys" so that Kai could not play with them, which caused Kai to begin stealing toys from other children's cubbies in the class and to lie about it when asked. After two years and seeing the toll it was taking on her child, Shappley changed tactics. Before Kai began kindergarten, Shappley went to visit the school to arrange for Kai to discreetly begin school as a girl. Shappley explains:

> We were going to be stealth. Because I'm not one of those LGBTQ people. Oh my God, no! Never had any gay friends. Why would I have gay friends? They're gonna go to hell, right? Because that's what I'd been taught. So I went to the school. I was like, "we're going to be stealth. No one needs to know except for the nurse, the principal, and the current teacher. My daughter is transgender. I don't want any issues; please don't use her dead name," you know, things that are really really important. And the way that I went about it, contacting the school psychologist and counselors, you know, I'm thinking I did great in my ultraconservative area. I'm amazing! And it seemed like it was going to be okay. Even the principal seemed okay.

Then, "in a whirlwind, the principal quit, asked to be transferred campuses," and the superintendent of the school district gave an interview to the *Houston Chronicle* in which he said that "trans kids would not be using whatever bathroom they want." The superintendent "equated trans kids to pedophiles and perverts and used all these scriptures to justify how this was not going to happen in their school district." At this point, Kimberly Shappley "started Googling and started asking, 'who do I call? What am I supposed to do?'" She was told to contact Equality Texas. Shappley recounts that at 11 o'clock on a Thursday she got in touch with Equality Texas activist Lou Weaver and at 4:00 PM she was "on a bar stool at Fox News with Lou Weaver giving an interview to Fox News." The following Tuesday, she says, she gave a press conference at the Texas capitol in Austin. Shappley says, "That's how we came out publicly. And that's when the wheels completely came off the bus." Until then, Shappley had concealed Kai's truth from her religious conservative family. Now, the whole world knew. Her grandmother wrote her out of her will. At the time of the interview, Shappley's mother—who was very ill—had not spoken to her in two years. Shappley says she has "one adult son who doesn't speak to us at all anymore because he is who he was raised to be." Her husband is no longer in the picture.

After coming out as having a trans kid, Kimberly Shappley earned two associate degrees, in health science and in applied science of nursing, and became an advocate of education and of women's education specifically. She is now involved not only in the LGBTQ+ movement but also in the women's movement and Black Lives Matter movement. In her words:

> It's one struggle, and . . . the different groups have started really being more integrated. Even with the Dreamers being under attack here in Texas, a lot of our trans activists, you'll see them show up in Austin. Even though they're not a Dreamer, they're there. Even though they're not black, they're at Black Lives Matter. Because more and more of us are realizing we're all responsible for equality. If we allow anyone's equality to be stripped away, everyone is vulnerable. And if you would have ever told me I would've gone to the march on Washington, that was totally not the person that I used to be. But I was totally there.

Kimberly Shappley bemoans what she perceives as infighting over the march: "I think we have to stop that. We have to stop that mentality. If we had properly channeled that anger and momentum of the Women's March, we would be further ahead."

Indeed, a risk of identity politics—of which coming out is a central part— is that people end up focusing more on how they are different than on their common interests. They turn their anger against each other instead of against the social-structural factors that keep them all oppressed.

Yet the research Juliet A. Williams and I are currently doing gives me hope. In interviews with white feminist and LGBTQ+ activists, we have been struck by how many bumper stickers we see in their office and on their laptops about the Black Lives Matter movement and how many speak about the importance of this movement in their own activist work. Unlike the white women who attended one or two of the Women's Marches but have not yet taken part in a Black Lives Matter movement, these are professional activists who are—by definition—more invested in activism and social change. Still, it is possible that a few of the one-time women's marchers will become more political and, as they do, have a broader understanding of the social issues that matter.

Indeed, the still-unrealized promise of coming out is that it will lead more people to affirm the common humanity and dignity of all people—despite differences from each other and from an abstract idea of what is normal. As more people come out to resist stigma and mobilize for civil rights, perhaps we can come together for a more just world.

Notes

Preface

1. Nicole Iturriaga and Abigail C. Saguy, "'I Would Never Want to be an Only Wife': The Role of Discursive Networks and Post-Feminist Discourse in Reframing Polygamy," *Social Problems* 64, no. 3 (2017); Laura E. Enriquez and Abigail C. Saguy, "Coming Out of the Shadows: Harnessing a Cultural Schema to Advance the Undocumented Immigrant Youth Movement," *American Journal of Cultural Sociology* 4, no. 1 (2016); Michael Stambolis-Ruhstorfer and Abigail C. Saguy, "How to Describe It? Why the Term *Coming Out* Means Different Things in the United States and France" *Sociological Forum* 29, no. 4 (2014); Rebecca DiBennardo and Abigail C. Saguy, "How Children of LGBQ Parents Negotiate Courtesy Stigma over the Life Course," *Journal of International Women's Studies* 4 (2018).
2. Abigail C. Saguy, *What Is Sexual Harassment? From Capitol Hill to the Sorbonne* (Berkeley: University of California Press, 2003); Abigail C. Saguy, "Employment Discrimination or Sexual Violence? Defining Sexual Harassment in American and French Law," *Law & Society Review* 34, no. 4 (2000); Abigail C. Saguy, "Europeanization or National Specificity? Legal Approaches to Sexual Harassment in France, 2002–2012," *Law & Society Review* 52, no. 1 (2018).
3. Dotan Saguy, *Venice Beach: The Last Days of a Bohemian Paradise* (Heidelberg, Germany: Kehrer Verlag, 2018).

Chapter 1

1. Catherine Connell, *School's Out: Gay and Lesbian Teachers in the Classroom* (Berkeley: University of California Press, 2015).
2. Abigail C. Saguy and Anna Ward, "Coming Out as Fat: Rethinking Stigma," *Social Psychology Quarterly* 74, no. 1 (2011).
3. Of course, people are complex and not easily encapsulated in a single "authentic self." In revealing some truths about themselves, people may intentionally or inadvertently gloss over other truths—a theme that is explored further in Chapter 2. My point here is that several people interviewed for this book spoke about finding a sense of liberation through the act of disclosing a stigmatized piece of their identity that they had previously kept hidden.
4. Erving Goffman, *Stigma: Notes on the Management of a Spoiled Identity* (New York: Prentice-Hall, 1963).

5. Indeed, the subtitle of Marilyn Wann's book *Fat! So?* is *Because You Don't Have to Apologize for Your Size*. Likewise, the undocumented immigrant youth movement has appended "unapologetic" to their original slogan of coming out as "undocumented and unafraid."

6. Serena Mayeri, *Reasoning from Race: Feminism, Law, and the Civil Rights Revolution* (Cambridge, MA: Harvard University Press, 2011).

7. Robert C. Bird, "More Than a Congressional Joke: A Fresh Look at the Legislative History of Sex Discrimination of the 1964 Civil Rights Act," *William and Mary Journal of Women and the Law* 3 (Spring 1997).

8. Saguy, *What Is Sexual Harassment? From Capitol Hill to the Sorbonne.*

9. David A. Snow and Robert D. Benford, "Ideology, Frame Resonance and Participant Mobilization," *International Social Movement Research* 1 (1988); Robert D. Benford, "Master Frame," in *The Wiley-Blackwell Encyclopedia of Social and Political Movements*, ed. David A. Snow et al. (Hoboken, NJ: Wiley, 2013).

10. David S. Meyer and Nancy Whittier, "Social Movement Spillover," *Social Problems* 41, no. 2 (1994); Saguy and Ward, "Coming Out as Fat; Doug McAdam, "'Initiator' and 'Spin-Off' Movements: Diffusion Processes in Protest Cycles," in *Repertoires and Cycles of Collective Action*, ed. Mark Traugott (Durham, NC: Duke University Press, 1995).

11. Charlotte Cooper, *Fat and Proud: The Politics of Size* (London: Women's Press, 1998); Charlotte, Cooper, "Fat Activism in Ten Astonishing, Beguiling, Inspiring and Beautiful Episodes," in *Fat Studies in the UK*, ed. Corinna Tomrley and Ann Kaloski (York, England: Raw Nerve Books, 2009); Marilyn Wann, *Fat!So? Because You Don't Have to Apologize for Your Size* (Berkeley, CA: Ten Speed Press, 1999); Saguy and Ward, "Coming Out as Fat"; Enriquez and Saguy, "Coming Out of the Shadows"; Veronica Terriquez, "Intersectional Mobilization, Social Movement Spillover, and Queer Youth Leadership in the Immigrant Rights Movement," *Social Problems* 62, no. 3 (2015).

12. More specifically, this book draws on 15 interviews Michael Stambolis-Ruhstorfer conducted with US lesbians, gay men, and bisexuals, 16 interviews I conducted with members of the fat acceptance movement, 33 interviews Laura E. Enriquez conducted with undocumented immigrant youth activists, 42 interviews Nicole Iturriaga conducted with Mormon fundamentalist polygamists, 21 interviews I conducted with French sexual harassment specialists, and 19 interviews that Juliet A. Williams and I conducted with feminist and LGBTQ+ rights activists. The book further draws on participant observation—from 2001–2012—on two fat-acceptance list servers and participant-observations of four "Coming Out of the Shadows" events held between 2010 and 2012 and of coming out language in undocumented organizational emails, social media, and popular news sites in 2010–2013. This book draws on analyses of autobiographies and anthologies focusing on fat identity, fat acceptance zines (self-published or online magazines), and National Association to Advance Fat Acceptance (NAAFA) newsletters. Finally, this book is informed by reading of the secondary literature, news reports, websites, and blogs.

13. George Chauncey, *Gay New York: Gender, Urban Culture, and the Making of the Gay Male World 1890–1940* (New York: Basic Books, 1994); Eric Garber, "A Spectacle in Color: The Lesbian and Gay Subculture of Jazz Age Harlem," in *In Hidden From History: Reclaiming the Gay and Lesbian Past*, ed. Martin Duberman et al. (New York: New American Library, 1989).

14. Larry Gross, *Contested Closets: The Politics and Ethics of Outing* (Minneapolis: University of Minnesota Press, 1993), 20.

15. Steven Seidman, *Beyond the Closet: The Transformation of Gay and Lesbian Life* (New York: Routledge, 2002).

16. Eve Kosofsky Sedgewick, *Epistemology of the Closet* (Berkeley: University of California Press, 2008).

17. Kathy Kiely, "Immigrant's Family Detained after Daughter Speaks Out," *USA Today*, October 16, 2007; Cindy Carcamo, "Relatives of Erika Andiola, Immigrant Activist, Detained," *Los Angeles Times*, January 11, 2013.

18. Nicholas Paul De Genova, "Migrant 'Illegality' and Deportability in Everyday Life," *Annual Review of Anthropology* 31 (2002); Nicholas De Genova and Nathalie Peutz, eds., *The Deportation Regime: Sovereignty, Space, and the Freedom of Movement* (Durham, NC: Duke University Press, 2010); Tanya Golash-Boza and Pierrette Hondagneu-Sotelo, "Latino Immigrant Men and the Deportation Crisis: A Gendered Racial Removal Program," *Latino Studies* 11, no. 3 (2013).

19. Walter J. Nicholls, *The Dreamers: How the Undocumented Youth Movement Transformed the Immigrant Rights Debate* (Stanford, CA: Stanford University Press, 2013); Laura E. Enriquez, "Undocumented and Citizen Students Unite": Building a Cross-Status Coalition Through Shared Ideology." *Social Problems* 61, no. 2 (2014)

20. Jeanne Batalova and Margie McHugh, "Dream vs. Reality: An Analysis of Potential Dream Act Beneficiaries" (Washington, DC: Migration Policy Institute, 2010).

21. Nicholls, *The Dreamers*; Josiah McC. Heyman, "'Illegality' and the U.S.-Mexico Border: How It Is Produced and Resisted," in *Constructing Immigrant "Illegality": Critiques, Experiences, and Responses*, ed. Cecilia Menjívar and Daniel Kanstroom (New York: Cambridge University Press, 2014); Leo R. Chavez, *The Latino Threat: Constructing Immigrants, Citizens, and the Nation* (Stanford, CA: Stanford University Press, 2008).

22. Sandra E. Garcia, "The Woman Who Created #Metoo Long before Hashtags," *New York Times*, October 20, 2017; Associated Press, "More Than 12m 'Me Too' Facebook Posts, Comments, Reactions in 24 Hours," news release, October 17, 2017, http://cbsn.ws/2ypyCET.

23. Lauren Elkin, "How French Libertines Are Reckoning with #Metoo," *Paris Review*, January 24, 2018.

24. The Clothesline Project, "The Clothesline Project: The Project: Survivor Stories: What Do the Shirts Mean? Gallery," http://www.clotheslineproject.info/project.html.

25. Jo Reger, "Micro-Cohorts, Feminist Discourse, and the Emergence of the Toronto Slutwalk," *Feminist Formations* 26, no. 1 (2014); Curtis Rush, "Cop Apologizes for 'Sluts' Remark at Law School," *Toronto Star*, February 18, 2011.

26. Miriam Valverde, "Timeline: DACA, the Trump Administration and a Government Shutdown," *Politifact*, January 22, 2018; National Immigration Law Center, "Status of Current DACA Litigation," https://www.nilc.org/issues/daca/status-current-daca-litigation/.

27. Amanda Taub, "'White Nationalism,' Explained," *New York Times*, November 21, 2016; Jack Smith, "The Women of the "Alt-Right" Are Speaking Out against Misogyny. They'd Prefer Absolute Patriarchy," *Mic*, December 8, 2017.

Chapter 2

1. Chauncey, *Gay New York*.

2. Ibid., 7.

3. Ibid.

4. John D'Emilio, "Capitalism and Gay Identity," in *Powers of Desire: The Politics of Sexuality*, ed. Ann Snitow, Christine Stansell, and Sharan Thompson, New Feminist Library Series (New York: Monthly Review Press, 1983); Alan Berubé, "Marching to a Different Drummer: Lesbian and Gay GIs in World War II," in *Hidden From History: Reclaiming the Gay and Lesbian Past*, ed. Martin Duberman et al. (New York: New American Library, 1989).

5. D'Emilio, "Capitalism and Gay Identity"; Berubé, Marching to a Different Drummer."

6. Gross, *Contested Closets*, 12.

7. Josh Howard, "April 27, 1953: For LGBT Americans, a Day That Lives in Infamy," *Huffpost*, April 27, 2012.

8. Warren Johansson and William A. Percy, *Outing: Shattering the Conspiracy of Silence* (New York: Haworth Press, 1994).

9. John D'Emilio, *Sexual Politics, Sexual Communities: The Making of a Homosexual Minority in the United States* (Chicago: University of Chicago Press, 1983), 67.

10. Ibid.

11. Johansson and Percy, *Outing*.

12. D'Emilio, *Sexual Politics, Sexual Communities*, 64.

13. Johansson and Percy, *Outing*.

14. Ibid.

15. Ibid., 96.

16. Steve Valocchi, "The Class-Inflected Nature of Gay Identity," *Social Problems* 46, no. 2 (1999).

17. Gross, *Contested Closets*, 14.

18. Chauncey, *Gay New York*, 286.

19. Gross, *Contested Closets*.

20. Ibid., 116; see also Johansson and Percy, *Outing*.

21. Johansson and Percy, *Outing*.

22. D'Emilio, *Sexual Politics, Sexual Communities*, 81.

23. Larry Van Dyne, "Is D.C. Becoming the Gay Capital of America?," *Washingtonian*, September 1980, cited in Gross, *Contested Closets*, 18.

24. D'Emilio, *Sexual Politics, Sexual Communities*, 153.

25. Van Dyne, "Is D.C. Becoming the Gay Capital of America?," 100, cited in Gross, *Contested* Closets, 18.

26. D'Emilio, *Sexual Politics, Sexual Communities*, 163–164.

27. Elizabeth A. Armstrong, *Forging Gay Identities: Organizing Sexuality in San Francisco, 1950–1994* (Chicago: University of Chicago Press, 2002).

28. Steven Epstein, "Gay Politics, Ethnic Identity: The Limits of Social Constructionism," *Socialist Review* 43/44 (1987): 139–140.

29. Gross, *Contested Closets*, 18.

30. Johansson and Percy, *Outing*, 98.

31. D'Emilio, *Sexual Politics, Sexual Communities*, 155–156.

32. Marc Stein, *The Stonewall Riots: A Documentary History* (New York: New York University Press, 2019).

33. Elizabeth A. Armstrong and Suzanna M. Crage, "Movements and Memory: The Making of the Stonewall Myth," *American Sociological Review* 71, no. 5 (2006).

34. The way we conceptualize sexual and gender identities shifts over time, creating a risk that we will view history through the lenses of contemporary categories. In the early 20th century, the line between same-sex desire and gender nonconformity was blurred in that "fairies" or "pansies" were not just men attracted to other men but feminine, indeed not entirely men at all. A female "invert" was not just attracted to other women but also "manly" in dress and behavior. Beginning in the 1950s, in large part in response to police control and violence, gay culture shifted to be gender conforming and transgender emerged as a separate identity. My use of LGBT here acknowledges that people who identified in this way or would be categorized as such today were all at Stonewall. The name of the movement would take a bit longer to acknowledge the diversity in its ranks. Originally, referred to simply as the "gay rights movement," in which gay was supposed to encompass both men and women, it was expanded to the "gay and lesbian" and then "lesbian and gay" movement as lesbians within the movement argued that they and their concerns were being subordinated within the movement. Later it was extended to include bisexuals and transgender people, becoming the LGBT movement, thereby linking as a single cause homophobia and transphobia. More recently, the collection of letters has been broadened to LGBTQ+ to include people who identify as queer, questioning, intersex, asexual, within the Native American category of two-spirited, and so on. When speaking of movements, marches, or demonstrations, I use the labels used at the time. See Nan Alamilla Boyd, *Wide-Open Town: A History of Queer San Francisco to 1965* (Berkeley: University of California Press, 2005); George Chauncey, "Christian Brotherhood or Sexual Perversion? Homosexual Identities and the Construction of Sexual Boundaries in the World War I Era," *Journal of Social History* 19, no. 2 (1985); Chauncey, *Gay New York*; Martin P. Levine, *Gay Macho: The Life and Death of the Homosexual Clone*, ed. Michael S. Kimmel (New York: New York University Press, 1998).

35. Stein, *The Stonewall Riots*.

36. Laud Humphreys, *Out of the Closets: The Sociology of Homosexual Liberation* (Englewood Cliffs, NJ: Prentice-Hall, 1972), 6.

37. Armstrong and Crage, "Movements and Memory."

38. Johansson and Percy, *Outing*, 115.

39. Humphreys, *Out of the Closets*, 2.

40. Louis Freedberg and Christopher Heredia, "Mixed Feelings about Gay March," *San Francisco Chronicle*, April 10, 2000, cited in Amin Ghaziani, *Dividends of Dissent* (Chicago: University of Chicago Press, 2008), 66.

41. Wainwright Churchill, *Homosexual Behavior among Males: A Cross-Cultural and Cross Species Investigation* (New York: Hawthorn Books, 1967); Johansson and Percy, *Outing*.

42. Churchill, *Homosexual Behavior among Males*; Johansson and Percy, "Outing."

43. Johansson and Percy, *Outing*, 6.

44. Ibid., 114.

45. D'Emilio, *Sexual Politics, Sexual Communities*, 235–236.

46. Ibid.

47. Joshua Gamson, *Freaks Talk Back: Tabloid Talk Shows and Sexual Nonconformity* (Chicago: Chicago University Press, 1998), 200.

48. Steve Valocchi, "Individual Identities, Collective Identities, and Organization Structure: The Relationship of the Political Left and Gay Liberation in the United States," *Sociological Perspectives 44*, no. 4 (2001): 457.

49. William Wilkerson, "Is There Something You Need to Tell Me? Coming Out and the Ambiguity of Experience," in *Reclaiming Identity: Realist Theory and the Predicament of Postmodernism*, ed. Paula M. Moya and Michael R. Hames-Garcia (Berkeley: University of California Press, 2000), 267.

50. Edward O. Laumann et al., *The Social Organization of Sexuality: Sexual Practices in the United States* (Chicago: University of Chicago Press, 1994); Alfred C. Kinsey, Wardell B. Pomeroy, and Clyde Martin, *Sexual Behavior in the Human Male* (Philadelphia: W. B. Saunders, 1948).

51. Johansson and Percy, *Outing*, 119.

52. Ibid.

53. Ibid.

54. Connell, *School's Out*.

55. Thomas M. Keck, "Beyond Backlash: Assessing the Impact of Judicial Decisions on LGBT Rights," *Law & Society Review 43*, no. 1 (2009).

56. Connell. *School's Out*.

57. Ibid., 71.

58. ChristineJorgensen.org, "Welcome to Christinejorgensen.Org," http://www.christinejorgensen.org/MainPages/Home.html.

59. Martina Navratilova, "Jason Collins a 'Game Changer,'" *Sports Illustrated*, April 23, 2013.

60. Johansson and Percy, *Outing*, 139.

61. Gross, *Contested Closets*, 38.

62. ACT-UP, "Capsule History—1989," http://www.actupny.org/documents/cron-89.html.

63. Johansson and Percy, *Outing*.

64. Gross, *Contested Closets*; Johansson and Percy, *Outing*.

65. Johansson and Percy *Outing*.

66. Johansson and Percy, *Outing*,112.

67. Gross, *Contested Closets*, 83.

68. Johansson and Percy, *Outing*.

69. Gross, *Contested Closets*.

70. Ibid., 37–38.

71. Johansson and Percy, *Outing*.

72. Gross, *Contested Closets*, 83.

73. Ibid.

74. William A. Henry, "Ethics: Forcing Gays Out of the Closet: Homosexual Leaders Seek to Expose Foes of the Movement," *Time*, January 29, 1990; Johansson and Percy, *Outing*.

75. Henry, "Ethics."

76. Johansson and Percy, *Outing*, 176.

77. Gross, *Contested Closets*, 24.

78. Ibid., 108.

79. Ibid., 126.

80. Johansson and Percy, *Outing*.

81. Ibid., 182.

82. Ibid., 186.

83. Gross, *Contested Closets*, 38.

84. Ibid., 57.

85. Ibid., 152.

86. Dick Kirby, *Outrage*, Magnolia Pictures, 2009.

87. Mark Chiang, "Coming Out into the Global System: Postmodern Patriarchies and Transnational Sexualities in the Wedding Banquet," in *In Q & A: Queer in Asian America*, ed. David L. Eng and Alice Y. Hom (Philadelphia: Temple University Press, 1998). For additional critiques of the notion of gay pride, see Connell, *School's Out*, 24.

88. Gross, *Contested Closets*.

89. Ghaziani, *Dividends of Dissent*.

90. Lisa C. Moore, *Does Your Mama Know? An Anthology of Black Lesbian Coming Out Stories* (Decatur, GA: RedBone Press, 1997), 203.

91. Ghaziani, *Dividends of Dissent*.

92. D'Emilio, "Capitalism and Gay Identity"; Lal Zimman, "'The Other Kind of Coming Out': Transgender People and the Coming Out Narrative Genre," *Gender and Language* 3, no. 1 (2009).

93. Catherine Connell, "Doing, Undoing, or Redoing Gender? Learning from the Workplace Experiences of Transpeople," *Gender & Society* 24, no. 1 (2010).

94. Darren Lenar Hutchinson, "Out yet Unseen: A Racial Critique of Gay and Lesbian Legal Theory and Political Discourse," *Connecticut Law Review* 29, no. 2 (1997).

95. Cathy J. Cohen, *The Boundaries of Blackness: AIDS and the Breakdown of Black Politics* (Chicago: University of Chicago Press, 1999); Mignon R. Moore, "'Black and Gay in L.A.': The Relationships Black Lesbians and Gay Men Have with Their Racial and Religious Communities," in *Black Los Angeles: American Dreams and Racial Realities*, ed. Darnell Hunt and Ana-Christina Ramon (New York: New York University Press, 2010).

96. Judith Halberstam, "Shame and White Gay Masculinity," *Social Text* 23 (2005); Jodi O'Brien, "Afterward: Complicating Homophobia," *Sexualities* 11 (2008); Salvador Vidal-Ortiz, "The Puerto Rican Way Is More Tolerant: Constructions and Uses of 'Homophobia' among Santeria Practitioners across Ethno-Racial and National Indentification," *Sexualities* 11 (2008): 476–495.

97. Amin Ghaziani, "Post-Gay Collective Identity Construction," *Social Problems* 58, no. 1 (2011): 117.

98. Sarah Holmes, ed., *Testimonies: A Collection of Lesbian Coming Out Stories* (Boston: Alyson, 1988); Lisa C. Moore;, *Does Your Mama Know?* Julia Penelope and Susan Wolfe, eds., *The Coming Out Stories* (Watertown, MA: Persephone Press, 1980); Meg Umans, *Like Coming Home: Coming-out Letters* (Austin, TX: Banned Books, 1988).

99. Eli Coleman, "Developmental Stages of the Coming Out Process," *Journal of Homosexuality* 7, no. 2/3 (1982); R. R. Troiden, "The Formation of Homosexual Identities," *Journal of Homosexuality 17* (1989).

100. Phillip L. Hammack and Bertram J. Cohler, eds., *The Story of Sexual Identity: Narrative Perspectives on the Gay and Lesbian Life Course* (Oxford: Oxford University Press, 2009). Rebecca F. Plante, *Sexualities in Context* (New York: W. W. Norton, 2006).

101. Gross, *Contested Closets*, 115.

102. Ibid.

103. Ibid.

104. Christina B. Hanhardt, *Safe Space: Gay Neighborhood History and the Politics of Violence* (Durham, NC: Duke University Press, 2013).

105. Bernadette Barton, *Pray the Gay Away: The Extraordinary Lives of Bible Belt Gays* (New York: New York University Press, 2012).

106. Gross, *Contested Closets*, 115.

107. Ibid.

108. Jason Orne, " 'You Will Always Have to "Out" Yourself': Reconsidering Coming Out through Strategic Outness," *Sexualities* 14, no. 6 (2011).

109. Gross, *Contested Closets*, 118.

110. Hammack and Cohler, *The Story of Sexual Identity*.

111. Seidman, *Beyond the Closet*.

112. Ibid.

113. Laura E. Durso and Gary J. Gates, *Serving Our Youth: Findings from a National Survey of Service Providers Working with Lesbian, Gay, Bisexual, and Transgender Youth Who Are Homeless or at Risk of Becoming Homeless* (Los Angeles: Williams Institute with True Colors Fund and Palette Fund, 2012).

Chapter 3

1. In an episode of *This American Life*, Lindy West talks about coming out as fat and describes being fat as simultaneously being way too visible and being invisible.

Ira Glass, National Public Radio, *This American Life*, podcast audio, "Tell Me I'm Fat," June 17, 2016. Similarly, writer Roxanne Gay writes that she hates being "extraordinarily visible but invisible." Roxanne Gay, *Hunger: A Memoire of (My) Body* (New York: Harper, 2017), 154.

2. Gay, *Hunger*, 120.
3. Wanda Sykes, *I'ma Be Me*, dir. Beth McCarthy-Miller (HBO, 2009).
4. Gay, *Hunger*, 139.
5. Wann, *Fat!So?*
6. Lesleigh Owen, Angela Buffington, and Kris Owen, "Boogeywoman Zine" (2000–2001).
7. Robert McRuer, *Crip Theory: Cultural Signs of Queerness and Disability* (New York: New York Universityp Press, 2006), 9.
8. Sedgewick, *Epistemology of the Closet*.
9. Christine Williams, *Still a Man's World: Men Who Do Women's Work* (Berkeley: University of California Press, 1995).
10. Amy M. Denissen and Abigail C. Saguy, "Gendered Homophobia and the Contradictions of Workplace Discrimination for Women in the Building Trades," *Gender & Society* 28, no. 3 (2014).
11. NAAFA, "Naafa Conferences," https://www.naafaonline.com/dev2/community/index.html.
12. Lisa Schoenfielder and Barb Wieser, eds., *Shadow on a Tightrope: Writings by Women on Fat Oppression* (Iowa City, IA: Aunt Lute, 1983); Wann, *Fat!So?*.
13. Schlomo Deshen, *Blind People: The Private and Public Life of Sightless Israelis* (Albany: State University of New York Press, 1992).
14. Harlan Lane, "Ethnicity, Ethics, and the Deaf-World," *Journal of Deaf Studies and Deaf Education* 10, no. 3 (2005).
15. Gina Kolata, *Rethinking Thin: The New Science of Weight Loss—and the Myths and Realities about Dieting* (New York: Farrar, Straus and Giroux, 2007); Jeffrey Friedman, "The Real Cause of Obesity," *Newsweek*, September 10, 2009.
16. Saguy and Ward, "Coming Out as Fat."
17. Saguy and Ward, "Coming Out as Fat"; Karen W. Stimson, "Fat feminist herstory, 1969-1993: A personal memoir." http://www.eskimo.com/~largesse/Archives/herstory.htm (n.d.). Accessed March 27.
18. Amy Erdman Farrell, *Fat Shame: Stigma and the Fat Body in American Culture* (New York: New York University Press, 2011).
19. Saguy and Ward, "Coming Out as Fat."
20. Schoenfielder and Wieser, *Shadow on a Tightrope*.
21. Thunder, "Coming Out: Notes on Fat Lesbian Pride," in *Shadow on a Tightrope: Writings by Women on Fat Oppression*, ed. Lisa Schoenfielder and Barb Wieser (Iowa City, IA: Aunt Lute, 1983), 210.
22. Ibid.
23. Ibid., 212.
24. Ibid.
25. On courtesy stigma, see Goffman, *Stigma*.

26. NAAFA, "Some Unusual Historical Notes about NAAFA," *NAAFA Newsletter*, April 1989, 2.

27. Kimm Bonner, "Spotlight on Kimm Bonner," *NAAFA Newsletter*, Spring/ Summer 1981.

28. Sally E. Smith, "A Message from Executive Director Sally E. Smith," *NAAFA Newsletter*, January/February, 1988, 3.

29. Saguy and Ward, "Coming Out as Fat," 64.

30. Barbara Altman Bruno, "Support What Supports You," *NAAFA Newsletter*, June/July 1993, 7.

31. "Disagree and Have a Great Life!," *NAAFA Newsletter*, July/August 1995, 4.

32. Saguy and Ward, "Coming Out as Fat," 64.

33. Armstrong. *Forging Gay Identities*.

34. Kathy Barron, "The Body Liberation Station," *NAAFA Newsletter*, Late Fall 2006, 1.

35. Saguy and Ward, "Coming Out as Fat," 64.

36. Wann email 9/30/09.

37. Wann email 9/ 30/09.

38. Wann email 9/30/09.

Chapter 4

1. Kiely, "Immigrant's Family Detained"; Carcamo, "Relatives of Erika Andiola."

2. Laura E. Enriquez, Martha Morales Hernandez, and Annie Ro, "Deconstructing Immigrant Illegality: A Mixed-Methods Investigation of Stress and Health among Undocumented College Students," *Race and Social Problems* 10, no. 3 (2018); Laura E. Enriquez, *Of Love and Papers: Forming Families in the Shadows of Immigration Policy* (Berkeley: University of California Press, forthcoming).

3. Golash-Boza and Hondagneu-Sotelo, "Latino Immigrant Men and the Deportation Crisis"; Amada Armenta, *Protect, Serve, and Deport: The Rise of Policing as Immigration Enforcement* (Berkeley: University of California Press, 2017).

4. Laura E Enriquez, "Multigenerational Punishment: Shared Experiences of Undocumented Immigration Status within Mixed-Status Families," *Journal of Marriage and Family* 77, no. 4 (2015); Marta María Maldonado, Adela C Licona, and Sarah Hendricks, "Latin@ Immobilities and Altermobilities within the U.S. Deportability Regime," *Annals of the American Association of Geographers* 106 (2016).

5. Batalova and McHugh, "Dream vs. Reality."

6. Hinda Seif, "'Wise Up': Undocumented Latino Youth, Mexican American Legislators, and the Struggle for Education Access," *Latino Studies* 2, no. 2 (2004).

7. Mary Louise Kelly and Cecilia Lei, *The Original Dreamer Recalls "All Pervasive" Fear as an Undocumented Child*, podcast audio, National Public Radio, *All Things Considered*, 7:582018, https://www.npr.org/2018/06/20/622002025/the-original-dreamer-recalls-all-pervasive-fear-as-an-undocumented-child.

8. Lauren Gambino, "Failed Deal over Dreamers at the Heart of Us Government Shutdown," *Guardian*, January 20, 2018.

9. Chris Nichols, "Do Three-Quarters of Americans Support the Dream Act? Nancy Pelosi Says So," http://www.politifact.com/california/statements/2017/sep/19/nancy-pelosi/nancy-pelosi-claims-three-quarters-americans-suppo/.

10. Nicholls, *The Dreamers*.

11. Douglas McGray, "The Invisibles," *Los Angeles Times*, April 23, 2006.

12. Gabriela Madera et al., eds., *Underground Undergrads: UCLA Undocumented Immigrant Students Speak Out* (Los Angeles: UCLA Center for Labor Research and Education, 2008).

13. Gaby Pacheco, "Trail of Dreams: A Fifteen-Hundred Mile Journey to the Nation's Capital," in *Undocumented and Unafraid: Tam Tran, Cinthya Felix, and the Immigrant Youth Movement*, ed. Kent Wong et al. (Los Angeles: UCLA Center for Labor Research and Education, 2012).

14. Immigrant Youth Justice League, "Who We Are," http://www.iyjl.org/whoweare/.

15. Terriquez, "Intersectional Mobilization"; Hinda Seif, "'Coming Out of the Shadows' and 'Undocuqueer': Undocumented Immigrants Transforming Sexuality Discourse and Activism," *Journal of Language and Sexuality* 3, no. 1 (2014); Enriquez and Saguy, "Coming Out of the Shadows."

16. Gary J. Gates, "LGBT Adult Immigrants in the United States," (Los Angeles: Williams Institute, 2013).

17. Terriquez, "Intersectional Mobilization."

18. Jeffrey S. Passel and D'Vera Cohn, *Unauthorized Immigrant Population: National and State Trends, 2010* (Washington, DC: Pew Hispanic Center, 2011).

19. Immigrant Youth Justice League, "National Coming Out of the Shadows Month 2013," http://www.iyjl.org/comingout2013/.

20. In 2010, dreamactivist.org and United We Dream had overlapping leadership. The founders of dreamactivist.org later separated from United We Dream and founded the National Immigrant Youth Alliance.

21. National Immigrant Youth Alliance, "A Guide to 'Coming Out' for Undocumented Youth" (2011). https://tinyurl.com/y3w5aqj6.

22. Enriquez and Saguy, "Coming Out of the Shadows."

23. The following description is based on Laura E. Enriquez's field notes from this event.

24. Lisa Christensen Gee, Matthew Gardner, and Meg Wiehe, *Undocumented Immigrants' State & Local Tax Contributions* (Washington, DC: Institute on Taxation and Economic Policy, 2016).

25. National Immigration Law Center, "Support for the Dream Act," https://www.nilc.org/issues/immigration-reform-and-executive-actions/dreamact/dreamsupport/.

26. Julianne Hing, "How Undocumented Youth Nearly Made Their Dreams Real in 2010," *Colorlines*, December 20, 2010.

27. Immigrant Youth Justice League, "Undocumented, Unafraid, Unapologetic," http://www.iyjl.org/undocumented-unafraid-unapologetic/.

28. Julianne Hing, "Dreamers Come Out: 'I'm Undocumented, Unafraid, and Unapologetic,'" *Colorlines*, March 8, 2011.

29. Pepe Lozano, "Immigrant Youth: Undocumented, Unafraid and Unapologetic," *People's World*, March 11, 2011.

30. Jose Antonia Vargas, "Not Legal Not Leaving," *Time*, June 25, 2012.
31. Roberto G. Gonzales, Veronica Terriquez, and Stephen P. Ruszczyk, "Becoming DACAmented: Assessing the Short-Term Benefits of Deferred Action for Childhood Arrivals (DACA)," *American Behavioral Scientist* 58, no. 14 (2014); Roberto G. Gonzales, "DACA at Year Three: Challenges and Opportunities in Accessing Higher Education and Employment" (Washington, DC: American Immigration Council, 2016); Tom K. Wong and Carolina Valdivia, "In Their Own Words: A Nationwide Survey of Undocumented Millennials," in *Working Paper 191* (San Diego, CA: Center for Comparative Immigration Studies, 2014).
32. Immigrant Youth Justice League, "National Coming Out of the Shadows Month 2013." http://www.iyjl.org/comingout2013/
33. Joel Sati, "How DACA Pits 'Good Immigrants' against Millions of Others," *Washington Post*, September 7, 2017. Tania A. Unzueta Carrasco and Hinda Seif, "Disrupting the Dream: Undocumented Youth Reframe Citizenship and Deportability through Anti-Deportation Activism," *Latino Studies* 12, no. 2 (2014).

Chapter 5

1. Polygamy refers to a marriage involving more than two partners. Polygyny refers specifically to the arrangement in which one man has two or more wives, while polyandry refers to a woman married to two or more men. This said, people often use the broader category of polygamy to refer to polygyny—the most common form of polygamy.
2. David Hinckley, " 'Sister Wives,' '19th Wife' and 'Big Love' Usher in Wave of Polygamy Programming," *NY Daily News*, September 13, 2010.
3. The 2013 ruling, which the state of Utah may appeal to the Tenth Circuit Court of Appeals, left standing the state's ability to prohibit multiple marriages in the literal sense of having two or more valid marriage licenses and made it a crime for a married man to try to legally marry a second woman.
4. Mary Batchelor, Marianne Watson, and Anne Wilde, eds., *Voices in Harmony: Contemporary Women Celebrate Plural Marriage* (Salt Lake City, UT: Principle Voices, 2000).
5. Ibid.; Greg Burton, "Political Polygamists Coming Out of the Closet," *Salt Lake Tribune*, December 11, 2000.
6. Eve Tushnet, "Polygamy Proponents Recycle Same-Sex 'Marriage' Arguments," *National Catholic Register*, March 25, 2001.
7. Judith Stacey, *Unhitched: Love, Marriage, and Family Values from West Hollywood to Western China* (New York: New York University Press, 2011), 114.
8. Ibid., citing National Public Radio, *Fresh Air*, podcast audio, Mark Olsen and Will Scheffer, "Feeling the 'Big Love,' " August 1, 2007.
9. Stacey, *Unhitched*, 116.
10. Ibid., citing Tapestry against Polygamy, "By 3rd Anniversary of 'Lawrence'—Polygamy Rights Accelerated," Pro-Polygamy.com, http://www.pro-polygamy.com/articles.php?news=0044.

11. Stacey, *Unhitched*, 117.

12. Tribune News Services, "Clan Leader Pleads Guilty to Incest," *Chicago Tribune*, November 7, 2003.

13. Amy Kathlyn Osmond, "Organizational Identification: A Case Study of the Davis County Cooperative Society, the Latter Day Church of Christ, or Kingston Order," Phd Dissertation in Communications (University of Utah, 2010).

14. Orne, "'You Will Always Have to "Out" Yourself'"; Gross, *Contested Closets*.

15. Lauren Davidson, "Is Your Daily Social Media Usage Higher Than Average?," *Telegraph*, May 17, 2015.

16. Jean M. Twenge, *IGen: Why Today's Super-Connected Kids Are Growing Up Less Rebellious, More Tolerant, Less Happy—and Completely Unprepared for Adulthood—and What That Means for the Rest of Us* (New York: Atria Books, 2017).

17. Jeffrey Michael Hayes, "Polygamy Comes Out of the Closet: The New Strategy of Polygamy Activists," *Stanford Journal of Civil Rights & Civil Liberties* 3 (2007).

18. Jaime M. Gher, "Polygamy and Same-Sex Marriage—Allies or Adversaries within the Same-Sex Marriage Movement," *William & Mary Journal of Women and the Law* 14, no. 3 (2008).

19. Angela McRobbie, "Top Girls? Young Women and the Post-Feminist Sexual Contract," *Cultural Studies* 1, no. 21 (2007).

20. Laura Hamilton and Elizabeth A. Armstrong, "Gendered Sexuality in Young Adulthood: Double Binds and Flawed Options," *Gender & Society* 23, no. 5 (2009).

21. Lisa Belkin, "What a Working Woman Needs: A Wife," *New York Times*, June 5, 2005.

22. Arlie Hochschild, *The Second Shift: Working Parents and the Revolution at Home* (New York: Viking Penguin, 1989).

23. Michael C. Dawson, *Behind the Mule: Race and Class in African-American Politics* (Princeton, NJ: Princeton University Press, 1994).

24. See also Hayes, "Polygamy Comes Out of the Closet."

25. National Public Radio, "In Major Shift, LDS Church Rolls Back Controversial Policies toward LGBT Members," *Religion*, April 4, 2019. https://tinyurl.com/yyhtp74u .

Chapter 6

1. Garcia, "The Woman Who Created #Metoo."

2. Ibid.

3. Ibid.

4. Elizabeth Wagmeister, "Tarana Burke on Hollywood, Time's Up and Me Too Backlash," *Variety*, April 10, 2018.

5. Nadja Sayej, "Interview: Alyssa Milano on the #Metoo Movement: 'We're Not Going to Stand for It Any More,'" *Guardian*, December 1, 2017. Facebook posts are informal writing and posts are thus often riddled with punctuation errors, spelling mistakes, and other editorial errors. I have corrected these in the accounts that follow but not in any way that changes the meaning of what is being said.

6. Garcia, "The Woman Who Created #Metoo"; Associated Press' "More Than 12m 'Me Too' Facebook Posts."

7. Associated Press, "More Than 12m 'Me Too' Facebook Posts."

8. Sheryl Estrada, "Time Magazine Excluding Tarana Burke from #Metoo Cover Speaks Volumes," *DiversityInc*, December 11, 2017.

9. Eleanor Beardsley, "Instead of #Metoo, French Women Say 'Out Your Pig,'" podcast audio, National Public Radio, *Morning Edition*, 4 minutes, November 3, 2017, http://n.pr/2CoI7qr.

10. Elkin, "How French Libertines Are Reckoning with #Metoo."

11. Alka Kurian, "#Metoo Is Riding a New Wave of Feminism in India," *Conversation*, February 27, 2018.

12. British Broadcasting Company (BBC), "Leta Hong Fincher, Author, Betraying Big Brother: The Feminist Awakening in China," BBC, March 5, 2018.

13. Choe Sang-Hun, "A Director's Apology Adds Momentum to South Korea's #Metoo Movement," *New York Times*, February 19, 2018.

14. Oleg Matsnev, "Russian News Outlets Boycott Parliament after Harassment Decision," *The New York Times,* March 22. https://tinyurl.com/yxgyqz62.

15. While the MeToo movement is global, the meaning and significance of the movement vary depending on the local legal context, a topic that is beyond the scope of this book but merits examination.

16. A study of how the #MeToo movement is unfolding differently in different nations based on varying national legal, political, and cultural contexts is beyond the scope of this book but merits investigation. In other work, I have shown how very different legal, political, and cultural contexts have led to distinct legal, corporate, and popular understandings of sexual harassment in France and the United States. Saguy, *What Is Sexual Harassment? From Capitol Hill to the Sorbonne*; Saguy, "Europeanization or National Specificity? Legal Approaches to Sexual Harassment in France, 2002–2012."

17. Sayej, "Interview: Alyssa Milano on the #Metoo Movement."

18. Jessica Levinson, "Non-Disclosure Agreements Can Enable Abusers. Should We Get Rid of NDAs for Sexual Harassment?," *NBCNews*, January 24, 2018.

19. Jessica Prois and Carolina Moreno, "The #Metoo Movement Looks Different for Women of Color. Here Are 10 Stories. Some of the Most Affected Have Been Left out of the Movement, and It's Time We Talk about It," *HuffPost*, January 2, 2018.

20. Ibid.

21. Ibid.

22. Ibid.

23. Ibid.

24. Ibid.

25. *The Daily Show* with Trevor Noah, Tarana Burke on What Me Too Is Really About—Extended Interview (2018).

26. Prois and Moreno, "The #Metoo Movement Looks Different."

27. Gary Langer, "Unwanted Sexual Advances Not Just a Hollywood, Weinstein Story, Poll Finds," *ABCNews*, October 17, 2017; RAINN, "Victims of Sexual Violence: Statistics," https://www.rainn.org/statistics/victims-sexual-violence.

28. Trav Mamone, "The #Metoo Conversation Erases Trans People," *HuffPost*, February 21, 2018.

29. Ibid.

30. Ibid.

31. Jennifer Earl and Katrina Kimport, *Digitally Enabled Social Change: Activism in the Internet Age (Acting with Technology)* (Cambridge, MA: MIT Press, 2011).

32. RAINN, "Key Terms and Phrases," https://www.rainn.org/articles/key-terms-and-phrases; Gwendolyn Wu, "'Survivor' Versus 'Victim': Why Choosing Your Words Carefully Is Important," *HelloFlo*, March 16, 2016; "Unpopular Opinion: I Am a Rape Victim, Not a Survivor," *XOJane*, April 27, 2016.

33. Reger, "Micro-Cohorts."

34. L. Yang, "Emma Sulkowicz: 2017's Sexual Assault Reckoning Is a 'Marker for Change'." *Vice*, December 3, 2017, from https://tinyurl.com/y34v9mez.

35. Soraya Nadia McDonald, "It's Hard to Ignore a Woman Toting a Mattress Everywhere She Goes, Which Is Why Emma Sulkowicz Is Still Doing It," *Washington Post*, October 29, 2014.

36. Nancy Whittier, "Activism against Sexual Violence Is Central to a New Women's Movement: Resistance to Trump, Campus Sexual Assault, and #Metoo," *Mobilizing Ideas*, January 22, 2018.

37. Rush, "Cop Apologizes for 'Sluts' Remark."

38. Andrea O'Reilly, "Slut Pride: A Tribute to Slutwalk Toronto," *Feminist Studies* 38, no. 1 (2012).

39. Reger, "Micro-Cohorts."

40. Jessica Valenti, "#Metoo Named the Victims. Now, Let's List the Perpetrators," *Guardian*, October 17, 2017.

41. Alana Massey, "Women Have Always Tried to Warn Each Other about Dangerous Men. We Have To," *Washington Post*, October 13, 2017.

42. Doree Shafrir, "What to Do with 'Shitty Media Men'?," *Buzzfeed*, October 11, 2017.

43. Jenna Wortham, "We Were Left Out," *New York Times Magazine*, December 13, 2017.

44. Moira Donegan, "I Started the Media Men List; My Name Is Moira Donegan," *The Cut*, January 10, 2018.

45. Ibid.

46. Wortham, "We Were Left Out."

47. Donegan, "I Started the Media Men List."

48. Ibid.

49. Ibid.

50. Ibid.

51. Ibid.

52. Ibid.

53. Ibid.

54. Shafrir, "What to Do with 'Shitty Media Men'?"

55. Jaclyn Peiser, "How a Crowdsourced List Set Off Months of #Metoo Debate," *New York Times*, February 3, 2018.

56. Ibid.

57. Ibid.
58. Ibid.
59. Ibid.
60. Donegan. "I Started the Media Men List."
61. Ibid.
62. Sapna Maheshwari, "Ad Agencies' Reckoning on Sexual Harassment Comes on Instagram, Anonymously," *New York Times*, March 7, 2018.
63. Ibid.
64. Ibid.
65. Ibid.
66. Elizabeth Harris, "Three Billboards Call Out Sexual Abuse," *New York Times*, March 23, 2018.
67. Saguy, "Europeanization or National Specificity? Legal Approaches to Sexual Harassment in France, 2002–2012."
68. Élise Karlin, "La Descente Aux Enfers De DSK," *L'Express*, May 17, 2011.
69. Bernard-Henri Levy, "Le Bloc-Notes De Bernard-Henri Levy," *Le Point*, May 17, 2011.
70. Philippe Boulet-Gercourt, "DSK Menotté: Le 'Perp Walk' Mode D'emploi," *Le Nouvel Observateur*, May 18, 2011 2011.
71. "Jean-François Kahn: Pas De Viol, Mais Un 'Troussage De Domestique,'" *Le Nouvel Observateur*, May 18, 2011,
72. Le Grand Barnum to Le Grand Barnum, May 16, 2011, http://www.le-grand-barnum.fr/de-laffaire-dsk-comme-troussage-de-domestique-jean-francois-kahn-et-linconscient-machiste-francais/.
73. Catharine MacKinnon, *Sexual Harassment of Working Women* (New Haven, CT: Yale University Press, 1979).
74. "#Metoo Has Done What the Law Could Not," *New York Times*, February 4, 2018.
75. "Who Is Larry Nassar? A Timeline of His Decades-Long Career, Sexual Assault Convictions and Prison Sentences," https://www.usatoday.com/pages/interactives/larry-nassar-timeline/.
76. Ibid.
77. Ibid.
78. Ibid.
79. Ibid.
80. Marisa Kwiatkowski, Mark Alesia, and Tim Evans, "A Blind Eye to Sex Abuse: How USA Gymnastics Failed to Report Cases," *IndyStar*, August 4, 2016.
81. Ibid.
82. Ibid.
83. Ibid.
84. Tim Evans, Marisa Kwiatkowski, and Mark Alesia, "Can USA Gymnastics Reform Itself under Current Leadership?," *IndyStar*, June 27, 2017.
85. Tim Evans, Mark Alesia, and Marisa Kwiatkowski, "A 20-Year Toll: 368 Gymnasts Allege Sexual Exploitation," *IndyStar*, December 15, 2016.
86. Evans, Kwiatkowski, and Alesia, "Can USA Gymnastics Reform Itself under Current Leadership?"

87. RAINN, "The Criminal Justice System: Statistics," https://www.rainn.org/statistics/criminal-justice-system.

88. Scott Cacciola, "Victims in Larry Nassar Abuse Case Find a Fierce Advocate: The Judge," *New York Times*, January 23 2108.

89. Ibid.

90. Ibid.

91. Ibid.

92. Ibid.

93. Ibid.

94. Ibid.

95. Ibid.

96. Eric Levenson, "Larry Nassar Will Never Get Out of Prison, No Matter His Sentence This Week," *CNN.com*, January 23, 2018.

97. Scott Cacciola and Victor Mather, "Larry Nassar Sentencing: 'I Just Signed Your Death Warrant,'" *New York Times*, January 24, 2018.

98. Thanks to Bruce Western for this point. For a provocative discussion of restorative justice in the #MeToo movement, see Katie J. M. Baker, "What Do We Do with These Men?," *New York Times*, April 27, 2018.

99. Howard Zehr and Ali Gohar, *The Little Book of Restorative Justice* (New York: UNICEF, 2003), 11.

100. Ibid.

101. Bryan Armen Graham, "Larry Nassar Is Locked Up for Life. Now the Real Work Begins," *Guardian*, January 25, 2018.

102. Nancy Hogshead-Maker, "Michigan State Will Pay $500 Million to Abuse Victims. What Comes Next?" *New York Times*, May 18, 2018.

103. Zach Schonbrun and Christine Hauser, "Larry Nassar, Sentenced in Sexual Abuse Case, Is Back in Court," *New York Times*, January 31, 2018.

104. Timothy Williams, "Did the #Metoo Movement Sway the Cosby Jury?," *New York Times*, April 26, 2018.

105. Ibid.

106. David Maialetti, "Cosby Juror Says He Didn't Believe 'Well-Coached' Constand," *Inquirer*, June 22, 2017.

107. Williams, "Did the #Metoo Movement Sway the Cosby Jury?"

108. Deborah Tuerkheimer, "The Cosby Jury Finally Believes the Women," *New York Times*, April 26, 2018; Timothy Williams, "Cosby Verdict Is Hailed a Breakthrough. Here's Why It Was an Anomaly," *New York Times*, April 27, 2018.

109. Gross, *Contested Closets*, 38.

Chapter 7

1. Samantha Allen, "Are Bisexuals Shut Out of the LGBT Club?," *Daily Beast*, January 3, 2015; Tangela S. Roberts, Sharon G. Horne, and William T. Hoyt, "Between a Gay and a Straight Place: Bisexual Individuals' Experiences with Monosexism," *Journal of Bisexuality* 15, no. 4 (2015).

2. Pew Research Center, "A Survey of LGBT Americans: Attitudes, Experiences and Values in Changing Times" (Washington, DC: Pew Research Center, 2013).

3. Ibid.

4. See also Mitch Kellaway, "Meet Obama's Newest Trans Appointee: Attorney Shannon Minter," *Advocate*, June 9, 2015.

5. Helene Cooper, "Critics See Echoes of 'Don't Ask, Don't Tell' in Military Transgender Ban," *New York Times*, March 28, 2018.

6. Ibid.

7. Editorial Board, "Trump's Heartless Transgender Military Ban Gets a Second Shot," *New York Times,* March 28, 2018.

8. Ben Protess, Danielle Ivory, and Steve Eder, "Where Trump's Hands-Off Approach to Governing Does Not Apply," ibid., September 10, 2017. The Supreme Court ruled 7–2 in favor of the baker on June 4, 2018. *Masterpiece Cakeshop, Ltd. v. Colorado Civil Rights Commission*, 584 U.S. ____.

9. Protess et al. "Where Trump's Hands-Off Approach to Governing Does Not Apply."

10. Ibid.; Alan Feuer, "Justice Department Says Rights Law Doesn't Protect Gays," *The New York Times*, July 27, 2017.

11. Melissa Hines, S. Faisal Ahmed, and Ieuan A. Hughes, "Psychological Outcomes and Gender-Related Development in Complete Androgen Insensitivity Syndrome," *Archives of Sexual Behavior* 32, no. 2 (2003).

12. StopIGM.org, " 'Inhuman Treatment': UN Committee against Torture (CAT) Condemns Intersex Genital Mutilations, Calls for Legislative Measures," news release, August 14, 2015, https://bit.ly/2uMLX7m; Chase Strangio, "Stop Performing Nonconsensual, Medically Unnecessary Surgeries on Young Intersex Children," *ACLU.org*, October 26, 2017; Human Rights Watch and InterACT, " 'I Want to Be Like Nature Made Me': Medically Unnecessary Surgeries on Intersex Children in the US," July 25, 2017, https://tinyurl.com/y8ez74gc.

13. In reviewing an earlier version of this chapter, Weigel requested that "transgender community" be revised to "LGBTQIA+ community." The I stands for intersex. The A can stand for both ally and asexual.

14. Newsday.com staff, "Donald Trump Speech, Debates and Campaign Quotes," *Newsday*, November 9, 2016.

15. Valverde, "Timeline."

16. Cesar Vargas, "Undocumented and Unafraid in the Face of Trump's Presidency," *Nation*, November 11, 2016.

17. Michael Scherer, "2016 Person of the Year Donald Trump," *Time*, 2016, https://time.com/time-person-of-the-year-2016-donald-trump/. .

18. Valverde, "Timeline."

19. Ibid.

20. Teresa Watanabe, "With News of DACA's End, UCLA Student Declares Herself 'Undocumented and Unafraid,'" *Los Angeles Times*, September 5, 2017.

21. Valverde, "Timeline."

22. National Immigration Law Center, "Status of Current DACA Litigation," https://www.nilc.org/issues/daca/status-current-daca-litigation/.

23. Kelly Heyboer, "'Undocumented and Unafraid' Immigrants March on I.C.E. Headquarters," *New Jersey Real-Time News*, March 6, 2018.

24. Alan Feuer, "Citing Trump's 'Racial Slurs,' Judge Says Suit to Preserve DACA Can Continue," *New York Times*, March 29, 2018.

25. Ibid.

26. David Lawler, "Trump on Fiorina: 'Look at That Face. Would Anyone Vote for That?,'" *Telegraph*, September 10, 2015;

27. Claire Cohen, "Donald Trump Sexism Tracker: Every Offensive Comment in One Place," *Telegraph*, July 14, 2017.

28. Ibid.

29. Stephen Collinson, "Can Donald Trump Recover from This?," *CNNPolitics*, October 8, 2016.

30. Jacqulyn Powell, "#Notokay Movement Encouraging Women to Share Sexual Assault Stories on Social Media," *WPTV*, October 11, 2016.

31. Ashwini Tambe, "Has Trump's Presidency Triggered the Movement against Sexual Harassment?," *Conversation*, November 28, 2017.

32. Gregory Krieg, "It's Official: Clinton Swamps Trump in Popular Vote," *CNNPolitics*, December 22, 2016.

33. CNNPolitics, "Exit Polls," https://www.cnn.com/election/2016/results/exit-polls.

34. Shankar Vedantam, *Hidden Brain*, podcast audio, Why Now?, National Public Radio, 52 minutes February 5, 2018.

35. Ibid.

36. Ibid.

37. Ibid.

38. Ibid.

39. Why #Metoo Happened in 2017, podcast audio, National Public Radio, February 7, 2018, https://www.npr.org/2018/02/07/583910310/why-metoo-happened-in-2017.

40. Tambe, "Has Trump's Presidency Triggered the Movement against Sexual Harassment?"

41. Ibid.

42. Ibid.

43. Jenna Wortham, "Who Didn't Go to the Women's March Matters More Than Who Did," *New York Times*, January 24, 2017.

44. Susan Chira, "Year of the Woman? In Arizona, It's Women, Plural, and It's Both Parties," *New York Times*, April 9, 2018.

45. Charlotte Alter, "A Year Ago, They Marched. Now a Record Number of Women Are Running for Office," *Time*, January 18, 2018.

46. Chira, "Year of the Woman?"

47. Tambe, "Has Trump's Presidency Triggered the Movement against Sexual Harassment?"

48. Michelle Goldberg, "The Teachers Revolt in West Virginia," *New York Times*, March 5. 2018; Emily Stewart, "All of West Virginia's Teachers Have Been on Strike for over a Week," *Vox*, March 4, 2018.

49. Goldberg, "The Teachers Revolt in West Virginia."

50. Paul Krugman, "The Force of Decency Awakens," *New York Times*, February 26, 2018.
51. Goldberg, "The Teachers Revolt in West Virginia."
52. Dana Goldstein, "Teachers in Oklahoma and Kentucky Walk Out: 'It Really Is a Wildfire,'" *New York Times*, April 2, 2018.
53. Simon Romero, Jack Healy, and Julie Turkewitz, "Teachers in Arizona and Colorado Walk Out over Education Funding," *New York Times*, April 26, 2018.
54. Paul Krugman, "The Force of Decency Awakens," *New York Times*, February 26, 2018.
55. Cindi Leive, "Let's Talk about My Abortion (and Yours)," *New York Times*, June 30, 2018.
56. Ibid.; Guttmacher Institute, "Abortion Is a Common Experience for U.S. Women, Despite Dramatic Declines in Rates" (Guttmacher Institute, 2017), https://tinyurl.com/ydaeb22f.
57. Leive, "Let's Talk about My Abortion."
58. Carol Sanger, *About Abortion: Terminating Pregnancy in Twenty-First-Century America* (Cambridge, MA: Harvard University Press, 2017).
59. Sarah K. Cowan, "Secrets and Misperceptions: The Creation of Self-Fulfilling Illusions," *Sociological Science* 1 (2014).
60. Amy J. Binder and Kate Wood, *Becoming Right: How Campuses Shape Young Conservatives*, ed. Paul J. DiMaggio et al., Princeton Studies in Cultural Sociology (Princeton, NJ: Princeton University Press, 2013), 2.
61. Monica Hesse and Dan Zak, "Does This Haircut Make Me Look Like a Nazi?," *Chicago Tribune*, December 6, 2016.
62. Christian S. Crandall, Jason M. Miller, and Mark H. White II, "Changing Norms Following the 2016 U.S. Presidential Election: The Trump Effect on Prejudice," *Social Psychology and Personality Science* 9, no. 2 (2018).
63. Ibid., 189.
64. Christian S. Crandall and Amy Eshleman, "A Justification-Suppression Model of the Expression and Experience of Prejudice," *Psychological Bulletin* 129, no. 3 (2003).
65. German Lopez, "Most Americans Agree Trump Has Made Race Relations Worse," *Vox*, April 9, 2019.
66. The Associated Press, "Trump Says White Nationalism Is Not on the Rise. Here Are the Facts," *Haaretz*, March 18, 2019.
67. Hesse and Zak, "Does This Haircut Make Me Look Like a Nazi?"
68. Lisa Mascaro, "David Duke and Other White Supremacists See Trump's Rise as Way to Increase Role in Mainstream Politics," *Los Angeles Times*, September 29, 2016.
69. Ibid.
70. FAIR (Federation for American Immigration Reform), "It's Time for Americans to Come Out of the Shadows," https://www.fairus.org/media/10096.
71. Taub, "'White Nationalism,' Explained"; Jack Smith.
72. Sociologist Michael Young argues that this tradition dates back to the 1830s, when political protest movements in the United States began to use public confession to address "special sins," or specific social problems. Michael Young, *Bearing Witness against Sin: The Evangelical Birth of the American Social Movement* (Chicago: University of Chicago Press, 2007).

73. Beatrice Dupuy, "Some Women of Color Are Boycotting the Women's March, Here's Why," *Newsweek*, January 20, 2018.

74. Marie Sollis, "Women of Color Are Being Blamed for Dividing the Women's March—and It's Nothing New," *Mic*, January 21, 2017.

75. Wortham, "Who Didn't Go to the Women's March Matters More Than Who Did."

76. Katherine Rodriguez, "Transgender Activists Complain Women's March Unfairly Linked Sex to Biology," *Breitbart*, January 24, 2017.

77. "The Importance of Women of Color at the Women's March 2018," *Glitter*, 2018, https://bit.ly/2suqm1j.

78. Wortham, "Who Didn't Go to the Women's March Matters More Than Who Did."

79. Kristin Luker, *Abortion and the Politics of Motherhood* (Berkeley: University of California Press, 1984); Phyllis Schlafly, "How the Feminists Want to Change Our Laws," *Stanford Law & Policy Review* 65 (1994).

80. Luker, *Abortion and the Politics of Motherhood*.

81. Lonnae O'Neil, "The 53 Percent Issue: This Time, the Problem in American Feminism Has a Name," *Undefeated*, December 20, 2016.

82. Sollis, "Women of Color Are Being Blamed."

83. Wortham, "Who Didn't Go to the Women's March Matters More Than Who Did."

84. S. T. Holloway, "Why This Black Girl Will Not Be Returning to the Women's March," *Huffington Post*, January 19, 2018.

85. Ibid.

Sources Cited

ACT-UP. "Capsule History—1989." http://www.actupny.org/documents/cron-89.html.

Allen, Samantha. "Are Bisexuals Shut Out of the LGBT Club?" *Daily Beast*, January 3, 2015.

Alter, Charlotte. "A Year Ago, They Marched. Now a Record Number of Women Are Running for Office." *Time*, January 18, 2018.

Armenta, Amada. *Protect, Serve, and Deport: The Rise of Policing as Immigration Enforcement*. Berkeley: University of California Press, 2017.

Armstrong, Elizabeth A. *Forging Gay Identities: Organizing Sexuality in San Francisco, 1950-1994*. Chicago: University of Chicago Press, 2002.

Armstrong, Elizabeth A., and Suzanna M. Crage. "Movements and Memory: The Making of the Stonewall Myth." *American Sociological Review* 71, no. 5 (October 2006): 724–751.

Associated Press. "More Than 12m 'Me Too' Facebook Posts, Comments, Reactions in 24 Hours." News release, October 17, 2017, http://cbsn.ws/2ypyCET.

Associated Press. "Trump Says White Nationalism Is Not on the Rise. Here Are the Facts." *Haaretz*, March 18, 2019.

Baker, Katie J. M. "What Do We Do with These Men?" *New York Times*, April 27, 2018.

Barron, Kathy. "The Body Liberation Station." *NAAFA Newsletter*, Late Fall (2006): 1.

Barton, Bernadette. *Pray the Gay Away: The Extraordinary Lives of Bible Belt Gays*. New York: New York University Press, 2012.

Batalova, Jeanne, and Margie McHugh. "Dream vs. Reality: An Analysis of Potential Dream Act Beneficiaries," 1–23. Migration Policy Institute, Washington, DC: 2010.

Batchelor, Mary, Marianne Watson, and Anne Wilde, eds. *Voices in Harmony: Contemporary Women Celebrate Plural Marriage*. Salt Lake City, UT: Principle Voices, 2000.

BBC. "Leta Hong Fincher, Author, Betraying Big Brother: The Feminist Awakening in China." *BBC*, March 5 2018.

Beardsley, Eleanor. Instead of #Metoo, French Women Say "Out Your Pig." Podcast audio. National Public Radio, *Morning Edition*, 4 minutes, 2017. http://n.pr/2CoI7qr.

Belkin, Lisa. "What a Working Woman Needs: A Wife." *New York Times*, June 5, 2005.

Benford, Robert D. "Master Frame." In *The Wiley-Blackwell Encyclopedia of Social and Political Movements*, edited by David A. Snow, Donatella della Porta, Bert Klandermans, and Doug McAdam: Hoboken, NJ: Wiley, 2013.

Berubé, Alan. "Marching to a Different Drummer: Lesbian and Gay GIs in World War II." In *Hidden from History: Reclaiming the Gay and Lesbian Past*, edited by Martin Duberman et al., 383–394. New York: New American Library, 1989.

Binder, Amy J., and Kate Wood. *Becoming Right: How Campuses Shape Young Conservatives*. Princeton, NJ: Princeton University Press, 2013.

Bird, Robert C. "More Than a Congressional Joke: A Fresh Look at the Legislative History of Sex Discrimination of the 1964 Civil Rights Act." *William and Mary Journal of Women and the Law* 3, Spring (1997): 137–161.

Bonner, Kimm. "Spotlight on Kimm Bonner." *NAAFA Newsletter*, Spring/Summer (1981): 2.

Boulet-Gercourt, Philippe. "DSK Menotté: Le 'Perp Walk' Mode D'emploi." *Le Nouvel Observateur*, May 18, 2011.

Boyd, Nan Alamilla. *Wide-Open Town: A History of Queer San Francisco to 1965*. Berkeley: University of California Press, 2005.

Bruno, Barbara Altman. "Disagree and Have a Great Life!". *NAAFA Newsletter*, July/August (1995): 4.

Bruno, Barbara Altman. "Support What Supports You." *NAAFA Newsletter*, June/July (1993): 7.

Burton, Greg. "Political Polygamists Coming Out of the Closet." *Salt Lake Tribune*, December 11, 2000, B1–B2.

Cacciola, Scott. "Victims in Larry Nassar Abuse Case Find a Fierce Advocate: The Judge." *New York Times*, January 23, 2108.

Cacciola, Scott, and Victor Mather. "Larry Nassar Sentencing: 'I Just Signed Your Death Warrant.'" *New York Times*, January 24, 2018.

Carcamo, Cindy. "Relatives of Erika Andiola, Immigrant Activist, Detained." *Los Angeles Times*, January 11, 2013.

Carrasco, Tania A. Unzueta, and Hinda Seif. "Disrupting the Dream: Undocumented Youth Reframe Citizenship and Deportability through Anti-Deportation Activism." *Latino Studies* 12, no. 2 (2014): 279–299.

Chauncey, George. "Christian Brotherhood or Sexual Perversion? Homosexual Identities and the Construction of Sexual Boundaries in the World War I Era." *Journal of Social History* 19, no. 2 (1985): 189–212.

Chauncey, George . *Gay New York: Gender, Urban Culture, and the Making of the Gay Male World 1890–1940*. New York: Basic Books, 1994.

Chavez, Leo R. *The Latino Threat: Constructing Immigrants, Citizens, and the Nation.* Stanford, CA: Stanford University Press, 2008.

Chiang, Mark. "Coming Out into the Global System: Postmodern Patriarchies and Transnational Sexualities in the Wedding Banquet." In *In Q & A: Queer in Asian America*, edited by David L. Eng and Alice Y. Hom. Philadelphia, PA: Temple University Press, 1998, 374–396.

Chira, Susan. "Year of the Woman? In Arizona, It's Women, Plural, and It's Both Parties." *New York Times*, April 9, 2018.

Christensen Gee, Lisa, Matthew Gardner, and Meg Wiehe. "Undocumented Immigrants' State & Local Tax Contributions." Washington, DC: Institute on Taxation and Economic Policy, 2016.

ChristineJorgensen.org. "Welcome to Christinejorgensen.Org." http://www.christinejorgensen.org/MainPages/Home.html.

Churchill, Wainwright. *Homosexual Behavior among Males: A Cross-Cultural and Cross Species Investigation*. Portland, OR: Hawthorn Books, 1967.

The Clothesline Project. "The Clothesline Project: The Project: Survivor Stories: What Do the Shirts Mean? Gallery." http://www.clotheslineproject.info/project.html.

CNNPolitics. "Exit Polls." https://www.cnn.com/election/2016/results/exit-polls.

Cohen, Cathy J. *The Boundaries of Blackness: AIDS and the Breakdown of Black Politics*. Chicago: University of Chicago Press, 1999.

Cohen, Claire. "Donald Trump Sexism Tracker: Every Offensive Comment in One Place." *Telegraph*, July 14, 2017.

Coleman, Eli. "Developmental Stages of the Coming Out Process." *Journal of Homosexuality* 7, no. 2/3 (1982): 31–43.

Collinson, Stephen. "Can Donald Trump Recover from This?" *CNNPolitics*, October 8, 2016.

Connell, Catherine. "Doing, Undoing, or Redoing Gender? Learning from the Workplace Experiences of Transpeople." *Gender & Society* 24, no. 1 (2010): 31–55.

Connell, Catherine. *School's Out: Gay and Lesbian Teachers in the Classroom.* Berkeley: University of California Press, 2015.

Cooper, Charlotte. "Fat Activism in Ten Astonishing, Beguiling, Inspiring and Beautiful Episodes." In *Fat Studies in the UK*, edited by Corinna Tomrley and Ann Kaloski, 19–31. York, UK: Raw Nerve Books, 2009.

Cooper, Charlotte . *Fat and Proud: The Politics of Size.* London: Women's Press, 1998.

Cooper, Helene. "Critics See Echoes of 'Don't Ask, Don't Tell' in Military Transgender Ban." *New York Times*, March 28, 2018.

Cowan, Sarah K. "Secrets and Misperceptions: The Creation of Self-Fulfilling Illusions." *Sociological Science* 1 (2014): 466–492.

Crandall, Christian S., and Amy Eshleman. "A Justification-Suppression Model of the Expression and Experience of Prejudice." *Psychological Bulletin* 129, no. 3 (May 2003): 414–446.

Crandall, Christian S., Jason M. Miller, and Mark H. White II. "Changing Norms Following the 2016 U.S. Presidential Election: The Trump Effect on Prejudice." *Social Psychology and Personality Science* 9, no. 2 (January 16, 2018): 186–192.

D'Emilio, John. "Capitalism and Gay Identity." In *Powers of Desire: The Politics of Sexuality*, edited by Ann Snitow, Christine Stansell, and Sharan Thompson. New Feminist Library Series. New York: Monthly Review Press, 1983.

D'Emilio, John. *Sexual Politics, Sexual Communities: The Making of a Homosexual Minority in the United States.* Chicago: University of Chicago Press, 1983.

The Daily Show with Trevor Noah. Tarana Burke on What Me Too Is Really About— Extended Interview. January 4, 2018.

Davidson, Lauren. "Is Your Daily Social Media Usage Higher than Average?" *Telegraph*, May 17, 2015.

Dawson, Michael C. *Behind the Mule: Race and Class in African-American Politics.* Princeton, NJ: Princeton University Press, 1994.

De Genova, Nicholas Paul. "Migrant 'Illegality' and Deportability in Everyday Life." *Annual Review of Anthropology* 31 (2002): 419–447.

De Genova, Nicholas, and Nathalie Peutz, eds. *The Deportation Regime: Sovereignty, Space, and the Freedom of Movement.* Durham, NC: Duke University Press, 2010.

"De l'Affaire DSK Comme 'Troussage De Domestique': Jean-François Kahn Et L'inconscient Machiste Français." *Le Grand Barnum*, May 16, 2011.

Denissen, Amy M., and Abigail C. Saguy. "Gendered Homophobia and the Contradictions of Workplace Discrimination for Women in the Building Trades." *Gender & Society* 28, no. 3 (2014): 381–403.

Deshen, Schlomo. *Blind People: The Private and Public Life of Sightless Israelis.* Albany: State University of New York Press, 1992.

DiBennardo, Rebecca, and Abigail C. Saguy. "How Children of LGBQ Parents Negotiate Courtesy Stigma over the Life Course." *Journal of International Women's Studies* 4 (2018): 1–20.

Donegan, Moira. "I Started the Media Men List; My Name Is Moira Donegan." *The Cut*, January 10, 2018.

Dupuy, Beatrice. "Some Women of Color Are Boycotting the Women's March, Here's Why." *Newsweek*, January 20, 2018.

Durso, Laura E., and Gary J. Gates. "Serving Our Youth: Findings from a National Survey of Service Providers Working with Lesbian, Gay, Bisexual, and Transgender Youth Who Are Homeless or at Risk of Becoming Homeless." Los Angeles: Williams Institute with True Colors Fund and the Palette Fund, 2012.

Earl, Jennifer, and Katrina Kimport. *Digitally Enabled Social Change: Activism in the Internet Age (Acting with Technology)*. 2011.

Editorial Board. "Trump's Heartless Transgender Military Ban Gets a Second Shot." *New York Times*, March 28, 2018.

Elkin, Lauren. "How French Libertines Are Reckoning with #Metoo." *Paris Review*, January 24, 2018.

Enriquez, Laura E. "Multigenerational Punishment: Shared Experiences of Undocumented Immigration Status within Mixed-Status Families." *Journal of Marriage and Family* 77, no. 4 (2015): 939–953.

Enriquez, Laura E. *Of Love and Papers: Forming Families in the Shadows of Immigration Policy*. Berkeley: University of California Press, forthcoming.

Enriquez, Laura E., Martha Morales Hernandez, and Annie Ro. "Deconstructing Immigrant Illegality: A Mixed-Methods Investigation of Stress and Health among Undocumented College Students." *Race and Social Problems* 10, no. 3 (September 2018): 93–208.

Enriquez, Laura E., and Abigail C. Saguy. "Coming Out of the Shadows: Harnessing a Cultural Schema to Advance the Undocumented Immigrant Youth Movement." *American Journal of Cultural Sociology* 4, no. 1 (August 12, 2016): 107–130.

Epstein, Steven. "Gay Politics, Ethnic Identity: The Limits of Social Constructionism." *Socialist Review* 43/44 (1987): 9–49.

Estrada, Sheryl. "Time Magazine Excluding Tarana Burke from #Metoo Cover Speaks Volumes." *DiversityInc*, December 11, 2017.

Evans, Tim, Mark Alesia, and Marisa Kwiatkowski. "A 20-Year Toll: 368 Gymnasts Allege Sexual Exploitation." *IndyStar*, December 5, 2016.

Evans, Tim, Marisa Kwiatkowski, and Mark Alesia. "Can USA Gymnastics Reform Itself under Current Leadership?" *IndyStar*, June 27, 2017.

FAIR (Federation for American Immigration Reform). "It's Time for Americans to Come Out of the Shadows." https://www.fairus.org/media/10096.

Farrell, Amy Erdman. *Fat Shame: Stigma and the Fat Body in American Culture*. New York: New York University Press, 2011.

Feuer, Alan. "Citing Trump's 'Racial Slurs,' Judge Says Suit to Preserve DACA Can Continue." *New York Times*, March 29, 2018.

Feuer, Alan . "Justice Department Says Rights Law Doesn't Protect Gays." *New York Times*, July 27, 2017.

Freedberg, Louis, and Christopher Heredia. "Mixed Feelings about Gay March." *San Francisco Chronicle*, April 10, 2000.

Friedman, Jeffrey. "The Real Cause of Obesity." *Newsweek*, September 10, 2009.

Gambino, Lauren. "Failed Deal over Dreamers at the Heart of US Government Shutdown." *Guardian*, January 20, 2018.

Gamson, Joshua. *Freaks Talk Back: Tabloid Talk Shows and Sexual Nonconformity.* Chicago: Chicago University Press, 1998.

Garber, Eric. "A Spectacle in Color: The Lesbian and Gay Subculture of Jazz Age Harlem." In *Hidden from History: Reclaiming the Gay and Lesbian Past,* edited by Martin Duberman et al. New York: New American Library, 1989.

Garcia, Sandra E. "The Woman Who Created #Metoo Long before Hashtags." *New York Times,* October 20, 2017.

Gates, Gary J. "LGBT Adult Immigrants in the United States." Los Angeles: Williams Institute, 2013.

Gay, Roxanne. *Hunger: A Memoire of (My) Body.* New York: Harper, 2017.

Ghaziani, Amin. *Dividends of Dissent.* Chicago: University of Chicago Press, 2008.

Ghaziani, Amin . "Post-Gay Collective Identity Construction." *Social Problems* 58, no. 1 (2011): 99–125.

Gher, Jaime M. "Polygamy and Same-Sex Marriage—Allies or Adversaries within the Same-Sex Marriage Movement." *William & Mary Journal of Women and the Law* 14, no. 3 (2008): 559–603.

Glass, Ira. *This American Life.* National Public Radio. Tell Me I'm Fat. Podcast audio, 2016.

Goffman, Erving. *Stigma: Notes on the Management of a Spoiled Identity.* New York: Prentice-Hall, 1963.

Golash-Boza, Tanya, and Pierrette Hondagneu-Sotelo. "Latino Immigrant Men and the Deportation Crisis: A Gendered Racial Removal Program." *Latino Studies* 11, no. 3 (2013): 271–292.

Goldberg, Michelle. "The Teachers Revolt in West Virginia." *New York Times,* March 5, 2018.

Goldstein, Dana. "Teachers in Oklahoma and Kentucky Walk Out: 'It Really Is a Wildfire.'" *New York Times,* April 2, 2018.

Gonzales, Roberto G. "DACA at Year Three: Challenges and Opportunities in Accessing Higher Education and Employment." Washington, DC: American Immigration Council, 2016.

Gonzales, Roberto G., Veronica Terriquez, and Stephen P. Ruszczyk. "Becoming DACAmented: Assessing the Short-Term Benefits of Deferred Action for Childhood Arrivals (DACA)." *American Behavioral Scientist* 58, no. 14 (December 1, 2014 2014): 1852–1872.

Graham, Bryan Armen. "Larry Nassar Is Locked Up for Life. Now the Real Work Begins." *Guardian,* January 25, 2018.

Gross, Larry. *Contested Closets: The Politics and Ethics of Outing.* Minneapolis: University of Minnesota Press, 1993.

Guttmacher Institute. "Abortion Is a Common Experience for U.S. Women, Despite Dramatic Declines in Rates." Guttmacher Institute, 2017. https://tinyurl.com/ydaeb22f.

Halberstam, Judith. "Shame and White Gay Masculinity." *Social Text* 23 (2005): 219–233.

Hamilton, Laura, and Elizabeth A. Armstrong. "Gendered Sexuality in Young Adulthood: Double Binds and Flawed Options." *Gender & Society* 23, no. 5 (October 2009): 589–616.

Hammack, Phillip L., and Bertram J. Cohler, eds. *The Story of Sexual Identity Narrative Perspectives on the Gay and Lesbian Life Course.* Oxford: Oxford University Press, 2009.

Hanhardt, Christina B. *Safe Space: Gay Neighborhood History and the Politics of Violence.* Durham, NC: Duke University Press, 2013.

Harris, Elizabeth. "Three Billboards Call Out Sexual Abuse." *New York Times*, March 23, 2018.

Hayes, Jeffrey Michael. "Polygamy Comes Out of the Closet: The New Strategy of Polygamy Activists." *Stanford Journal of Civil Rights & Civil Liberties* 3 (2007): 99–129.

Henry, William A. "Ethics: Forcing Gays Out of the Closet: Homosexual Leaders Seek to Expose Foes of the Movement." *Time*, January 29, 1990.

Hesse, Monica, and Dan Zak. "Does This Haircut Make Me Look Like a Nazi?" *Chicago Tribune*, December 6, 2016.

Heyboer, Kelly. "'Undocumented and Unafraid' Immigrants March on I.C.E. Headquarters." *New Jersey Real-Time News*, March 6, 2018.

Heyman, Josiah McC. "'Illegality' and the U.S.-Mexico Border: How It Is Produced and Resisted." In *Constructing Immigrant "Illegality": Critiques, Experiences, and Responses*, edited by Cecilia Menjívar and Daniel Kanstroom, 111–135. New York: Cambridge University Press, 2014.

Hinckley, David. "'Sister Wives,' '19th Wife' and 'Big Love' Usher in Wave of Polygamy Programming." *NY Daily News*, September 13, 2010.

Hines, Melissa, S. Faisal Ahmed, and Ieuan A. Hughes. "Psychological Outcomes and Gender-Related Development in Complete Androgen Insensitivity Syndrome." *Archives of Sexual Behavior* 32, no. 2 (April 2003): 93–101.

Hing, Julianne. "Dreamers Come Out: 'I'm Undocumented, Unafraid, and Unapologetic.'" *Colorlines*, March 8, 2011.

Hing, Julianne . "How Undocumented Youth Nearly Made Their Dreams Real in 2010." *Colorlines*, December 20, 2010.

Hochschild, Arlie. *The Second Shift: Working Parents and the Revolution at Home.* New York: Viking Penguin, 1989.

Hogshead-Maker, Nancy. "Michigan State Will Pay $500 Million to Abuse Victims. What Comes Next?" *New York Times*, May 18, 2018.

Holloway, S. T. "Why This Black Girl Will Not Be Returning to the Women's March." *Huffington Post*, January 19, 2018.

Holmes, Sarah, ed. "Testimonies: A Collection of Lesbian Coming Out Stories." Boston, MA: Alyson, 1988.

Howard, Josh. "April 27, 1953: For LGBT Americans, a Day That Lives in Infamy." *Huffpost Queer Voices*, April 27, 2012.

Human Rights Watch and InterACT. "'I Want to Be Like Nature Made Me': Medically Unnecessary Surgeries on Intersex Children in the Us." July 25, 2017. https://tinyurl.com/y8ez74gc.

Humphreys, Laud. *Out of the Closets: The Sociology of Homosexual Liberation.* Englewood Cliffs, NJ: Prentice-Hall, 1972.

Hutchinson, Darren Lenar. "Out Yet Unseen: A Racial Critique of Gay and Lesbian Legal Theory and Political Discourse." *Connecticut Law Review* 29, no. 2 (Winter 1997): 561–645.

Immigrant Youth Justice League. "National Coming Out of the Shadows Month 2013." http://www.iyjl.org/comingout2013/.

Immigrant Youth Justice League. "Undocumented, Unafraid, Unapologetic." http://www.iyjl.org/undocumented-unafraid-unapologetic/.

Immigrant Youth Justice League. "Who We Are." http://www.iyjl.org/whoweare/.

"The Importance of Women of Color at the Women's March 2018." *Glitter*, 2018, https://bit.ly/2suqm1j.

Iturriaga, Nicole, and Abigail C. Saguy. "'I Would Never Want to be an Only Wife': The Role of Discursive Networks and Post-Feminist Discourse in Reframing Polygamy." *Social Problems*, 64, no. 3 (August 2017): 333–350.

"Jean-François Kahn: Pas de Viol, Mais un 'Troussage de Domestique.'" *Le Nouvel Observateur*, May 18, 2011.

Johansson, Warren, and William A. Percy. *Outing: Shattering the Conspiracy of Silence.* New York: Haworth Press, 1994.

Karlin, Élise. "La Descente aux Enfers de DSK." *L'Express*, May 17, 2011.

Keck, Thomas M. "Beyond Backlash: Assessing the Impact of Judicial Decisions on LGBT Rights." *Law & Society Review* 43, no. 1 (2009): 151–186.

Kellaway, Mitch. "Meet Obama's Newest Trans Appointee: Attorney Shannon Minter." *Advocate*, June 9, 2015.

Kelly, Mary Louise, and Cecilia Lei. The Original Dreamer Recalls "All-Pervasive" ' Fear as an Undocumented Child. Podcast audio. National Public Radio, *All Things Considered* 7:582018. https://www.npr.org/2018/06/20/622002025/the-original-dreamer-recalls-all-pervasive-fear-as-an-undocumented-child.

Kiely, Kathy. "Immigrant's Family Detained after Daughter Speaks Out." *USA Today*, October 16, 2007.

Kinsey, Alfred C., Wardell B. Pomeroy, and Clyde Martin. *Sexual Behavior in the Human Male*. Philadelphia: W. B. Saunders, 1948.

Kirby, Dick. "Outrage." 87 minutes. New York: Magnolia Pictures, 2009.

Kolata, Gina. *Rethinking Thin: The New Science of Weight Loss—and the Myths and Realities about Dieting*. New York: Farrar, Straus and Giroux, 2007.

Krieg, Gregory. "It's Official: Clinton Swamps Trump in Popular Vote." *CNNPolitics*, December 22, 2016.

Krugman, Paul. "The Force of Decency Awakens." *New York Times*, February 26, 2018.

Kurian, Alka. "#Metoo Is Riding a New Wave of Feminism in India." *Conversation*, February 27, 2018.

Kwiatkowski, Marisa, Mark Alesia, and Tim Evans. "A Blind Eye to Sex Abuse: How USA Gymnastics Failed to Report Cases." *IndyStar*, August 4, 2016.

Lane, Harlan. "Ethnicity, Ethics, and the Deaf-World." *Journal of Deaf Studies and Deaf Education* 10, no. 3 (Summer 2005): 291–310.

Langer, Gary. "Unwanted Sexual Advances Not Just a Hollywood, Weinstein Story, Poll Finds." *ABCNews*, October 17, 2017.

Laumann, Edward O., John H. Gagnon, Robert T. Michael, and Stuart Michaels. *The Social Organization of Sexuality: Sexual Practices in the United States*. Chicago: University of Chicago Press, 1994.

Lawler, David. "Trump on Fiorina: 'Look at That Face. Would Anyone Vote for That?'" *Telegraph*, September 10, 2015.

Leive, Cindi. "Let's Talk about My Abortion (and Yours)." *New York Times*, June 30, 2018.

Levenson, Eric. "Larry Nassar Will Never Get Out of Prison, No Matter His Sentence This Week." CNN.com, January 23 2018.

Levine, Martin P. *Gay Macho: The Life and Death of the Homosexual Clone*. Edited by Michael S. Kimmel. New York: New York University Press, 1998.

Levinson, Jessica. "Non-Disclosure Agreements Can Enable Abusers. Should We Get Rid of NDAs for Sexual Harassment?" NBCNews, January 24, 2018.

Levy, Bernard-Henri. "Le Bloc-Notes De Bernard-Henri Levy." *Le Point*, May 17, 2011.

Lopez, German. "Most Americans Agree Trump Has Made Race Relations Worse." *Vox*, April 9, 2019.

Lozano, Pepe. "Immigrant Youth: Undocumented, Unafraid and Unapologetic." *People's World*, March 11, 2011.

Luker, Kristin. *Abortion and the Politics of Motherhood*. Berkeley: University of California Press, 1984.

MacKinnon, Catharine. "#Metoo Has Done What the Law Could Not." *New York Times*, February 4, 2018.

MacKinnon, Catharine . *Sexual Harassment of Working Women*. New Haven, CT: Yale University Press, 1979.

Madera, Gabriela, Angelo A. Mathay, Armin M. Najafi, Hector H. Saldivar, Stephanie Solis, Alyssa Jane M. Titong, Gaspar Rivera-Salgado, et al., eds. *Underground Undergrads: UCLA Undocumented Immigrant Students Speak Out*. Los Angeles: UCLA Center for Labor Research and Education, 2008.

Maheshwari, Sapna. "Ad Agencies' Reckoning on Sexual Harassment Comes on Instagram, Anonymously." *New York Times*, March 7, 2018.

Maialetti, David. "Cosby Juror Says He Didn't Believe 'Well-Coached' Constand." *Inquirer*, June 22, 2017.

Maldonado, Marta María, Adela C. Licona, and Sarah Hendricks. "Latin@ Immobilities and Altermobilities within the U.S. Deportability Regime." *Annals of the American Association of Geographers* 106 (2016): 321–329.

Mamone, Trav. "The #Metoo Conversation Erases Trans People." *HuffPost*, February 21, 2018.

Mascaro, Lisa. "David Duke and Other White Supremacists See Trump's Rise as Way to Increase Role in Mainstream Politics." *Los Angeles Times*, September 29, 2016.

Massey, Alana. "Women Have Always Tried to Warn Each Other about Dangerous Men. We Have To." *Washington Post*, October 13, 2017.

Matsnev, Oleg. "Russian News Outlets Boycott Parliament after Harassment Decision." *New York Times*, March 22, 2018.

Mayeri, Serena. *Reasoning from Race: Feminism, Law, and the Civil Rights Revolution*. Cambridge, MA: Harvard University Press, 2011.

McAdam, Doug. "'Initiator' and 'Spin-Off' Movements: Diffusion Processes in Protest Cycles." In *Repertoires and Cycles of Collective Action*, edited by Mark Traugott, 217–239. Durham, NC: Duke University Press, 1995.

McDonald, Soraya Nadia. "It's Hard to Ignore a Woman Toting a Mattress Everywhere She Goes, Which Is Why Emma Sulkowicz Is Still Doing It." *Washington Post*, October 29, 2014.

McGray, Douglas. "The Invisibles." *Los Angeles Times*, April 23, 2006.

McRobbie, Angela. "Top Girls? Young Women and the Post-Feminist Sexual Contract." *Cultural Studies* 1, no. 21 (2007): 718–737.

McRuer, Robert. *Crip Theory: Cultural Signs of Queerness and Disability*. New York: New York University Press, 2006.

Meyer, David S., and Nancy Whittier. "Social Movement Spillover." *Social Problems* 41, no. 2 (1994): 277–298.

Moore, Lisa C. "Does Your Mama Know? An Anthology of Black Lesbian Coming Out Stories." Decatur, GA: RedBone Press, 1997.

Moore, Mignon R. "'Black and Gay in L.A.': The Relationships Black Lesbians and Gay Men Have with Their Racial and Religious Communities." In *Black Los Angeles: American Dreams and Racial Realities*, edited by Darnell Hunt and Ana-Christina Ramon. New York: New York University Press, 2010.

NAAFA (National Association to Advance Fat Acceptance). "NAAFA Conferences." https://www.naafaonline.com/dev2/community/index.html.

NAAFA (National Association to Advance Fat Acceptance). "Some Unusual Historical Notes about NAAFA." *NAAFA Newsletter*, April (1989): 2.

National Immigrant Youth Alliance. "A Guide to 'Coming Out' for Undocumented Youth." 2011.

National Immigration Law Center. "Status of Current DACA Litigation." https://www.nilc.org/issues/daca/status-current-daca-litigation/.

National Immigration Law Center . "Support for the Dream Act." https://www.nilc.org/issues/immigration-reform-and-executive-actions/dreamact/dreamsupport/.

National Public Radio. "In Major Shift, LDS Church Rolls Back Controversial Policies toward LGBT Members." *Religion*. April 4, 2019. https://tinyurl.com/yyhtp74u

Navratilova, Martina. "Jason Collins a 'Game Changer.'" *Sports Illustrated*, April 23, 2013.

Newsday.com staff. "Donald Trump Speech, Debates and Campaign Quotes." *Newsday*, November 9, 2016.

Nicholls, Walter J. *The Dreamers: How the Undocumented Youth Movement Transformed the Immigrant Rights Debate*. Stanford, CA: Stanford University Press, 2013.

Nichols, Chris. "Do Three-Quarters of Americans Support the Dream Act? Nancy Pelosi Says So." http://www.politifact.com/california/statements/2017/sep/19/nancy-pelosi/nancy-pelosi-claims-three-quarters-americans-suppo/.

O'Brien, Jodi. "Afterward: Complicating Homophobia." *Sexualities* 11 (2008): 496–512.

Olsen, Mark, and Will Scheffer, Feeling the "Big Love." Podcast audio. National Public Radio. *Fresh Air*. August 1, 2007.

O'Neil, Lonnae. "The 53 Percent Issue: This Time, the Problem in American Feminism Has a Name." *Undefeated*, December 20, 2016.

Orne, Jason. "'You Will Always Have to 'Out' Yourself': Reconsidering Coming Out through Strategic Outness." *Sexualities* 14, no. 6 (2011): 681–703.

O'Reilly, Andrea. "Slut Pride: A Tribute to Slutwalk Toronto." *Feminist Studies* 38, no. 1 (2012): 245–250.

Osmond, Amy Kathlyn. "Organizational Identification: A Case Study of the Davis County Cooperative Society, the Latter Day Church of Christ, or Kingston Order." Phd Dissertation in Communications (University of Utah, 2010).

Owen, Lesleigh, Angela Buffington, and Kris Owen. "Boogeywoman Zine." 2000–2001.

Pacheco, Gaby. "Trail of Dreams: A Fifteen-Hundred Mile Journey to the Nation's Capital." In *Undocumented and Unafraid: Tam Tran, Cinthya Felix, and the Immigrant Youth Movement*, edited by Kent Wong, Janna Shadduck-Hernandez, Fabiola Inzunza, Julie Monroe, Victor Narro, and Abel Valenzuela Jr. Los Angeles: UCLA Center for Labor Research and Education, 2012.

Passel, Jeffrey S., and D'Vera Cohn. *Unauthorized Immigrant Population: National and State Trends, 2010*. Washington DC: Pew Hispanic Center, 2011.

Peiser, Jaclyn. "How a Crowdsourced List Set Off Months of #Metoo Debate." *New York Times*, February 3, 2018.

Penelope, Julia, and Susan Wolfe, eds. *The Coming Out Stories*. Watertown, MA: Persephone Press, 1980.

Pew Research Center. *A Survey of LGBT Americans: Attitudes, Experiences and Values in Changing Times*. Washington, DC: Pew Research Center, 2013.

Plante, Rebecca F. *Sexualities in Context*. New York: W. W. Norton, 2006.

Powell, Jacqulyn. "#Notokay Movement Encouraging Women to Share Sexual Assault Stories on Social Media." *WPTV*, October 11, 2016.

Prois, Jessica, and Carolina Moreno. "The #Metoo Movement Looks Different for Women of Color. Here Are 10 Stories. Some of the Most Affected Have Been Left out of the Movement, and It's Time We Talk about It." *HuffPost*, January 2, 2018.

Protess, Ben, Danielle Ivory, and Steve Eder. "Where Trump's Hands-Off Approach to Governing Does Not Apply." *New York Times*, September 10, 2017.

RAINN (Rape, Abuse & Incest National Network). "The Criminal Justice System: Statistics." https://www.rainn.org/statistics/criminal-justice-system.

RAINN (Rape, Abuse & Incest National Network). "Key Terms and Phrases." https://www.rainn.org/articles/key-terms-and-phrases.

RAINN (Rape, Abuse & Incest National Network). "Victims of Sexual Violence: Statistics." https://www.rainn.org/statistics/victims-sexual-violence.

Reger, Jo. "Micro-Cohorts, Feminist Discourse, and the Emergence of the Toronto Slutwalk." *Feminist Formations* 26, no. 1 (2014): 49–69.

Roberts, Tangela S., Sharon G. Horne, and William T. Hoyt. "Between a Gay and a Straight Place: Bisexual Individuals' Experiences with Monosexism." *Journal of Bisexuality* 15, no. 4 (2015): 554–569.

Rodriguez, Katherine. "Transgender Activists Complain Women's March Unfairly Linked Sex to Biology." *Breitbart*, January 24, 2017.

Romero, Simon, Jack Healy, and Julie Turkewitz. "Teachers in Arizona and Colorado Walk Out over Education Funding." *New York Times*, April 26, 2018.

Rush, Curtis. "Cop Apologizes for 'Sluts' Remark at Law School." *Toronto Star*, February 18, 2011.

Saguy, Abigail C. "Employment Discrimination or Sexual Violence? Defining Sexual Harassment in American, and French Law." *Law & Society Review* 34, no. 4 (2000): 1091–1128.

Saguy, Abigail C. "Europeanization or National Specificity? Legal Approaches to Sexual Harassment in France, 2002–2012." *Law & Society Review* 52, no. 1 (2018): 140–171.

Saguy, Abigail C. *What Is Sexual Harassment? From Capitol Hill to the Sorbonne*. Berkeley: University of California Press, 2003.

Saguy, Abigail C., and Anna Ward. "Coming Out as Fat: Rethinking Stigma." *Social Psychology Quarterly* 74, no. 1 (March 2011): 53–75.

Saguy, Dotan. *Venice Beach: The Last Days of a Bohemian Paradise*. Heidelberg, Germany: Kehrer Verlag, 2018.

Sang-Hun, Choe. "A Director's Apology Adds Momentum to South Korea's #Metoo Movement." *New York Times*, February 19, 2018.

Sanger, Carol. *About Abortion: Terminating Pregnancy in Twenty-First-Century America*. Cambridge, MA: Harvard University Press, 2017.

Sati, Joel. "How DACA Pits 'Good Immigrants' against Millions of Others." *Washington Post*, September 7, 2017.

Sayej, Nadja. "Interview: Alyssa Milano on the #Metoo Movement: 'We're Not Going to Stand for It Any More.'" *Guardian*, December 1, 2017.

Scherer, Michael. "2016 Person of the Year Donald Trump." *Time*, 2016.

Schlafly, Phyllis. "How the Feminists Want to Change Our Laws." *Stanford Law & Policy Review* 65 (Spring 1994): 65–73.

Schoenfielder, Lisa, and Barb Wieser, eds. *Shadow on a Tightrope: Writings by Women on Fat Oppression*. Iowa City: Aunt Lute, 1983.

Schonbrun, Zach, and Christine Hauser. "Larry Nassar, Sentenced in Sexual Abuse Case, Is Back in Court." *New York Times*, January 31, 2018.

Sedgewick, Eve Kosofsky. *Epistemology of the Closet*. Berkeley: University of California Press, 2008.

Seidman, Steven. *Beyond the Closet: The Transformation of Gay and Lesbian Life*. New York: Routledge, 2002.

Seif, Hinda. "'Coming Out of the Shadows' and 'Undocuqueer:' Undocumented Immigrants Transforming Sexuality Discourse and Activism." *Journal of Language and Sexuality* 3, no. 1 (2014): 87–120.

Seif, Hinda. "'Wise Up': Undocumented Latino Youth, Mexican American Legislators, and the Struggle for Education Access." *Latino Studies* 2, no. 2 (2004): 210–230.

Shafrir, Doree. "What to Do with 'Shitty Media Men'?" *Buzzfeed*, October 11, 2017.

Smith, Jack. "The Women of the 'Alt-Right' Are Speaking Out against Misogyny. They'd Prefer Absolute Patriarchy." *Mic*, December 8, 2017.

Smith, Sally E. "A Message from Executive Director Sally E. Smith." *NAAFA Newsletter*, January/February (1988): 3.

Snow, David A., and Robert D. Benford. "Ideology, Frame Resonance and Participant Mobilization." *International Social Movement Research* 1 (1988): 197–217.

Sollis, Marie. "Women of Color Are Being Blamed for Dividing the Women's March—and It's Nothing New." *Mic*, January 21, 2017.

Stacey, Judith. *Unhitched: Love, Marriage, and Family Values from West Hollywood to Western China*. New York: New York University Press, 2011.

Stambolis-Ruhstorfer, Michael, and Abigail C. Saguy. "How to Describe It? Why the Term Coming Out Means Different Things in the United States and France." *Sociological Forum* 29, no. 4 (2014): 808–829.

Stein, Marc. *The Stonewall Riots: A Documentary History*. New York: New York University Press, 2019.

Stewart, Emily. "All of West Virginia's Teachers Have Been on Strike for over a Week." *Vox*, March 4, 2018.

StopIGM.org. "'Inhuman Treatment': UN Committee against Torture (CAT) Condemns Intersex Genital Mutilations, Calls for Legislative Measures." News release, August 14, 2015. https://bit.ly/2uMLX7m.

Strangio, Chase. "Stop Performing Nonconsensual, Medically Unnecessary Surgeries on Young Intersex Children." ACLU.org, October 26, 2017.

Sykes, Wanda. "I'ma Be Me." Director Beth McCarthy-Miller. HBO, 2009.

Tambe, Ashwini. "Has Trump's Presidency Triggered the Movement against Sexual Harassment?" *Conversation*, November 28, 2017.

Tapestry against Polygamy. "By 3rd Anniversary of 'Lawrence'—Polygamy Rights Accelerated." Pro-Polygamy.com. http://www.pro-polygamy.com/articles.php?news=0044.

Taub, Amanda. "'White Nationalism' Explained." *New York Times*, November 21, 2016.

Terriquez, Veronica. "Intersectional Mobilization, Social Movement Spillover, and Queer Youth Leadership in the Immigrant Rights Movement." *Social Problems* 62, no. 3 (2015): 343–362.

Thunder. "Coming Out: Notes on Fat Lesbian Pride." In *Shadow on a Tightrope: Writings by Women on Fat Oppression*, edited by Lisa Schoenfielder and Barb Wieser. Iowa City: Aunt Lute, 1983.

Tribune News Services. "Clan Leader Pleads Guilty to Incest." *Chicago Tribune*, November 7, 2003.

Troiden, R. R. "The Formation of Homosexual Identities." *Journal of Homosexuality* 17 (1989): 43–73.

Tuerkheimer, Deborah. "The Cosby Jury Finally Believes the Women." *New York Times*, April 26, 2018.

Tushnet, Eve. "Polygamy Proponents Recycle Same-Sex 'Marriage' Arguments." *National Catholic Register*, March 25, 2001.

Twenge, Jean M. *IGen: Why Today's Super-Connected Kids Are Growing Up Less Rebellious, More Tolerant, Less Happy—and Completely Unprepared for Adulthood—and What That Means for the Rest of Us*. New York: Atria Books, 2017.

Umans, Meg. "Like Coming Home: Coming-out Letters." Austin, TX: Banned Books, 1988.

"Unpopular Opinion: I Am a Rape Victim, Not a Survivor." *XOJane*, April 27, 2016.

Valenti, Jessica. "#Metoo Named the Victims. Now, Let's List the Perpetrators." *Guardian*, October 17, 2017.

Valocchi, Steve. "The Class-Inflected Nature of Gay Identity." *Social Problems* 46, no. 2 (May 1999): 207–224.

Valocchi, Steve . "Individual Identities, Collective Identities, and Organization Structure: The Relationship of the Political Left and Gay Liberation in the United States." *Sociological Perspectives* 44, no. 4 (2001): 445–467.

Valverde, Miriam. "Timeline: DACA, the Trump Administration and a Government Shutdown." *Politifact*, January 22, 2018.

Van Dyne, Larry. "Is D.C. Becoming the Gay Capital of America?" *Washingtonian*, September 1980, 96–101, 133.

Vargas, Cesar. "Undocumented and Unafraid in the Face of Trump's Presidency." *Nation*, November 11, 2016.

Vargas, Jose Antionia. "Not Legal Not Leaving." *Time*, June 25, 2012, 4.

Vedantam, Shankar. Hidden Brain. Podcast audio. Why Now? 52 minutes. National Public Radio February 5, 2018. https://tinyurl.com/ybbyq3s7.

Vedantam, Shankar. Morning Edition. Podcast audio. Why #Metoo Happened in 2017. 52 minutes. National Public Radio February 7, 2018. https://tinyurl.com/y2x8kdxq.

Vidal-Ortiz, Salvador. "The Puerto Rican Way Is More Tolerant: Constructions and Uses of 'Homophobia' among Santeria Practitioners across Ethno-Racial and National Indentification." *Sexualities* 11 (2008): 476–495.

Wagmeister, Elizabeth. "Tarana Burke on Hollywood, Time's Up and Me Too Backlash." *Variety*, April 10, 2018.

Wann, Marilyn. *Fat!So?: Because You Don't Have to Apologize for Your Size*. Berkeley, CA: Ten Speed Press, 1999.

Watanabe, Teresa. "With News of DACA's End, UCLA Student Declares Herself 'Undocumented and Unafraid.'" *Los Angeles Times*, September 5, 2017.

Whittier, Nancy. "Activism against Sexual Violence Is Central to a New Women's Movement: Resistance to Trump, Campus Sexual Assault, and #Metoo." *Mobilizing Ideas*, January 22, 2018.

"Who Is Larry Nassar? A Timeline of His Decades-Long Career, Sexual Assault Convictions and Prison Sentences." https://www.usatoday.com/pages/interactives/larry-nassar-timeline/.

Wilkerson, William. "Is There Something You Need to Tell Me? Coming Out and the Ambiguity of Experience." In *Reclaiming Identity: Realist Theory and the Predicament of Postmodernism*, edited by Paula M. Moya and Michael R. Hames-Garcia, 251–278. Berkeley: University of California Press, 2000.

Williams, Christine. *Still a Man's World: Men Who Do Women's Work*. Berkeley: University of California Press, 1995.

Williams, Timothy. "Cosby Verdict Is Hailed a Breakthrough. Here's Why It Was an Anomaly." *New York Times*, April 27, 2018.

Williams, Timothy . "Did the #Metoo Movement Sway the Cosby Jury?" *New York Times*, April 26, 2018.

Wong, Tom K., and Carolina Valdivia. "In Their Own Words: A Nationwide Survey of Undocumented Millennials." In *Working Paper 191*. San Diego, CA: Center for Comparative Immigration Studies, 2014.

Wortham, Jenna. "We Were Left Out." *New York Times Magazine*, December 17, 2017.

Wortham, Jenna . "Who Didn't Go to the Women's March Matters More Than Who Did." *New York Times*, January 24, 2017.

Wu, Gwendolyn. "'Survivor' versus 'Victim': Why Choosing Your Words Carefully Is Important." *HelloFlo*, March 16, 2016.

Young, Michael. *Bearing Witness against Sin: The Evangelical Birth of the American Social Movement*. Chicago: University of Chicago Press, 2007.

Zehr, Howard, and Ali Gohar. *The Little Book of Restorative Justice*. New York: UNICEF, 2003.

Zimman, Lal. "'The Other Kind of Coming Out': Transgender People and the Coming Out Narrative Genre." *Gender and Language* 3, no. 1 (2009): 53–80.

Index

For the benefit of digital users, indexed terms that span two pages (e.g., 52–53) may, on occasion, appear on only one of those pages.